I WANNA BE ME

Sound Matters

a series edited by Michael Jarrett

I WANNA BE ME

ROCK MUSIC AND

THE POLITICS

OF IDENTITY

Theodore Gracyk

 Temple University Press
PHILADELPHIA

Temple University Press, Philadelphia 19122
Copyright © 2001 by Temple University
All rights reserved
Published 2001
Printed in the United States of America

⊗ The paper used in this publication meets the requirements of the
American National Standard for Information Sciences—Permanence
of Paper for Printed Library Materials, ANSI Z39.48-1984

Library of Congress Cataloging-in-Publication Data

Gracyk, Theodore.
  I wanna be me : rock music and the politics of identity / Theodore
  Gracyk.
     p.   cm. — (Sound matters)
  Includes bibliographical references and index.
  ISBN 1-56639-902-5 (cloth : alk. paper) — ISBN 1-56639-903-3
  (pbk. : alk. paper)
     1. Rock music—History and criticism.   2. Identity (Psychology)—
  Political aspects.   I. Series.

ML3534 .G69 2001
781.66–dc21   2001023766

This one's for Athena

Contents

Preface

This book focuses on a range of issues about personal and political identity in popular music. The three parts of this book can be read independently of one another. However, many of the arguments in the second and third parts are informed by the position developed in Part One.

The first part of the book recommends approaching rock music as a type of mass art and not merely as a mode of popular culture (Chapter 1). I explore consequences of rock's status as mass art that can prevent rock songs from communicating invariant messages about identity. The music's mass replication and its ease of understanding spread the music to diverse audiences located at times and places remote from its original production. The inevitable result is that many listeners will respond to some, but only some, of its allusions and intended messages. As a result, all meaning in recorded popular music is simultaneously open-ended and constrained (Chapters 2 and 3). Recorded popular songs have no specific, singular meaning. Nevertheless, diverse examples are provided to show how the interplay of music and lyrics places limits on any reasonable interpretation of the identities communicated in specific cases. These interpretations are facilitated by reference to musical paradigms in the form of recordings embraced by a widespread audience without establishing agreement on what they mean or what is valuable about them (Chapter 4).

The second part of the book examines the construction of identity that arises through musical appropriation. Beginning with four case studies that illustrate four distinct modes of appropriation, I highlight some of the conflicts that arise when music with a distinct "racial" identity becomes associated with a different culture or subculture. Examining several common objections to this musical appropriation (Chapter 5), I highlight but challenge the suggestion that certain forms of appropriation amount to cultural genocide (Chapter 6), a charge that is found to have some merit when reinterpreted as a question of listener responsibility (Chapter 8). Many arguments against appropriation overlook the degree to which each individual can make a claim to diverse cultural identities. While mass art and popular forms of culture are highly accessible, their pleasures and meanings demand a certain level of "cultural capital" from the audience. Informed musicians and listeners can "own" many different styles of music, inviting us to consider how much understanding is required to grasp and identify with the music as the music that it is (Chapters 7 and 8).

The third part of this book examines gender identity in rock music. Although gender identity is always socially constructed, popular culture routinely reinforces prevailing and conservative ideas that locate gender in sexual difference (Chapter 9). I challenge several analyses that try to locate an essential or compelling tie between rock music and an ideology of patriarchy (Chapter 10). Rock music is an important forum for communicating subversive ideas about gender identity, and mainstream rock may do a better job at communicating such ideas than musicians and styles whose music and gender identity are directly confrontational (Chapter 11). Finally, I propose that the musical rewards of rock are an important but unacknowledged element in delivering subversive ideas about gender identity to an otherwise resistive audience (Chapter 12).

Acknowledgments

This book reflects the kind help, support, and advice of a number of friends and scholars. I would particularly like to extend my thanks to Philip Alperson, Bruce Baugh, Lee B. Brown, Noël Carroll, Stephen Davies, Claire Detels, Laura Fasick, John Andrew Fisher, Janet Francendese, Barbara Claire Freeman, Tim Gracyk, Tom Gracyk, Kathleen Higgins, Michael Jarrett, Tom Kennedy, Renée Lorraine, Edward Macan, and Joel Rudinow. I must also thank Minnesota State University–Moorhead for providing a faculty improvement grant that supported some of the research behind Part Three.

Introduction

The Sex Pistols' "I Wanna Be Me"

It gave us an identity.

—Tom Petty on Beatlemania

Wherever the relevance of speech is at stake, matters become political by definition, for speech is what makes man a political being.

—Hannah Arendt, *The Human Condition*

here fortune tellers sometimes read tea leaves as omens of things to come, there are now professionals who scrutinize songs, films, advertisements, and other artifacts of popular culture for what they reveal about the politics and the feel of daily life at the time of their production. Instead of being consumed, they are historical artifacts to be studied and "read." Or at least that is a common approach within cultural studies. But dated pop artifacts have another, living function.

Throughout much of 1973 and early 1974, several working-class teens from west London's Shepherd's Bush district struggled to become a rock band. Like tens of thousands of such groups over the years, they learned to play together by copying older songs that they all liked. For guitarist Steve Jones and drummer Paul Cook, that meant the short, sharp rock songs of London bands like the Small Faces, the Kinks, and the Who. Most of the songs had been hits seven to ten

1

years earlier. They also learned some more current material, much of it associated with the band that succeeded the Small Faces, the brash "lad's" rock of Rod Stewart's version of the Faces. Ironically, the Rod Stewart songs they struggled to learn weren't Rod Stewart songs at all. They were Stewart's re-creation of his own youth, covers of American rhythm and blues songs like "It's All Over Now" and Sam Cooke's "Twistin' the Night Away." In 1974, Cook and Jones added another Faces fan, Glen Matlock, on bass. In all but name, the Sex Pistols had formed.

In late November 1976, the Sex Pistols released one of rock's great debut singles, "Anarchy in the UK." Lyrically, the song is little more than a string of defiant but unconnected political slogans that promise an anarchic collapse of consumer society. The singer, sounding very young and very shrill, reveals his wish to be the instrument of change: "I wanna be anarchy." Musically, the band is strictly business: little more than a rhythm guitar in lockstep with solid but unremarkable drumming. The overall effect is of a shotgun marriage of frustration and intelligence. Even today, one can hear in "Anarchy" the traces of a society so rigidly class-bound that its youth felt they had no options but resignation or defiance.

The single met a strange fate. Within days of its release, the band was invited to appear on the British *Today* television program, a teatime talk show. The rock band Queen had been scheduled to appear to promote their new single, "Somebody to Love," but canceled only a few hours before the show's live broadcast. Their record label, EMI, offered the Sex Pistols as a substitute. Since punk was heralded as rock's do-it-yourself challenge to the pompous rock of Queen's "Bohemian Rhapsody" (and because EMI arranged for a limousine to pick them up), the young upstarts grabbed the opportunity. Once it got beyond its tepid start, the resulting broadcast was roughly equivalent to the "Anarchy" single.

At first, host Bill Grundy tried to provoke the band by pointing out the conflict between their anti-materialist politics and their large advance from EMI. Finding little response, he offered several other topics. Inspired by Johnny Rotten's use of mild profanity, followed by another from Steve Jones, Grundy challenged the band to say something outrageous. Jones obliged with the "fuck" Grundy had been fishing for, and the show ended in chaos. Their exchange took a little less than two minutes.

Establishment shock and outrage dominated the next day's press: "The Foul-Mouthed Yobs," screamed a typical tabloid headline. Waiting on the platform for the morning train that would take him to his job as a computer programmer, Declan McManus (soon to become Elvis Costello) laughed with delight about the ruckus it all created among his fellow commuters. A small music scene in London was now the talk of England. But if the behavior of both Grundy and the members of the band was largely calculated for show (Grundy as the establishment's policeman, the band as the ugly face of disaffected youth), the rest of British society took very real sides.

Afraid of the controversy, promoters canceled bookings. Deprived of the immediate income of live performance, the Sex Pistols and its management company found themselves in serious trouble, and when EMI offered to buy out their contract early in the new year, the band eagerly jumped ship. Less than two months after its release, "Anarchy in the UK" was no longer available, withdrawn from circulation. Most of the rock world would not hear it until the release of *Never Mind the Bollocks Here's the Sex Pistols* at the end of 1977. By then, punk had become highly ritualized, with fans and bands playing the part first enacted on *Today*.

Lost in the shuffle and EMI's termination of the vinyl single was its flip side, "I Wanna Be Me." (Greil Marcus wrote a massive book, *Lipstick Traces*, devoted to the question of the sources of the gesture of "Anarchy in the UK." Yet there's not a single word about the B-side.) Too crude to be re-released on *Never Mind the Bollocks*, "I Wanna Be Me" is almost literally a reversal of "Anarchy." "Anarchy" is the anthem of the early punk movement, an overwhelming renunciation of the social forces acting on British youth. "I Wanna Be Me" is about the personal cost of belonging to the nascent punk movement. Since the song was hardly the strongest in the Sex Pistols' bag of tunes in late 1976 (certainly no match for "Pretty Vacant" or "Problems"), the decision to feature it on their first single suggests that the band had a personal stake in "I Wanna Be Me."

The impersonal threat behind "I wanna be anarchy"—the punk as a natural, destructive force—gives way to a very different idea of identity. For "I Wanna Be Me" is perhaps one of only two or three songs written by the Pistols that can be construed as personal. The rest of their seventeen original songs divide into two groups. One batch emphasizes the role of disaffected youth: "Pretty Vacant" and "No Feelings" top this list. Then there are their topical social critiques, loaded with Situationist slogans: songs about consumerism, the British monarchy ("God Save the Queen"), and the legacy of fascism ("Holidays in the Sun" and, less so, "Belsen Was a Gas"). Like so many of their songs, both "Bodies" and "I Wanna Be Me" are tirades set to music. Yet this pair is different, if only because the narrator's rant actually positions him against someone else, one-to-one, so that Rotten's fury has a target. He sounds less like a blustering, posturing youth and more like a real person addressing someone else.

"Bodies" is one of the Sex Pistol's strongest songs. While the passing of years makes it apparent how *conventional* most of their songs really were, this track retains all of the fury and inchoate passion that punk promised. These three minutes of rock are truly sublime. "Bodies" also explicitly calls attention to issues of race and gender. The music starts out sluggishly and then lunges forward with the arrival of the vocal; the music pummels the listener for three minutes as the vocalist berates a young woman for choosing an abortion over bearing the child of a "black" who's gotten her pregnant. More misogynist than anti-abortion, he becomes nearly inarticulate with profanity as he contemplates an outsider (she's "from Birmingham") who is so aware of identity that she aborts the child rather than bring forth a body with an undesirable racial identity. As the music hurtles along, the band's unswerving drive heightens the sense that the vocalist is losing control. At the end, his real revulsion surfaces. The issue is not the girl so much as himself. The lyric suddenly shifts its target. He repeatedly insists that he's not an animal, that he's not a body. With a final cry, we learn that he's not even addressing us. We are merely overhearing him—he calls out for his "mummy."

Whereas "Bodies" responds to the young woman's shallow sense of identity and then redirects that anger inward over the question of the vocalist's own body and the relationship he thus bears to his mother, "I Wanna Be Me" is conflicted in quite a different way. Musically, the song isn't very memorable. Opening with a staccato riff that sounds derivative of Steppenwolf's "Born to Be Wild," the arrangement quickly settles into a general background roar punctuated by wooden drumming. Its one interesting moment is the false ending—a trick that Matlock, Jones, and Cook perfected by copying Rod Stewart arrangements. The singer's increasing hysteria cuts off, perfectly synchronized with the band's sudden silence: it feels like a speeding motorcycle that's suddenly reached the end of a dead-end street. Three seconds later, Cook smacks his snare drum and the song crashes forward again. (Their direct model for this gesture may very well be the Faces' "Had Me a Real Good Time." But the Sex Pistols could never admit to having a good time, hiding behind cover versions like the Stooges' "No Fun.")

The lyrics of "I Wanna Be Me" are another matter. Other punks positioned themselves against all that rock had come to represent. The Sex Pistols realized that the burden of making music in the shadow of the Beatles and Led Zeppelin included the critical apparatus supporting the modern entertainment industry. The lyrics are oddly prophetic about the band's coming struggle to define themselves in a world where their own image would be mediated by a hostile press—ignorant listeners who later found it among the debris of *The Great Rock 'n' Roll Swindle* (1979) or on subsequent song collections could easily conclude that it was written about the Grundy incident. In its initial context, as the flip side to a song that repeats the slogan "I wanna be anarchy," the words to "I Wanna Be Me" are perhaps most striking for *failing* to repeat the title phrase. In this song, the title phrase is heard only at the very end. (Neil Young uses the same trick for "Last Dance" [1973]—but then Johnny Rotten was quite the Neil Young fan.) Pop songs, after all, are supposed to have titles that capture the "hook" or chorus. This general rule lends a tremendous power to Bob Dylan songs that so obviously violate it, such as "Positively Fourth Street" and "Rainy Day Women."

The words to "I Wanna Be Me" address members of the press who will fabricate and distort their story in search of a "scoop." But the singer's complaint takes a more interesting turn in the one phrase that *is* repeated again and again: "you wanna be me." Writers and photographers were codifying punk in the national press and, soon enough, on television. Their real interest in punk, the catch phrase suggests, is their own desire to live on the edge, to see, the lyrics proclaim, through "real eyes." As the situation unfolds in fragments, the singer comes to some recognition that the media's vicarious interest in his position as the bellwether of a fringe music scene threatens to strip him of his own identity. The media succeed in defining their own position by positioning *him*. Having satisfied Rotten's desire to make a name for himself in the public realm, the media threaten to turn him into the purely symbolic figurehead of a movement he is not allowed to define. For if the media control the process of familiarizing the public with punk's visual code, punk's familiarity will erase anything individual about his message.

As with "Bodies," the singer's final utterance is crucial. At the very end we finally hear "I wanna be me," as if it has only just occurred to him that he needs to assert his own precarious personal identity, an identity that, until now, he took for granted. If punk performance was all about the risk of being ridiculed for being yourself, so that questions of craft were shoved aside as irrelevant to musical expression, then "I Wanna Be Me" is a symptom that the singer knows he must always remain subject to larger social forces. It might take some work to be who he was.

"I Wanna Be Me" displays a level of critical thought and self-awareness that shames such punk contemporaries as, say, the Clash. The Clash produced only one early song on a similar theme, "What's My Name." But their song reduces the problem of identity to the system's failure to recognize the individual. That recognition, in turn, is reduced to having the world know one's name. (Not that the singer can name the various representatives of the system paraded through the song.) The vocalist's cry of "I'm not who I want to be" turns out to be a fairly routine complaint that consumer society is based on hollow promises; the pimple creams and other products he's tried have not made him "who I want to be." (It hasn't yet occurred to the singer that he's peddling a product; in real life his fans would someday turn this complaint back on him.) "What's My Name" ends with the threat that his anonymity gives him power, since "you" won't know who he is when he breaks into your home and gets you. The Clash were still a long way from the self-critical reflections about the struggle for self that emerge on parts of *Give 'Em Enough Rope* (1978), where songs such as "Safe European Home" begin to question their naive perspective on youth and class.

A deeper irony is at work in early punk. For just as the lyrics of "I Wanna Be Me" express outrage that media have used them so that "you" (the press? the audience?) can live vicariously, many Sex Pistols songs are obviously derived from earlier rock songs that they encountered through the mass media. Much has been written about the visual code of punk, with far too little said about punk's musical code. The architects of the Sex Pistols sound were Jones, Cook, and their original bass player, Glen Matlock. Even as the Pistols rose to national fame in the British media, cover versions dominated their live sets. Songs by the Small Faces and the Who were staples. Although contemporary bands like Queen and Pink Floyd made the "Anarchy in the UK" single sound like music from another planet, audiences for the live show were provided a larger context. Where a Small Faces song like "Watcha Gonna Do About It" provided punk attitude, the Who's "Substitute" gave them their first real anthem about confusions over personal identity. Snatches of the instrumental parts that Jones and Matlock had learned together were used as riffs and chord changes for their own compositions. The Pistols' topical response to the Grundy fiasco, "EMI," is one of the catchiest things on *Never Mind the Bollocks*— all the more so to the record-buying public who'd ignored the obscure Modern Lovers track it copies. Their only appropriation from a British contemporary was the opening riff to "Holidays in the Sun," copped from the Jam's "In the City." Jones and Matlock knew enough to steal from the one other London band whose arrangements paid homage to the Who and the Small Faces.

The pop sensibilities of Matlock and Jones ensured that Johnny Rotten had an interesting platform for his ravings. Rotten often claimed that his primary mission in the Sex Pistols was to destroy rock 'n' roll. The presence of Matlock and Jones insured that every performance was infused with irony: the leader pillaged the castle as the workers tried to shore it up around him. It also meant that their version of punk emerged through a manipulation of the identities constructed by other, earlier rock bands. In rock, there is no virgin birth, no year zero. In the case of the Sex Pistols, the political defiance of "God Save the Queen" is simply a substitution of class resentment for the casual misogyny of their 1960s prototypes. The target was different but the attitude was the same.

"I wanna be me," wailed Rotten, threatened by the awareness that someone else wanted to be him. Away from the microphone, John Lydon—the person who'd become Johnny Rotten by joining the band—felt threatened by his dependence on others in assuming that role. Less than three months after the Grundy interview catapulted the Sex Pistols to national and even international fame, Rotten drove Glen Matlock out of the band. Accounts differ as to why Matlock left, but the consensus points to Rotten's inability to share power; the Sex Pistols were to be an expression of his sensibility, and his alone. Replacing Matlock with a friend, Sid Vicious, Rotten unwittingly provided a new symbol of the punk movement: punks were inarticulate, untalented, and self-destructive. Worse, Rotten no longer had a writing partner. Only three new songs entered the band's repertoire after Matlock's departure. Asserting his own identity by destroying the democracy of the working band, Rotten found that he no longer had the means to express himself. Stuck with a bass player of limited competence, the game of rote performance became oppressive and the band fell apart within nine months. Johnny Rotten reverted to John Lydon.

This is not a book about the Sex Pistols. It does, however, explore the dilemma of "I Wanna Be Me." Questions of identity hinge on an individual's position within a larger culture. If personal identity involves a constant struggle against the impositions and assumptions of others, then it also seems to depend on appropriations from a larger cultural apparatus that is beyond our individual comprehension. That cultural apparatus includes popular culture and mass media. Foreshadowing what has become known as standpoint theory, Hannah Arendt drew on ancient Greek thought to observe that we cannot be direct spectators of our own action. Our perspective on our situation is inherently partial. We never achieve the critical distance to see and grasp our own situation with adequate understanding. Yet our actions always position us in relation to others whose opinions frame the meaning of our conduct. As actors in our own culture, we must play a part—as if adopting a role in a game or in a play.

At the same time, every attempt to gain the distance and understanding of spectators—seeing oneself from their standpoint—is similarly self-defeating. To judge oneself from a standpoint that is not one's own is to trade one's own prejudices for someone else's. Thus every attempt to grasp one's own identity arrives at an impasse. If personal identity is constantly threatened by the hegemony of culture, then it is simultaneously announced through a subordination of self to culture. If I make music for a spectator who wants to be me, Johnny Rotten realizes, it endlessly complicates the "me" I'm striving to be.

But issues of identity in the sphere of popular music are further complicated by more abstract problems about music and meaning. For if musical meaning is always a matter of a code of discourse, then individual participants will inevitably encode unintended meanings. With those unforeseen meanings there can be an unexpected moral weight. In drawing on the musical codes of 1960s British pop, the Sex Pistols' defiant assaults on the British system implicate them in the very ideologies that they repudiate. Railing against British society from a perspective of economic and political impotence, the Sex Pistols bought into the ideology of white privilege and male privilege. Rooting through other traditions for fresh materials, Lydon's post-Pistols band, Public Image, implicates him in the ideology of colonialism.

Or so we are to believe if we accept the emerging consensus on such matters. The oldest ideas about art locate its power in its capacity to imitate the world, holding out the promise that each new work of art can by itself show us the world anew. Looking at a picture book, a preverbal child can distinguish the doggie from the ducky simply by seeing the difference. But as a specifically *musical* gesture, a guitar riff or a melody or a dissonant voice is strangely mute. It represents nothing at all. Its capacity to mean anything, to convey one meaning rather than another or to support one ideology rather than another, rests on its relationship to previous music. Johnny Rotten hoped to exploit the arrogance and raw power of earlier rock without accepting anything else from it. To succeed in this project he needed something that he did not have. He needed a musical vocabulary that would mean whatever he shaped it to mean. He wanted, in other words, to be the Rolling Stones at the beginning of their career, not the Rolling Stones of the 1970s and of records like *Goats Head Soup* and *It's Only Rock 'n' Roll*. Looking back after twenty years on his decision to quit the Sex Pistols, Rotten summed up the group's failure, especially their horrific tour of the United States: "it had become a Rolling Stones affair."

PART

Frameworks

1

Like a Rolling Stone

A Community of Consumption

If you ask some people why they go for R&B you get pretentious answers. . . . For me it's merely the sound. . . . It doesn't express damn-all to me, really. . . . But I like the sound.

—Brian Jones

Mick Jagger and Keith Richards were occasional playmates as young children, growing up only two blocks from each other in Dartford, one of London's outermost suburbs. Both attended Wentworth County Primary School, and in some school photographs they stand near each other in their matching school uniforms. Richards remembers the uniforms vividly: "the cap, very strange contraption, like a skull-cap with a peak on it, school badge on the front. And a dark blazer with a badge on the breast pocket, a tie, and gray flannel trousers."[1] Richards despised the uniforms and everything they stood for: as a younger child he had liked to dress up as an American cowboy.

The English class system effectively separated the boys when they completed their primary education in 1954. Encouraged by his parents, Jagger passed the Eleven Plus examination, winning a place in grammar school and, with it, the possibility of a university education. Richards received a miserable score and was steered to Dartford's technical

school. Jagger's family moved to a more prestigious middle-class neighborhood, while the less affluent Richards family accepted a place in a
subsidized housing project, the dreary "council estates" of Spielman
Road. Six years passed before they talked to each other again. In the
summer of 1960, Richards bought an ice cream at an outdoor stand
staffed by Jagger. They acknowledged knowing each other, then
Richards left. The two youths seemed to have nothing in common
besides their distant childhood.

More than a year passed before they met once more. This time
they found themselves taking the same morning train to London.
This encounter was different, but not because Richards was carrying
his acoustic guitar. Richards identifies the spark that rekindled their
friendship:

> I get on this train one morning and there's Jagger and under his arm he has
> four or five albums. . . . He's got Chuck Berry and Little Walter, Muddy
> Waters. "You're into Chuck Berry, man, really?" That's a coincidence. He
> said, "Yeah, I got few more albums. Been writin' away to this, uh, Chess
> Records in Chicago." . . . So I invited him up to my place for a cup of tea.
> He started playing me these records and I really turned on to it.[2]

Richards renewed his friendship with Jagger because of those records.
One LP in that batch of Chess recordings gave Richards his first taste
of Muddy Waters: the 1958 compilation album *The Best of Muddy Waters*
included "Rolling Stone" and "I Just Want to Make Love to You." It
was not long before Jagger invited Richards to sit in with some friends
to recreate the Chicago electric blues they both loved. Still playing
together six months later, they went to see Alexis Korner and Blues
Incorporated at a West London jazz club and were impressed with the
Elmore James licks of a young slide guitarist who played on the same
bill. They soon convinced him to share their squalid Chelsea flat. With
the addition of Brian Jones, the Rolling Stones were a band in search
of a stable rhythm section.

At this point, Richards and Jagger had never seen a Muddy Waters
performance (Brian Jones had). Yet they became preoccupied with imitating the sound of his Chess recordings. We must credit the formation of the Rolling Stones to the role of recordings as the primary texts
of rock. Even after the basic quintet coalesced at the beginning of

1963, their early career was dominated by performing and recording cover versions of blues and R&B songs they learned from records, particularly tunes by Muddy Waters and Jimmy Reed. "When we started the Rolling Stones," Richards once observed, "our aim was to turn other people on to Muddy Waters."[3] Jagger and Richards felt that they'd really arrived as R&B musicians when Otis Redding and then Aretha Franklin cut cover versions of "(I Can't Get No) Satisfaction." Although he now denies it, one must imagine that Peter Green, another Brit bitten by the blues bug, experienced a similar sense of having arrived when "Black Magic Woman" became a signature tune for Carlos Santana, just as Jimmy Page must have been delighted when both King Curtis and Tina Turner covered "Whole Lotta Love," itself derived from Muddy Waters's version of Willie Dixon's "You Need Love."

All of this took place four decades ago, so long ago that the popular success of the British rhythm and blues explosion can easily be taken for granted, like the Allied victory in World War II or the possibility that a Hollywood actor could really be President of the United States. Elvis Presley, the Beatles, and Johnny Rotten get more historical attention than Mick Jagger and Keith Richards, in part because Mick and Keith are still at it, releasing new albums and taunting the public with yet another chance to see them before they retire.[4] Yet the success of such music, Peter Van Der Merwe observes, is "one of musical history's best jokes." Suppose you are a European musician and the year is 1900 rather than 2000: "If anyone had told you that the most potent musical force of the twentieth century was to be American gutter music, you would have doubted his sanity."[5]

Even within the context of the time, the early 1960s, the success of such music could not have been predicted. In 1963, the era of "Be My Baby" and "Blowin' in the Wind," it looked as if the main directions of popular music would be the studio craft of Phil Spector and Motown. Or, for the more bohemian crowd, it would be the acoustic authenticity of Bob Dylan and Joan Baez—or, on the radio, the smoother "folk" of Peter, Paul, and Mary, who actually had the popular hit with "Blowin' in the Wind." In 1964, everything changed. The musicians of the so-called British Invasion solidified a cluster of conventions for rock music and its performance that remain more or less intact: the band as unit of creativity, the charismatic lead singer, and the guitar as primary instrument. It is what we mean by "rock" music, for instance, in press reports that rock is losing ground to sales of pop and rap and country music.

But a second set of conventions arose within these: rock music is white music, rock performers are male, and rock songs express men's feelings, especially men's feelings about women. These generalizations are stereotypes, of course, but such stereotypes usually find their way into the official record: "Songs such as Muddy Waters's 'Rock Me' are pleas for comfort, for sanctuary in a cruel world. When they were taken over by the rock generation, they came to be about the domination of women, leading to the heavy metal threat to 'nail your ass to the floor.'"[6] The Rolling Stones were born too late to be accused of direct collusion with British colonialism and Victorian codes of sexuality, but in an emerging theoretical and historical revisionism, they risk becoming poster boys for everything reprehensible and reactionary in rock.

This book will often return to the Rolling Stones, but it is not a study of any one group. It examines some complex questions that have emerged in the wake of their astounding success and continuing appeal. In an era where popular music is understood to be a major source of identity, what sort of identity can that be? "There's nobody singing to me now," sings Richard Ashcroft in the Verve's "Bitter Sweet Symphony" (1997), a song constructed over a sample of a fragment of a melody by Jagger and Richards. When I first caught these words to "Bitter Sweet Symphony," I immediately flashed to the first Smiths song that showed me there was more to the Smiths than initially met my American ears. The song was "Panic" (1986), and what grabbed me was its absurd, repeated exhortation to "Hang the DJ" for constantly playing music that "says nothing to me about my life." What does it mean when I feel that the song on the radio does speak for me? How can the music made by someone else, someone like the Smiths' Morrissey, say anything to me about my life? And what does it mean to complain that it doesn't?

Like a Long Distance Call: Popular Music as Mass Art

We don't want to make a record that three-quarters of the world is going to snub their nose at just so I can jerk off and play guitar solos. The biggest thrill is driving around and hearing your song on the radio between Led Zeppelin and the Stones. That's what we fucking got in this for.

—Aerosmith's Joe Perry[7]

We don't want to be found only in the specialty bin at the record store. We want to be in your face.

—2 Nice Girls on being pigeonholed as "women's music"[8]

The meeting of Jagger and Richards on a train in 1961 reverberates with most of the major themes explored in this book. Although physically reunited by mass transit, their real connection was mass art. They lived in the same suburb but commuted to different schools in London, reflecting the different futures that English society had decided for them: Jagger was in his first year at the London School of Economics while Richards was in his third and final year at Sidcup Art College. Jagger had a Chuck Berry album, and Richards was a Chuck Berry fanatic. They both belonged to a select brotherhood of English blues fans, a very small fraternity united by a rabid appreciation of American music that was known almost exclusively from recordings. (The Stones' first manager, Giorgio Gomelsky, may not have been too far off in estimating that in 1960 only forty people in London were seriously interested in authentic blues.) As Richards sums it up, Jagger "had all these American records, flash son of a bitch, because he comes from a better side of town from me. It's the music I'm trying to listen to. I've got a few singles, but he's got the bloody albums."[9] It was not merely a question of cost; one of the most impressive things about the LPs under Jagger's arm was that they were simply not available in British shops. Jagger got the albums by writing directly to Chess Records in Chicago (an early Rolling Stones instrumental was named with the address, "2120 South Michigan Avenue"). Here was a serious blues fan, whose partnership with Richards is of continuing interest for the ways that their involvement with the blues would play a major role in creating another music, rock.

Rock is only one among many types of popular music to circulate in the twentieth century.[10] In all that follows, I assume that rock is historically rooted in a type of American popular music that came to international prominence in the 1950s: "rock 'n' roll, rock and other kinds of music, mostly derived from the music of one of the minority cultures in America, that have become part of and revolutionized the popular music scene in America."[11] But genealogy is not the whole story. It is equally important to understand that rock arose as mass art, and a distinction between popular art and mass art underlies the arguments that follow. Had rock not been distributed as mass art and had it remained the "people's art" celebrated by *Rock 'n' Roll Is Here to Pay*, it might join the popular music of India or Nigeria as topics for discussion by ethnomusicologists, but it would not be a central area of concern in cultural studies.[12]

Let us begin by comparing mass art with popular culture. Popular culture embraces every imaginable sort of cultural activity, from nursery rhymes to games to fast food to pornography to holiday celebrations. However, a cultural practice belongs to "popular" culture only in contrast to the cultural practices favored by a distinct, more privileged class. (A classless society does not have popular culture, although it almost certainly has folk art.) Thus, among sports currently found in the United States, we can identify basketball and hockey as belonging to popular culture, but not polo or rowing. Popular art is likewise the art of the masses—think here of line dancing contrasted with ballet—and some form of popular music is found in every society in which different sorts of music are identified with different classes.

In order to be popular, popular art must be both economically and cognitively accessible to most people in a given society. People with no specialized background will understand and appreciate a popular work "virtually without effort . . . almost on first contact."[13] In short, mass art must employ a familiar vernacular code. A new recording of J. S. Bach's "Goldberg Variations" costs roughly the same as a new release by the Beastie Boys or Mariah Carey—and back catalogue of Classical labels is usually cheaper than back catalogue of the Beatles and Led Zeppelin.

Yet cognitively, as something to grasp and appreciate, Bach's music is inaccessible to most people at the start of the twenty-first century. Unlike Bach's European contemporaries, relatively few people have the musical background to understand and appreciate the brilliance of Bach's keyboard variations. Bach is a popular composer, so far as classical music goes, but his music is not popular art. Kitsch-classical music by George Winston and Yanni is more "user friendly" and comes closer to counting as popular music.

Only some popular arts are also mass arts. Another necessary condition is the element of mass production. Besides economic and cognitive accessibility, a popular art form will not count as mass art unless it also exists within a framework of modern mass industrial production and is aimed at a far-flung audience: "Like the mass manufacture of automobiles, mass art is a form of mass production and distribution, designed to deliver a multiplicity of artworks to geographically remote mass consuming audiences. Mass art is the art of mass society, predicated on addressing mass audiences by means of the opportunities afforded by mass technologies."[14] To put it crudely, mass art exists only when members of the audience can interact with specific works even when they have no access to anything directly created by the artist responsible for the work. Access to the work comes through its mass reproduction. While on a road trip a thousand miles from home, one of my windshield wiper blades broke. Thanks to modern mass production and distribution of identical auto parts, in a few minutes I had a replacement on my car from the nearest auto parts store. In much the same way, when my wife wanted some new music for the tape player in the car, we found the nearest music store and quickly returned to the interstate, listening to the Lyle Lovett album that she wanted to hear.

What follows from recognizing that mass art is a special sort of popular art? There are at least four important consequences. First, an existing popular art can be transformed into a mass art when it is adapted to the demands of industrial mass technology. Thus, Jagger and Richards would not have been connected by the music of Muddy Waters that fateful day had Waters remained content to make *popular music;* he could have stayed on the Mississippi plantation, playing weekend dances with the occasional foray into nearby Clarksdale, Mississippi, to play on street corners. But Waters wanted to create *mass art*. He did not head north merely to be a professional musician; the Delta offered plenty of examples of such men. He went to Chicago because it held the promise of "opportunities to get into the big record field."[15] Mass art was the key to status, to being "a known person." "To get a name," Muddy Waters observed, "you got to get a record. People lived right up under me [in Chicago], they didn't know who I was until I got a record out. Then they say, 'He live right there!'—got to get a record."[16] Through his recordings, he became known far beyond Stovall's plantation or Fourth Street in nearby Clarksdale. Two decades later, his sound enthralled two English teens in a London suburb.

The second consequence is that mass art can be simultaneously accessible to geographically remote individuals. Its "spatial mobility" and rapid diffusion *creates* rather than *expresses* community.[17] Among the budding Rolling Stones, only Brian Jones had seen Muddy Waters perform live. Jones was even allowed to sit in with the blues legend on one of his forays to England because Jones already knew the music from the records. But at this point Jones did not yet know Jagger or Richards, and the latter pair would not see Chuck Berry and Muddy Waters in the flesh until they arrived at Chess Records in Chicago for two days of recording in June 1964. On the day Jagger and Richards met on the train, they lived on opposite sides of the same town, separated by class more effectively than by geography. Jones lived nearly a hundred miles from London, in the resort town of Cheltenham. Yet before they came together in the same place to make music together, and before they came face to face with the musical models they emulated, the three already participated in a common mass audience. Their "common ground," Richards remembers, "was Elmore James and Muddy Waters."[18] Ironically, when Jagger and Richards finally met Muddy Waters, they arrived at Chess Studios to record "It's All Over Now" only to find that the man painting the studio ceiling was their hero.

The same process that informed the musical sensibilities of Richards, Jagger, and Jones is at work today, only on a more massive scale. After hundreds of thousands of ethnic Albanians fled the war in Kosovo in the late spring and early summer of 1999, massive refugee camps were assembled in Albania and Macedonia. Once the refugees' most basic needs were satisfied, relief workers faced the question of how to occupy the refugees' time. Among other ventures, Relief International provided the Albanian camps with a karaoke machine and some forty karaoke CDs. When the machine arrived in one of the camps, many of the delighted refugees demanded to know which Elton John songs were available.[19]

Many musicologists still believe in the superiority of classical music, rooted in its autonomy. ("Classical" is here used in the everyday sense of being music typical of the European concert, opera, and liturgical traditions.) That is, they think that classical music is better than popular music because the appeal of the former is "timeless," purely musical, and independent of the social situation of the audience. But wouldn't mass art, whose very existence is predicated on distribution to diverse audiences and across gaps of space and time, have a stronger claim to autonomy than classical?[20]

A third consequence is that a work of mass art is radically different in kind from the "works" or artistic products of traditional art forms like oil paintings and sculpture. The creations of mass art are meant to be distributed to audiences as *multiple* instances. Geographically separated individuals can read different copies of the same book, see different prints of the same film, and listen to different copies of the same recording. But unless a copy contains errors of some sort, each copy gives equal access to the same work. While a CD has better sound quality than a cassette or most files downloaded from the Internet, a CD copy of Madonna's *Music* or *The Immaculate Collection* is no more genuine or authentic than a black market cassette copy or an MP3 file. This situation contrasts sharply with such artworks as Titian's *Madonna with Rabbit* (painted in 1530). If one wants to experience that painting, one has to go to the one and only place where the genuine instance can be found. With traditional patterns of culture, the audience quite literally converges on the art. With mass art, the art makes its way to the audience.

With mass art, the audience does not respond to what artists directly create. This gap is not just a time gap between the process of production and the moment of reception. The gap is more radical: in mass art, artists create types but audiences interact with tokens.[21] Opening my wallet I find some dollar bills. Any of these slips of paper is as much a dollar bill as any other. They are all tokens or instances of the same thing, provided that we understand that that "same thing" is really a type of thing. "The" dollar bill is a denomination of money. Because it is not identical with any specific physical object, "the" dollar bill continues to exist so long as there is a legitimate process for generating new tokens. Thus, individual tokens may be destroyed, as when my brother borrowed my vinyl copy of Neil Young's *Zuma* and then left it in a car on a hot day. It became too warped to play. Yet the musical achievement, *Zuma*, was not destroyed. *Zuma* is a type of thing, but audiences know it through its concrete instances or tokens.

Rather obviously, mass art is not the only sphere of art in which we can distinguish the work, as a type, from its instances or tokens. Any kid who's ever suffered through "Kumbayah" or "Michael Row the Boat Ashore" during a sing-along understands what it means to produce a new token of an existing type. Here, the tokens are *performances* or individual interpretations of a basic type. With performances, each new token interjects further interpretation of the type. I might sing "Here we are now, entertain us" to find out if you know Nirvana's "Smells Like Teen Spirit," but this produces a token of a fragment of the song and not another token of Nirvana's *Nevermind*. *Nevermind* is an album and not just a set of songs. As mass art, instances of *Nevermind* are created and distributed through mass technologies, involving a multistage production and distribution process.

To be genuine instances of works of mass art, end-product tokens (the tokens that consumers pay to experience) must be physically derived from an appropriate first-stage object or template responsible for the physical characteristics of the end-products. Genuine tokens of a mass art—the film *Jailhouse Rock* or a CD of Neil Young's *Zuma*—must be derived by mechanical or electronic transfer from some original master.[22] The sounds that actually reach our ears may be many times removed from their source. Until digital sound became the norm, many fans shared music through home taping, a transfer technique that ensured a deterioration of sound quality with each transfer. Nonetheless, every copy remained an equally genuine instance of the same artistic creation. An original, physically embodied sequence of digital coding is the source of all the CDs, vinyl copies, digital downloads, and cassettes of digitally recorded music. But the end-products are the products of a technological process, and the resulting music is played on machines rather than performed. If you choose to sing the song "Jailhouse Rock" in the shower, it's no more Elvis than reciting lines from one of his movies while in the shower would be a piece of cinema. One person can tell others about a movie or sing them a song learned from a recording, but neither of these activities provides a genuine instance of the text in the way that reciting a poem can.[23]

The distinction between mass art and other art forms with multiple instances implies that when Brian Jones first saw a performance by Muddy Waters, he was experiencing popular music but not mass art. Live performance of popular music is not itself a case of mass art.[24] Similarly, the original Broadway production of the musical *Grease* was not mass art. The 1978 film version, with John Travolta and Olivia Newton-John, is mass art. So is the soundtrack recording that continues to sell a steady pace. A concert performance by the Rolling Stones is not mass art, while their appearances on the *Ed Sullivan Show* and in their many videos are mass art. This point would hardly be worth emphasizing were it not for the fourth consequence of recognizing that mass art is a special sort of popular art.

A fourth consequence is that whether something is mass art is not, like popularity, a matter of degree. *Actual* popularity is not a prerequisite for a piece of popular art to count as mass art, and Madonna is no more a mass artist than Anne Richmond Boston (whose name will ring few bells). Vocalist for the Swimming Pool Q's, Richmond Boston first appeared on records about the same time as Madonna. Richmond Boston may be a footnote to rock history, but she is no less a mass artist for that fact. Rock is mass art because it is a specific tradition of music making that employs technologies of mass media and *is intended for* a mass audience, and not because it actually succeeds by being appreciated by large numbers of people who are geographically remote from one another and from the artist. Thus any music falling within this tradition is mass art, even if it reaches few places and few people.

Failed mass distribution has been the bane of many a struggling rock artist. The Velvet Underground were livid when they got good reviews in the rock press for their third album, *The Velvet Underground* (1969), and then found that record stores were not receiving the copies they ordered from MGM. Little Feat had exactly the same experience with Warner Bros. Records when promoting their self-titled debut album. Other times the music is in the stores but audiences do not respond. One could easily find albums by the Swimming Pool Q's, Let's Active, and the Fleshtones in record stores throughout the United States during the 1980s, but their music did not fit the prevailing radio formats, they didn't break through on MTV, and their sales went nowhere. Their recorded music is mass art anyway.

The history of rock is strewn with influential musicians who never gained the mass audience they sought. Prominent cases include Richard Hell and the Ramones. As the musicians who initially defined punk at the start of the punk era, both Hell and the Ramones *wanted* to reach an audience and were puzzled to find that their aesthetic choices alienated most rock fans. Hell (Richard Meyers) went so far as to self-publish a poetry magazine in order to create a forum for the poems he and a friend, Tom Miller, were writing. He gave up after four issues: "it felt very futile. I wanted to shake up the world. I wanted to make noise, but nobody reads.... I could see reading could be very boring if you weren't conditioned to enjoy it.... About 1972–73 we decided we were going to make a band."[25]

Seeking an audience, Hell had found that his poetry was doubly inaccessible. Self-publishing is not an efficient means of mass distribution, and poetry is not user friendly for most Americans in the late twentieth century. Inspired by 1960s garage bands and by the New York Dolls and the Stooges, Hell and Miller formed the Dead Boys. Two years later, with Miller rechristened Tom Verlaine, they formed Television; convincing the seedy Manhattan club CBGBs to give them a regular Sunday gig, they created a venue for Blondie, Talking Heads, and the other bands that formed a core of the New York punk scene. Then, like Muddy Waters some thirty years before, they all sought record deals that would make them known.

In contrast to Hell and Verlaine, the Ramones always knew that mass art was the way to go. They saw themselves as pop musicians, peers of Aerosmith and Kiss, rather than as avant-garde or underground artists. Their early performances revealed the limitation that forced them to play only their own material: they hadn't been playing very long and they weren't very proficient technicians. The Ramones shopped a demo tape to record companies but found it difficult to sustain serious interest once talent scouts saw them play. But they kept trying, eventually securing a record deal with Sire. When albums one through three got them raves from the press but little else, they tried to get on the radio with a remake of an oldie, "Needles and Pins." But *Road to Ruin* (1978) sold only marginally better than its predecessor, and vocalist Joey Ramone complained bitterly about their situation: "I'm *sick* of not selling records. I want to draw more people to the shows, make *something* happen." Guitarist Johnny Ramone was equally puzzled by their lack of mass acceptance: "we try to be entertaining and bring back the feeling of kids coming and having a good time."[26]

The Ramones made records and sought a mass audience, and so made mass art. But they were something more: they were musicians within the mass art *tradition*. They saw themselves as squarely within the tradition of the early Beatles: their haircuts were Beatle cuts, their leather jackets hark to the Beatles' dress code before Brian Epstein cleaned them up, and the name "Ramon" was a pseudonym used by Paul McCartney when he checked into hotels. The extreme stereo separation of early Beatles recordings served as the model for the sound mix on the first Ramones album. Another pivotal inspiration for their career was a specific product of mass art, *Nuggets* (1972), an anthology of 1960s garage rock compiled by Lenny Kaye. In turn, most of the bands represented on *Nuggets* were copying previous mass art, in this case the harder sounds of the British Invasion, particularly the Stones and the Yardbirds. Those British artists were, in their formative period, influenced by the mass art products of American electrified blues. The Ramones, surprisingly, owe a debt to Muddy Waters.

Generalizing, mass art is the dominant mode in which rock artists produce and distribute their music. Only a tiny fraction of it ever reaches a genuinely mass audience. One study examined the sales of ninety thousand different titles over three years in the 1990s. Just over two-thirds of the ninety thousand sold less than a thousand copies. So how does the music industry make a profit? From the tiny handful of best-selling releases: 72 percent of sales came from 3 percent of those titles.[27]

Whether we consider the Ramones or Metallica or Madonna, the music's status as mass art depends on its distribution through mass media. In contrast, its status as rock music depends on its genealogy. Similarly, physical accessibility for the mass audience depends on recording the music, while cognitive accessibility requires some fidelity to widely familiar forms. Tensions created by the twin features of accessibility and geographic disbursement will emerge as major issues of Part Two and Part Three.

Not Fade Away: Phonographic Influence

All the albums I ever liked were albums that delivered a great song, one after another. Aerosmith's *Rocks*, the Sex Pistols' *Never Mind the Bollocks*, *Led Zeppelin II*, *Back in Black*, by AC/DC.
—Nirvana's Kurt Cobain[28]

The question of ancestry in culture is spurious. Every new manifestation in culture rewrites the past, changes old maudits into new heroes, old heroes into those who should have never been born. . . . But in all times forgotten actors emerge from the past not as ancestors but as familiars.
—Greil Marcus[29]

One of the most important features of commercially recorded music is that later generations have access to the very same texts that were produced for the original audience. Of course, works are sometimes lost when no copies are preserved. But when music takes the form of mass art and tokens are preserved and circulated, we have continuous access to that music without the obscuring intervention of additional artistic interpretation. "What's the point in listening to us doing 'I'm a King Bee,'" Jagger mused, "when you can listen to Slim Harpo doing it?"[30] Part of the pleasure, of course, is that we can compare the two versions. We can determine for ourselves what is slavishly imitated and what is freshly interpreted. Jagger may have felt inadequate in comparison to Muddy Waters and Slim Harpo, but in hindsight we can appreciate the cultural difference.

Significantly, these blues sources are not just reference points for appreciating the Rolling Stones. They continue to circulate as music in their own right: the recordings that so excited Mick Jagger and Keith Richards continue to circulate, inspiring others. P. J. Harvey's *To Bring You My Love* (1995) comes to mind as a recent updating of the Chess sound. Of course, this phenomenon has been crucial to the development of hip-hop, as tracks are constructed around samples of older music; old tracks by Sly and the Family Stone, Ann Peebles, James Brown, and Roberta Flack are suddenly relevant again. Stetsasonic weren't kidding when their lyrics boasted that "Rap brings back old R&B."

If hip-hop tends to use the technology of sampling when recycling the tradition, white rock musicians tend to use cover versions. Even after the Rolling Stones developed into a self-sufficient group writing their own material, their albums continued to feature songs they learned from recordings. They seem to have acted with considerable deliberation, with one per album, to remind listeners of their sources. *Beggars Banquet* (1968) has the Reverend Robert Wilkins's "Prodigal Son." Yazoo Records immediately returned the favor by issuing a Wilkins collection entitled *The Original Rolling Stone*. *Let It Bleed* (1969) has Robert Johnson's "Love in Vain" (wrongly credited to someone named "Payne"). *Sticky Fingers* (1971) has Mississippi Fred McDowell's "You Gotta Move." *Exile on Main Street* (1972) returns to Robert Johnson for "Stop Breaking Down" (again miscredited). Breaking the pattern with *Goats Head Soup* (1973), the Stones resumed the practice of placing one classic blues or rhythm and blues cover on each of their next three studio albums, and then again on *Dirty Work* (1986). Their generally soporific live album from 1977, *Love You Live*, is redeemed only by its four cover tunes, all drawn from the same club performance in Toronto. Once again, they returned to their roots with Muddy Waters, Bo Diddley, Slim Harpo, and Chuck Berry.

As in the case of the parlor game of identifying samples, tracing cover versions to their sources can also reveal a good deal about an artist's own experience with mass art, providing the audience with a framework and context for understanding the music. Consider the Cowboy Junkies' lovely *The Trinity Sessions* (1988), especially their haunting cover of Lou

Reed's "Sweet Jane," brought to the attention of a larger audience by its inclusion in Trent Reznor's soundtrack to *Natural Born Killers* (1994). The soft, wistful song is something of an oddity on a soundtrack album dominated by techno, hip-hop, and rap, and many buyers must have wondered about its inclusion. Those with longer memories already knew it to be a Lou Reed song. Thus, more specific questions arose. Was that the Cowboy Junkies' own arrangement of the song? And where did they get those lyrics, credited to Lou Reed?

The song's first appearance was the Velvet Underground's *Loaded* (1970). But some of the words sung by Margo Timmons are not to be found there, and the arrangement is quite different. Lou Reed's subsequent recordings of the song, on *Rock n Roll Animal* (1974) and *Live in Italy* (1984), follow the Loaded arrangement and lyrics. Yet there is no great mystery. Like any Velvets aficionado, Margo and her brothers went to the Velvet's posthumous release *1969 Velvet Underground Live* (1974), where we find all of the lyrics—together with the tempo and the distinctive "wine and roses" segment—of the Cowboy Junkies' version. Played back to back, the resemblance is striking, right down to the ambiance of the recorded sound. But within a year of incorporating the song into the Velvets' live show, Reed began to push the tempo of "Sweet Jane," and the "wine and roses" segment was chopped from the recorded song when Reed quit the band before *Loaded* was finished.

The Cowboy Junkies' source is clear. We found it by following a trail of vinyl (now preserved on compact discs). Each marker along the trail is a creation of mass art. (If Margo Timmons did not learn it from *1969 Velvet Underground Live*, whoever taught it to her certainly did.) Mott the Hoople, on the other hand, did not have the 1969 live recording available when they cut "Sweet Jane" for *All the Young Dudes* (1972). Mott took *Loaded* for their text.[31] In turn, both Mott's version and *Loaded* were sources for the arrangement used by Lone Justice when they toured with U2 in the early 1980s. As Maria McKee traded verses with Bono, she preserved the phrase "all you protest kids" that Mott's Ian Hunter deleted; meanwhile, lead guitarist Tony Gilkyson drew from the Mott the Hoople arrangement, supplying Mick Ralph's signature guitar line on the chorus. Yet by singing a Velvet Underground song with Bono, Lone Justice acknowledged a common and perhaps surprising source of inspiration. McKee could thus erase the audience's questions about Lone Justice's obvious stylistic differences from U2 and "modern rock."

There is nothing elusive about any of this. Both professional and amateur rock musicians become acquainted with the music by listening to it rather than by reading a score.[32] In this very limited respect, rock falls within an "oral/aural tradition" in a way that classical music does not. The standard theoretical options of notated and oral traditions should be supplemented with a third category, that of phonographically aural music.[33]

These points are offered in the hope that they will curb the tendency to treat mass art as just another mode of oral tradition. Earlier generations of popular musicians learned their techniques directly and personally from their predecessors, whose music then gave way to the next generation's "rereading." All sorts of contingencies prompt performers to introduce variations into the tradition, constantly updating it. Lacking any independent record of their practices, the oral tradition continually obliterates its past: constantly erasing the distinction between original and imitation, songs within an oral tradition have no standard or authentic versions.

In oral tradition, anything irrelevant to the present "simply falls away."[34] As a result of this artistic amnesia, the reconstructed history of an oral tradition is largely speculation. Such is the case with the early history of jazz and blues. These oral traditions may be the roots of rock, but they are precisely what *mass* art replaces. The conversion from folk tradition to mass art generates a very different form of cultural memory, in which our documentation of a "frozen" past comes back to haunt us in the guise of authenticity. Harry Smith's *Anthology of American Folk Music* (1952, reissued 1997) features a moving country-blues performance of "Expressman Blues" by Sleepy John Estes. There is an obvious influence of the sound of Memphis jug band music in this 1930 recording, but this is dance music from a Mississippi juke joint, played by a trio of piano, mandolin, and guitar. Muddy Waters recalled the many times he played the Delta blues backed by mandolin and violin, but the only recorded evidence comes from his second performance at a microphone, on Stovall's plantation as a member of the Son Simms Four in 1942 ("Ramblin' Kid Blues" and "Rosalie" in particular). He embraced electric guitar when he went to Chicago and found that he needed more volume to cut through the din of urban clubs.[35] Yet how many blues fans—particularly fans of recent blues music—think of a mandolin as an authentic blues instrument? Thus Keb' Mo', multiple winner in the acoustic blues category of the W. C. Handy Blues Awards, poses for publicity photographs while embracing his resonator guitar. Keb' Mo' certainly knows that a mandolin would be just as authentic, but he cannot yet risk confusing the general audience he hopes to attract.

Rather than continually rewrite the past, mass art tends to confuse its own history with the continuing presence of past work. Advertisements for albums like *Pure Funk, Heavy Metal Ballads,* and *Solid Gold Disco* hawk 1970s popular hits during commercials between music videos on cable television. Meanwhile, shows like VH1's *Behind the Music* revitalize the careers of bands like Fleetwood Mac and Lynyrd Skynyrd. In the British pop charts of 1976, the Sex Pistols competed with both the Bay City Rollers and decade-old Beatles singles; in 1997, the Spice Girls competed in the same charts with compilations of 1970s disco and reggae music and a new European compilation of Bob Dylan's greatest hits. Dylan had a tremendous influence on musicians in the 1960s, but Dylan's recordings are still there thirty years later, influencing Beck. So are the 1960s recordings of Mance Lipscomb. If Beck's sideburns (circa 1996) recall rockabilly (circa 1955), it turns out that Elvis Presley's appeal is not just to aging baby-boomers; the Cranberries' Delores O'Riordan became hooked on both Elvis and Patsy Cline when she was twelve. Presley was ten years dead, Cline more than twenty. As popular music is disseminated through recordings, linear change gives way to an endless series of epicycles.

Since before the music was called "rock and roll," rock musicians learned and perfected their art by studying records. If Delores O'Riordan learned to sing by accompanying records, so did Elvis. Elvis's Sun recordings are one and all adapted from his close study of specific records, and the vocal nuances of many of his early RCA hits were "practically an exact copy" of Otis Blackwell's demo recordings of the songs.[36] So the rock aesthetic is fundamentally a mass art aesthetic: its products are created for mass distribution, the musicians themselves rely on mass art for their models, and the audience understands these products in light of other mass art. When John Lydon auditioned to be singer for the Sex Pistols, he did so by standing in front of a jukebox and screeching along to an Alice Cooper record.

Such patterns of musical influence could not occur in a genuinely oral tradition. Why did the Beatles, from Liverpool, have broader rock 'n' roll roots than similar musicians in England's capital and industrial heartland? The most plausible explanation is that the economy of Liverpool was more closely tied to the port and so there was greater access to the latest hit records from America, regularly brought home by merchant seamen. Although attending school in London, Mick Jagger had to send away to the United States to get the recordings he wanted. While both the Beatles and the Rolling Stones filled their early performances with cover versions of American recordings, the Beatles' set list included few straight blues tunes. The members of the Beatles, poorer and less sophisticated, had to rely on whatever turned up in Liverpool itself. So their sources tended to be more overtly commercial than were the Chess recordings that interested Jagger and Richards. We can date the Beatles' live Hamburg recording as late December 1962 because some of the songs they're performing had only just been released and become American (but not British) hits. The Rolling Stones were seldom so current in their choices.

Yet through a trail of recordings, the music played by the Beatles in their formative years traces back to some of the country blues sources used by the Stones. Carl Perkins happened to join the Beatles in the studio when they recorded his "Matchbox Blues," but Perkins did not have to show them how to play it. It was already in their performing repertoire in Hamburg—they were copying Perkins's 1956 rockabilly hit. Perkins, in turn, had adapted the song from Blind Lemon Jefferson's 1927 recording, or possibly from Larry Henseley's 1934 copy of Jefferson.

Growing up in Belfast, Van Morrison got started in much the same way. Like Liverpool, Belfast was a busy port where the latest American recordings were readily available. Van's father George, an electrician employed at the local shipyard, had traveled in the United States and was interested in many things American, including the singing of Muddy Waters and Mahalia Jackson. The elder Morrison supplemented his purchases of popular jazz with a small collection of American folk and blues recordings that could be ordered through a Belfast record shop that specialized in jazz. Observing his son's response to the imported music, George Morrison bought Van an acoustic guitar and instruction book, *The Carter Family Style*. Van Morrison relates that he "grabbed as many Leadbelly and [Woody] Guthrie and Hank Williams records as I could and tried to learn something." Their recordings "made me start singing."[37] Abandoning school at fifteen, he was a professional musician at sixteen, playing saxophone in a "show" band. His early Them recording of "Baby Please Don't Go" (1964) became the opening theme of *Ready Steady Go* and thus became a staple of British Invasion bands, only to be revived again in the 1990s by figuring prominently in the David Lynch film *Wild at Heart*. Van Morrison's source is a version cut by John Lee Hooker for Chess Records in 1952. Others in the British blues movement learned the song from *Muddy Waters at Newport, 1960*. In the United States it was something of a Delta blues standard, popularized by Big Joe Williams (from whom Waters, uncharacteristically, learned it firsthand when Williams performed at Stovall's plantation). Williams, in turn, had rewritten and renamed "Don't You Leave Me Here," a song he'd learned from a 1927 recording.[38]

But if Van Morrison could connect himself with the primitive authority of another tradition by covering "Baby Please Don't Go," and *Ready Steady Go* could use Them's recording to convey an awareness of the contemporary pulse, and then a David Lynch film can use the same recording to generate nostalgic associations, it begins to look as if mass art is as unstable as the oral tradition it replaces. Such arguments are my next concern.

2

Don't Let Me Be Misunderstood: Issues of Meaning

Don't Look Back: Musical History and Identity

What we hear a Tyrolean peasant singing, into which seemingly no trace of art penetrates, is artistic music through and through.

—Eduard Hanslick

You can't have lived your life in a musical void; it's impossible.

—R.E.M.'s Mike Mills

Unfamiliar music cannot be understood unless it is positioned against other, already familiar music.[1] Eduard Hanslick realized well over a century ago that every piece of music reflects a specific tonal system, and so there is no such thing as genuinely primitive music. Rock's abrasive noise becomes music only to appreciative listeners, that is, listeners for whom rock sounds like a "natural" musical language. To listen from within a tradition is to adjust one's listening to the kind of music heard, to hear it in terms of appropriate listening habits, and to listen imaginatively, with the expectations or imaginative projections appropriate to the style of music in question.[2] In sociological terms, such listening requires participation in a specific musical culture, demanding distinct cultural capital.[3]

Listening to the Rolling Stones or the Sex Pistols with understanding demands rather different cultural capital than listening to Wagner's *Parsifal* or *Lohengrin* with understanding. Perhaps the rock music is easier to understand. Nonetheless, spending a rewarding hour with rock music demands considerably more cultural capital than an hour playing jump rope or the card game Go Fish. The situation is *not* that classical music yields its pleasures only to those who acquire the right cultural capital, with no cultural capital needed to enjoy rock. No music is meaningful or valuable except in light of appropriate cultural capital. As Patricia Herzog puts it, musical meaning "exists in an intentional space created by the critical or evaluative interests of the listener."[4] The phrasing, intonation, instrumentation, and other aesthetic properties of a musical performance are meaningful only to those for whom such features *matter*. Music's significance and value are functions of its use by appropriately knowledgeable listeners.

None of this is to suggest that value distinctions play no role in the continuing power and interest of central figures, such as the Rolling Stones. For if we were to repudiate all value distinctions (if our rejoinder to every value judgment is "Who are you to say it's no good?"), the resulting "democracy" would render music meaningless. Every dismissal is a proposal that something else merits our attention. We don't judge music against an ideal standard of good music, but against other music actually made and heard. The same principle holds for interpretation. We grasp the meaning of musical activity only by reference to other music actually made and heard.

By way of illustration, someone who thinks that Elvis Presley was a no-talent pretty boy who ripped off African American music for personal gain—in short, someone who regards Elvis as of negative value—is not in a position to regard the rockabilly explosion of the 1950s as an intelligent, meaningful expression of white Southern culture. Among other things, that response misses Elvis's profound debt to "white" country music, something he never hid. His early singles on Sun Records were evenly divided between cover versions of "black" and "white" songs.

Yet Public Enemy advances the simplistic Elvis-as-rip-off-artist position. In "Fight the Power" (1989), they dismiss Presley as "Straight-up racist that sucker was simple and plain." They insist that *their* activity is not to be assimilated to the standard rock tradition. Public Enemy wants to make it clear that they reject the integrationist impulses of Run-D.M.C., whose "Rock Box" (1984) mixed rap and metal—paving the way for the Beastie Boys—and whose cover of Aerosmith's "Walk This Way" (1986) paved the way for Aerosmith's second coming. Of course, the success of the "Walk This Way" cover depended on audience perception of the respective races of the participants. Immensely successful from 1973 through 1978 with a hard rock sound that reminded everyone of the Rolling Stones, Aerosmith fell on hard times both critically and commercially when guitarist Joe Perry left to attempt a solo career. Perry soon returned to the fold, but the band seemed to be little more than a live oldies act when Run-D.M.C. reached back more than a decade for a cover song and then, in an inspired move, invited its originators to join them on the remake. If the presence of Steve Tyler and Joe Perry made rap palatable to white consumers who were suspicious of the form, then their pairing with two originators of hard-core rap gave Tyler and Perry a credibility that they'd long since squandered. At the same time, Public Enemy's rejection of white rock only works to the extent that Chuck D can assume that the audience has a superficial idea of Elvis. If Public Enemy excludes what Run-D.M.C. embraces, both strategies succeed only because a certain musical history can be taken for granted, as known by a sizeable portion of those who'll hear it.

So we arrive at a sort of crossroads. Musicians project an identity by situating themselves in relation to other musicians. Listeners derive meaning and value from popular music by contributing cultural capital to the process—which seems to imply that their own identity as members of a certain audience depends on the ability of others to employ cultural capital situating them properly. For both musicians and audience, the construction of a meaningful identity demands a historical perspective on the music as a dialogue with the past, not just with the present scene. But with mass art, there is no stability in the process. No cultural capital is common throughout the audience. Historical perspective is often lacking, or seriously misguided. Meanings aren't contested so much as muddled, lost, misunderstood. The Sex Pistols supposedly represent that moment when rock became complex and self-conscious enough to destabilize the popular music mainstream, creating a space in popular music for expressing a radically alternative identity.[5] But as mass art, floating free of English society circa 1976, what coherent mainstream continues to frame and sustain the meaning of "Anarchy in the U.K." or "God Save the Queen"? In short, I want to explore what it means to be an appropriately knowledgeable listener of rock music.

If You See It as Male or Female: Open-Ended Meaning

You're not pushing it too far, you're just making it *specific*. And you're making it specific to what's going on today. But what's going on today isn't gonna last, you know?

—Bob Dylan responding to Kurt Loder's interpretation of a song[6]

A lot of Dylan's work, the music was writing the words. But there's meaning there, too—a lot of meaning. . . . People are just being lazy if they can't find meaning in words like that. Be creative! I don't want to fill out the picture. You fill in the blanks. That's the way it should be.

—Beck[7]

Attributions of influence are important, I have suggested, because rock musicians are themselves fans who study and imitate recordings. By situating a piece of music against a backdrop of such influences, listeners have a surer grasp of a musician's musical intentions. Yet influences are not the same thing as a coherent community. As Deena Weinstein rightly observes when defending heavy metal against its abuse from critics, "it [is] no longer fair for critics to assume a community with shared standards to which they [can] contribute enlightenment."[8] Recorded music fractures space and time: virtually identical sounds emerge again and again, at practically any time or place. Yet the sheer profusion of recorded music works against there being any consistent, integrated core that is shared by everyone who participates. Without the backdrop of a stable community and common musical tradition, musicians have little basis for predicting how different listeners will respond to their efforts.

While the gap between authorial intention and audience comprehension bedevils all performers, few have articulated it as directly as members of the Los Angeles punk band X. On the one hand, John Doe discovered, it was difficult to attract an audience because "people didn't want to know about what we were talking about." On the other hand, "I've seen too many nineteen and twenty year old boys—men, boy-men—going like this [raised fist pumped in the air] during 'Johny Hit and Run Paulene' and don't understand that it's an anti-rape song. And they're like into it for the wrong reasons. So we don't play that any more."[9]

Employing techniques of realist literature and beat poetry, X's tactic of holding a mirror up to Los Angeles did not have the intended effect of inviting critical self-reflection. Exene Cervenka, Doe's then wife and partner in X, locates much of the problem in an audience that wanted its music to serve as little more than a badge of subcultural identity: "At some point the audiences went from being relatively intelligent and understanding, interesting people to kind of scary young kids who like to spit at the bands a lot, who wielded chains and beat up people who had long hair and it became kind of a war between what was and this new hardcore scene. . . . It gave punk a bad name."[10] But punk already had a bad name, and the American masses largely ignored it.

Ignorant of X's literary influences, the emerging hardcore audience assumed that X was celebrating them in its portraits of misogyny and casual racism. Seeking a confirmation of identity in the music, misogynist "boy-men" found what they sought. They simply did not experience the tensions that X intended to create by combining the music (rooted in Chuck Berry and rockabilly) with verbal portrayals of the sordid side of Southern California (heavily influenced by beat literature). If such bands hoped to serve as an antidote to the smooth, "inauthentic" Southern California sound that dominated FM radio at the time, the final irony must be that the Eagles' "Hotel California" and "Life in the Fast Lane" are still features of "classic rock" radio. It remains an open question whether most listeners have understood the Eagles' message, which is not so different from that of X's *Los Angeles* (1980).

Why is it so difficult for musicians to send a clear message to the audience? Do we take the easy way out and simply grant that the music's identity and meaning is infinitely plastic, taking on whatever interpretation an audience presses on it? Peter Manuel endorses a version of this position when he examines a relatively simple Bob Marley song, "Small Axe" (1969).[11] Urging upright living, Marley's song alternates two verses and a chorus, repeating the second verse three times. The verses highlight the general theme that we reap what we sow. The chorus advises that a small axe will cut down a big tree if the axe is sharp enough. Set to a chugging mid-tempo reggae pulse, the sketchy lyric has much the quality of a fable. One can almost hear the moral at the end (if at first you don't succeed . . .).

Trying to dig beneath the shallow surface of "Small Axe," Manuel links Marley's Rastafarian beliefs with Jamaica's political climate at the time. He concludes that the lyric "lent itself" to an overtly utopian political message. Several of Marley's biographers read it in a far more mundane way, as a warning from producer Lee Perry to the three larger record companies that dominated Jamaica's music scene. Whichever reading was originally intended for this elliptical lyric, "By the late 1990s we are in a different world order, in which Jamaica's heady aspirations to economic autonomy have been definitively quashed. . . . With the changing milieu comes a new hermeneutic, reflected by the interpretation of 'Small Axe' insisted upon by one Jamaican student, that the song referred to 'a man in bed with a big woman.' "

Almost every conjoining of dance music to an elliptical lyric, Manuel observes, leads to "ribald (mis)reading of the text." But a sharp deviation from authorial intention has "a certain legitimacy" when the reading "coheres to extant interpretive norms." In other words, different audiences approach the text in terms of their own interpretive framework. If they can make sense of it from within that framework, their reading is no better than the reading of someone employing a different framework, *even if these frameworks differ from the ones governing interpretation in the musical community of the originating musician.*

In order to regard a range of interpretations as equally legitimate, Manuel asks us to set aside two of our most basic pragmatic principles for interpreting any communication. The first principle is that each choice reflected in a text is relevant to its meaning. The second principle is that the relevance of a specific choice requires seeing it as the decision of a historically placed individual. The latter principle requires us to approach each text against a horizon of others produced by the same historically and culturally located group. Ignorance about a song's originating context will generate misreading of the specific message or distinctive identity that the song is designed to convey.[12]

Manuel asks us to dodge the question of which musical community has the original and thus "definitive" framework for interpreting a song correctly. He secures a plurality of reasonable interpretations by positioning every interpretation within a coherent local community and its norms. But that community may be the listener's community rather than the music's originating community.[13] Responding as others respond is the basis for legitimacy. The individual who responds to the message and finds an identity in music only does so through group conformity. To discover an identity that no one else finds is to misunderstand the music. This seems rather peculiar to me. It suggests that even when I respond to commercial music as a reflection of my own identity, that identity isn't mine if it's genuinely personal or idiosyncratic. Suppose I interpret Marley's "Small Axe" in more or less the political way that it struck his Jamaican contemporaries, but my own contemporaries hear it as a sexual metaphor. Although I will respond to Marley's intentions, my interpretation will be idiosyncratic and therefore illegitimate within Manuel's principles of legitimate "reading."

I want to suggest something rather different, avoiding both the suggestion of "legitimate (mis)reading" and the belief that reference to communal norms is sufficient to distinguish plausible readings from incorrect ones. My suggestion is that the original situation of the mass art already implies that multiple interpretations will be equally legitimate, and this indeterminacy of meaning arises because fans are individuals and not just members of a semantic community. Granted, song lyrics sung in a natural language will have relatively clear meaning, because there are basic semantic norms within linguistic communities. To be fair to popular music, its lyrics also contain a fair amount of nonsense, from Little Richard's "Awopbopaloobop" to Otis Redding's "Fa Fa Fa Fa Fa" to the screams punctuating so many of Nirvana's performances—not that such nonsense is without meaning. But nothing of this sort happens with "Small Axe" or "Johny Hit and Run Paulene."

I want to explore the indeterminacy that arises because products of mass art are relatively permanent objects that provide multiple playbacks (e.g., cassette tapes, CDs, records), created to appeal to audiences who remain otherwise remote from their originating contexts. They are designed for a geographically dispersed audience and they are designed to accommodate *future* audiences. They are, in short, *intended* for audiences who cannot be expected to share a common framework for interpreting them. As E. D. Hirsch puts it, the artistic decision to work within a certain media entails that the communication "refuses to fix itself in its originating moment." The artist's intention is open-ended. It must include "an intention to communicate effectively in the future," sanctioning its adjustment to the situations of different future audiences.[14] This way of viewing author's intentions is precisely what Beck observes about Dylan. In Dylan's liner notes to his own *World Gone Wrong* (1993), an acoustic collection of "traditional" material, Dylan employs the thesis of open-ended meaning as a way into his interpretations of the songs; he emphasizes how the old songs relate to our "New Dark Ages."

In making records and publishing songs, popular musicians plan on the future reception of their music. Discussing poetry, Hirsch proposes an analogy with other plans that people make about future events. One can purchase a claw hammer and plan to use it without knowing whether the nails will be threepenny or tenpenny. Similarly, the poet's plan in choosing words will have some fixity and some "areas of inexplicitness."[15] Hirsch concludes that a "future-directed intention" must always refuse to commit itself to many details. One implication for song lyrics is that the audience has considerable flexibility in "reading" anything that the author does not make explicit. Whatever the *original* meanings might be for a song, such meanings may demand many distinct and even conflicting readings when, as mass art, the song makes its way into other contexts for interpretation. Otherwise, our common recognition of ourselves in a song, the feeling that a song speaks so powerfully to me because it is about me, would have to be dismissed as a misreading—for of course a Led Zeppelin song recorded before a Zeppelin fan was born can't have been written about that particular fan. Unless, that is, it was put forth with an open-ended intention.

This recognition of open-ended intentions stems from a discussion of the ongoing relevance of texts—"of literature (and law, and religion)"—to our own lives. If texts from the past have no such application, they will have minimal "present value." I made this same point much earlier, when I emphasized that most fans don't relate to older music for its historical value. Most fans relate passionately to older music just as they relate to current music: as living texts embroiled with our lives. But unless we grant that an artist's intentions for a text allow for its later application to our situations (details of which are not known to the artist), those later applications will be unrelated to anything that can be regarded as its real, intended meaning.

George Lipsitz similarly emphasizes the "openness" of mass communication as the only way to convey ideas and experiences to audiences situated in diverse contexts and who bring "diverse frames of interpretation" to a song or video.[16] The influence of mass art demands texts that remain "open to interpretation, capable of being related to personal values and experiences . . . in the contexts of their own experiences and aspirations." Lipsitz and Hirsch differ on the key to this openness. Lipsitz thinks that it enters mass art "through allusion rather than exact representation." Since I don't think that any communication is ever an exact representation, Lipsitz's opposition strikes me as unhelpful. I prefer Hirsch's notion that audiences make connections to their own experience by recognizing very specific images and references rather than by responding to allusions.

Consider Lipsitz's extended analysis of the "sedimented" layer of politics in a seemingly innocuous video for Musical Youth's "Pass the Dutchie" (1982). Point by point, his interpretation emphasizes specific verbal and visual cues upon which to rest a subtext of black nationalism. True, the musical style (highly commercialized reggae) and the video's image of a black man wearing dreadlocks will signal oppositional messages to many listeners and viewers. But Lipsitz acknowledges that the song and video were interpreted along different lines by most of the audience: the kinetic appeal of the group's leader, Kelvin Grant, signaled energy and youth in a way that had nothing to do with racial politics. Openness seems to rest on historical and contemporary connections with discrete elements of "Pass the Dutchie," but stylistic and representational elements must be initially presented and understood by the audience as a precondition for that activity.

To the extent that an artist really does intend for the audience to grasp a message through some combination of narrative, thematic, and musical decisions, those intentions are never more than exemplary: "Stories are deeply interesting to us only when we can make some *analogy* between the story and our knowledge and experience. The basis for any such analogy is a concept, either stated or implied. Hence 'exemplified concepts' in literature can be further exemplified."[17] This transition from details to exemplified concepts accounts for the open-ended nature of the communicative process. When the details mentioned in the lyrics are taken as exemplary—as placeholders for the general concepts thus illustrated—then the audience is quite free to imaginatively substitute their own examples of the same conceptual content.[18] A misreading is an interpretation that ignores or overlooks the placeholders supplied by the music and lyrics.

Consider the simple case of the Replacements' "Answering Machine" (1984) and its plaintive question, "How do you say 'goodnight' to an answering machine?" The audience does not know the specific references made to real things and events: I don't know whose answering machine inspired the song. If I want to apply "Answering Machine" to my life—and sometimes I do—I cannot fret about whatever person and whatever answering machine inspired Paul Westerberg. When a writer describes a situation, even an autobiographical one, it serves as an example, as "a member of a class which exemplifies the class."[19] I understand "Answering Machine" when I relate it to times I was away from home, missed my wife, called her, and only got the answering machine. But the responsible audience does not simply free-associate; if I somehow think of toasters instead of answering machines, I misinterpret Westerberg's song.

In an interesting interview, Van Morrison protests that he *cannot* explain the cryptic "Madame George" (from *Astral Weeks*, 1968). The problem is not that Morrison doesn't know how it relates to his own life. On the contrary, Morrison sees it as so rooted in his own life in East Belfast ("a real place, with definite people and it's true") that only someone who experiences *the very same things* will benefit from his explanation: "Just imagine we had a sponsor ... and we went from here to Belfast, and we hung out and came back, then you would know the song. But I don't think I could tell you about the song if we didn't do that." Because he and his listener will never share these experiences, Morrison offers his own version of Hirsch's open-ended intention: "What's Madame George look like? . . . It all depends on what you want, that's all, how you want to go. If you see it as a male or a female or whatever, it's your trip. How do I see it? I see it as a . . . Swiss cheese sandwich. Something like that."[20]

In the same interview, Morrison expresses deep regret that he no longer functions as a popular singer rooted in a community, as he did when Them was the house band at the Maritime Hotel in 1963. Since few listeners will visit Belfast, Morrison knows that his recorded music must function differently for different listeners. When Van Morrison wrote "Cyprus Avenue" for *Astral Weeks*, he was thinking of a specific tree-lined street near where he grew up; when John Lennon wrote "Strawberry Fields Forever" (1967), he was remembering a real place in Liverpool. For any listener not raised in those specific neighborhoods of Belfast or Liverpool, some other childhood street and play area must be imaginatively substituted. Yet we still lack norms, operating across all communities of interpretation, to put clear limits on this process of imaginative substitution.

It appears that a great deal of the meaning of popular, mass art music is only present through audience engagement with future-directed intentions. Most of what passes as the "meaning" of popular music is simply not inherent in the music: not its effects on the audience, not its expression of identity, not its ideological slant.[21] The audience doesn't extract additional meaning that the text already "has." That way of putting it wrongly suggests that its meanings are somehow built into it, as if it "has" the meanings in much the same way that a vending machine "has" candy or soda pop in it, waiting to be discharged and made visible. I don't mean that popular music is insignificant or lacking in meaning. After all, it is subject to interpretation. However, if we equate meaning with the interpretations or "decoding" of the music's various audiences, there can be no presumption that superior readings emerge from a *historical* or author-centered perspective on the music. I'd be dishonest to pretend that all of these points are original. I'm not satisfied, however, that their consequences are adequately grasped, particularly when it comes to the question of whether anyone's interpretation ever counts as better than anyone else's. Like Lisa Lewis, I want a model of audience response that recognizes "a complex and dynamic interaction of decoding *and* encoding practices."[22] This approach emphasizes that the possession of cultural capital positions the audience to recognize artistic intentions. One of the most important elements that audiences learn to *recognize* during "decoding" is the social or political identity that a creative musician "encodes" into the music's message.

They Don't Know: Ignorance and Misunderstanding

It's very different once the record is made and it's out to the general public. The listener is outside of the creative process. Actually it becomes a peripheral force of that creative process because they enter themselves into the music and they interpret it to fit their lives and to fit their needs.
—R.E.M.'s Michael Stipe[23]

Many writers celebrate the "power" that the audience has in using popular art to suit their own needs. What they are really talking about is the audience's tendency to engage mass and popular art with highly selective attention, or sometimes they want to call attention to the willful reversals of meaning involved in "perverse" readings.[24] But even a willful reversal presumes that the audience grasps some core of correct meaning. Many writers propose that the meanings of popular music are rich and multiple (the popular text as polysemic or multiple in meaning).[25] Many others propose that a more enlightened and critical perspective will reveal previously hidden meanings (the popular text as univocal but hermetic).

I want to explore a much simpler proposal. Successful music for a mass audience must invite multiple interpretations by being future-directed and open-ended. As such, it will speak to diverse audiences, conveying different but related meanings and identities to different groups and to different individuals within the same group. Consequently, there's limited room to complain when the audience "misunderstands" the message. The flip side is that we can't valorize the audience for misreading reactionary songs in progressive ways. That activity is no different in kind from that of the misogynist who hears a celebration of his misogyny in "Johny Hit and Run Paulene." These conclusions seem inescapable even if we presume that the audience responds to the music intelligently and as "authored" by a specific person, appreciating the full range of intentions encoded in the music.

Imaginative substitution is further complicated when we notice that inexplicitness may arise with specific elements, or it may arise at the point of connecting different elements into a coherent message. There are verbal elements and there are specifically musical elements, a point too often ignored in deciding what a song means:

> [David Susskind] invited Phil Spector to the *Open End* television program one evening to talk about the record business. Suddenly Susskind and William B., station WNEW's old-nostalgia disc jockey, were condemning Spector. . . . Susskind sits there on his show reading one of Spector's songs out loud—no music, just reading the words, from the Top 60 or whatever it is—"Fine Fine Boy," to show how banal rock & roll is. The song just keeps repeating, "He's a fine fine boy." So Spector starts drumming on the big coffee-table there with the flat of his hands in time to Susskind's voice and says, "What you're missing is the beat." Blam blam.[26]

Any number of well-meaning rock fans tried to counter these dismissals by praising the "rock poetry" that arose from Bob Dylan, Paul Simon, and similarly ambitious lyricists that started to appear on the pop charts around 1965. But that tactic simply reinforced the same misunderstanding that Susskind brought to Darlene Love's "A Fine, Fine Boy." As Spector pointed out to Susskind, lyrics alone don't convey meaning.[27]

Popular music is primarily an art form concerned with delivering songs, and a song's meaning involves the interplay of musical and verbal elements. Here was X's problem with "Johny Hit and Run Paulene." Its tempo and exuberant guitar riff recall songs like Chuck Berry's "Carol" and "Little Queenie," songs that celebrate the male sex drive. The music sets the song's emotional tone, and X's creepy lyrics don't override that message of celebration. Something more has to happen within the musical setting of those lyrics. But there's no dark edge to the music of "Johny Hit and Run Paulene."

Let's examine a better known example. The song "Born in the U.S.A." was first made public as the opening track of Bruce Springsteen's

Born in the U.S.A. album (1984), the best selling of his career. But the song was written in 1981 and first recorded in 1982. Other recordings from those informal sessions became the *Nebraska* album, but producer Jon Landau quickly removed that particular song from consideration for that project. The original version has since surfaced on the four-CD set *Tracks* (1998).

While the two versions have identical lyrics and chord changes, they differ radically in duration, texture, arrangement, tempo, vocal timbre, and in the melody of the verses. The more famous version is mid-tempo, deliberate, and solid; the early version is fast without being aggressive. The famous version is one of the most gloriously *full* arrangements that Springsteen has ever produced, showcasing the E Street Band at its peak. The performance is extended with instrumental passages, including a false ending that generates a tremendous thrill that contributes to the feeling of triumph in the coda. Through much of it, Springsteen bellows the vocal. The acoustic version is foursquare, fleshed out by some wordless vocal counterpoint near the end. The main vocal is tough but conversational. The E Street Band version swallows a key lyric: "had a buddy ... they're still there, he's all gone." The early demo version spits it out clearly, only to bury the closing lines: "I'm a cool rocking daddy in the U.S.A." These differences generate quite distinct tensions within two sets of verbally identical lyrics. Viewed as deliberate choices, such differences convey distinct meanings and identities. In the full-band version, the protagonist is angry and defiant. In the acoustic version, he is bitter and resigned.

So while a song's most rudimentary meaning lies in the interplay of lyric and music, the basic song is further interpreted in performance and as featured in different recordings. The recording process itself can make a difference. The limited dynamics of the Teac Tascam tape deck used for Springsteen's home recording of the acoustic "Born in the U.S.A." contributed to its subdued emotional feel, while the state-of-the-art studio used for the full-band version generated a richer, brighter, and more expansive sound. In mass art it makes no sense to discuss the song, for the basic unit of meaning is a recording. For this very reason, however, we might suppose that musicians ought to be able to convey their intentions with considerable specificity. After all, they can "encode" all of their musical decisions in the recording, so that all of it reaches the audience intact, without the mediation of further artistic interpretation.

But saying that a recorded song is open-ended already assumes that it conveys enough information to generate questions about the significance of various details and about the interaction of such details: not everything can be up for grabs! The fictional narrator of "Born in the U.S.A." joins the U.S. military to avoid jail time, experiences combat in Vietnam, then returns home and suffers unemployment. However inexplicit it is about a host of details, it is not about whatever the audience wants it to be about. (An audience that ignores the lyric is an audience that responds to the music but not to the song.) Let us reconsider X's "Johny Hit and Run Paulene." *Johny* is a male name and a male pronoun is used. *Paulene* is a female name and it is used generically: Johny aims to violate "all Paulenes." The lyric supplies just enough detail to make it clear that to identify with Johny is to identify with a rapist: "Beside the bed he found clumps of hair / The last Paulene wouldn't cooperate." But how is the audience supposed to feel about Johny? Is Johny to blame? Does he stand for all men? Even if the rush of the music is there to convey how Johny feels, its gleeful, even celebratory tone undercuts the idea that this is a straightforward anti-rape message. In contrast, Bob Marley's "Small Axe" has no coherent narrative thread and thus places considerable burden on the audience to connect the verse and chorus in a meaningful way.

Audience ignorance generates a different complication, for it blocks access to artists' intentions about imaginative substitution. A listener may grasp too little to count as understanding a song, either from a lack of familiarity with the musical style or through ignorance regarding some (or all) of the words. Plastic Bertrand's "Ca Plane pour Moi" was a new wave novelty hit in 1978, but nobody that I knew ever translated it for me. I didn't care. The music was energetic and it was fun—its basic pulse and start-stop beat reminded me of Eddie Cochran songs like "Come On Everybody" and "Nervous Breakdown." I understood the musical dimension: no questions yet arose. My attraction to the song involved a bracketing out of elements that were present but that I did not grasp.[28] It was only much later, when I learned "ca plane pour moi" means "this life's for me," that I faced the open-ended meanings of the line in relation to the musical gesture that accompanies it each time it's shouted out. I could start to grasp the *song*.

Whatever Plastic Bertrand's situation, I presumed that his European lifestyle was considerably different from my college lifestyle in California. Did this mean that I misunderstood it? Was I in the same category as the kids who misunderstood "Johny Hit and Run Paulene"? I'm a native English speaker and a cultural contemporary of John Doe and Exene. Therefore, the lyrics to "Johny Hit and Run Paulene" are completely accessible to me. But the lyrics were also accessible to the fans who shocked John Doe and Exene by identifying with Johny. There is nothing explicitly in the music and words to block their identification with Johny. There's a narrative, but the anti-rape message has to be inferred by asking what moral concepts are exemplified by Johny's behavior. The audience correctly understood that his behavior exemplifies a brutal misogyny. The problem arose when a sizable part of the audience didn't share the band's moral vision and made a different inference at the point where the audience must be trusted to make their own inferences.[29] In its arty cleverness, X confuses matters by using music that invites the audience to celebrate. While it's possible to encourage the audience to engage in a more complex reflection of the narrative's implications, this is hardly the music to encourage such reflection.

On one level, then, I was at a greater disadvantage with Plastic Bertrand than were the X fans who ruined the song for its authors: I grasped fewer details of the whole construct. They may have been available to many Europeans, but not to me. What were the other lines about? How do they relate to the one line that I now understood? I was not yet in a position to raise such questions. I could dance to it and it infused me with energy, but as long as the lyrics were unavailable to me, the song remained too open-ended to convey any specific point of view.

A rather different sort of ignorance arises for a listener who understands the language but lacks background information that the author might regard as obvious. Consider the popular Lynyrd Skynyrd song "Sweet Home Alabama" (1974). Even if one grasps the line "In Birmingham they love the Governor," some listeners won't know that Birmingham is in Alabama. Today, much of Skynyrd's audience is unlikely to know that the governor of that state at that time was George Wallace and that Wallace once represented overt racism in American politics. Since the song does not mention Wallace by name, the line will not provide an open-ended reading to those who are ignorant of American political history.

Fully understanding its political references, Robert Christgau identifies a very different problem with the verse. The problem is in the song's construction. At a crucial point, it fails to convey part of the band's higher-level intentions, intentions conveyed through the combination of musical and lyrical parts.[30] Puzzled about the background singers' prominent chant of "boo boo boo" at the end of the line about Wallace, Christgau tried to get Skynyrd frontman and lyricist Ronnie Van Zant to explain the political message of "Sweet Home Alabama."[31] Christgau got nothing useful out of Van Zant.

A successful execution of lower-level intentions aims at communicating higher-level intentions. The most basic of lower-level intentions are those guiding a performer to do specific things at specific points in a piece. They include the aim of putting across the right noises in the right places while keeping with the beat, or the singer's aim of conveying the right words in English while singing them with the pitch demanded by the melody. But in mass art, musicianship is seldom an end in itself. It is usually done for the sake of the higher-level intentions, among which are the music's emotive and affective dimensions. At least one higher-level intention of "Sweet Home Alabama" is hard to miss: the song asserts Southern pride. The problem with the verse in question is that its higher-level intention seems to undercut rather than to support the rest of the song.

Attracted to the music and independently understanding each of the three lines that follow the one about Governor Wallace, Christgau attempts to link them together but cannot find a coherent way to do so. Taken as a unit (the musical unit of the verse suggesting the written unit of the paragraph), nothing emerges from the four lines. If they indicate that the song's expression of Southern pride is to be tempered by a certain shame at having a popular governor like Wallace, then their famous slam at Neil Young's "Southern Man" becomes quite a bit more complex. One reading would be that their Southern pride is no longer knee-jerk boosterism. Another reading is that they're hypocrites. (Yet another is that they're sloppy craftsmen.) The problem stands, nonetheless, for there is nothing in the lower-level intentions to send us one way rather than another.

For this verse of "Sweet Home Alabama," the combination of lines and music are suggestive without being clear enough to be genuinely open-ended. The same holds for the overall effect of "Johny Hit and Run Paulene." In both cases an existing musical style serves as a base for lyrics that are out of line with expectations for the theme and the musical style, compounded by the fact that in each case the lyric implies far more than it says. George Wallace stands for something here, but what? Johny's behavior exemplifies something, but what?

Even if we cannot say, a general point emerges concerning the distinction between lower-level and higher-level intentions. Music can be difficult to understand when it demands (even of a knowing audience) conscientious attention to the musicians' higher-level artistic intentions. Where the words create a narrative, we anticipate that a moral or political message will dominate its higher-level intentions. When a lyric relates something concrete, describing particular events without explicitly moralizing or drawing general conclusions, its message must be found in "implied" concepts. In "Sweet Home Alabama," both the indirect reference to George Wallace (a specific person) and the direct reference to Watergate (a political crisis) take on the burden of standing for other politicians and other political crises. But having grasped those references, there aren't any norms or rules or frameworks determining how to apply them when they come over the radio twenty-five years later. Well-defined norms or rules wouldn't solve the problem of separating acceptable readings from wild ones, because as products of mass art they already involve the higher-level intention of being open-ended. Because song lyrics are meant to be adapted to future cases whose features are not fully anticipated, they remain subject to individualized interpretation even where there is agreement about their literal meaning.

3

Heard It Through the Grapevine

Around and Around:
Texts and Intertextuality

**Here's a song that Charles Manson stole from the Beatles.
We're stealing it back.**

—U2's Bono before launching into "Helter Skelter," *Rattle and Hum*

ntil now I have talked mainly of songs and recordings. But
occasionally I've been forced to mention something a bit
more abstract, something that many theorists call "the text."
Texts are opposed to the highly contextualized utterances of
daily life, for which the identity of speaker and the context
of communication go a long way toward establishing meaning.

Reflecting on "the effect on stage" compared to "the
effect on record," Mick Jagger makes the obvious point that
live performance brings performer and audience together in
a shared place and time:

> How can you understand a worldwide audience? Of God knows
> how many million people? How can you expect a pop singer to
> analyze his audience or his effect or anything? . . . You don't
> know what the effect is: the effect on stage is different from the
> effect on record. You can see what the effects on stage are, but
> that's all. . . . I always think that's more superficial than the
> effect you have when somebody plays it at home. Because
> you get more into their head.[1]

Live performance bears an obvious similarity to the direct communications that dominate daily life. In these cases the listener almost always understands the communication as originating from specific persons at a specific time and place. Sound recordings and videos are more like books and films. The audience may appreciate these fixed but endlessly replicable texts as highly contextualized utterances, produced by specific persons addressing the circumstances of a specific time and place. Or the audience may approach the same material with little or no concern for such matters. As contextualized utterances, songs and recordings convey specific higher-level intentions. Decontextualized and taken as mere texts, they do not. As texts are cut adrift from historical authors and specific historical origins, listeners are presumed to be free to attach any meaning to them.[2]

As a performer, Jagger is an uneven singer but a master showman, manipulating the audience by observing their responses and constantly adjusting his performance to bring about a desired effect. In the early years, however, it was Brian Jones who seemed to take a particular delight in heightening tension by baiting the audience. Alexis Korner describes Jones's extreme aggression: "He used to jump around with a tambourine and smash it in your face and sneer at you at the same time ... inciting every male in the room to hit him.... He would deliberately play at someone's chick, and when the bloke got stroppy, he'd slap a tambourine in his face."[3]

But all of this happened when the Stones were first starting out. Jones the performer is now forgotten, superseded by the recorded evidence of Jones as the superlative studio sideman and the visual evidence of Jones as the androgynous beauty.[4] In one sense, then, Jagger is right to say that the effect of the stage performance is relatively superficial. Details of performance behavior may overpower the actual music. The audience "at home" has the option of listening to the same recording over and over again, appreciating all its details. Songs that seemed slight or throwaway on first listening to an album will often emerge as the album's true gems. But this is only possible because the audience can return repeatedly to the same invariable text.

Yet to emphasize that a song or poem or story is a text is to point to the pattern of words, images, sounds, or other features that reoccur in its many tokens. It is to call attention to the way that meaning-bearing entities circulate with no reference back to the authorial activity and intentions of whoever created them. Or as a certain generation of theorists likes to put it, the text is independent of its author. The author is dead.[5] Texts are thus differentiated from the musical, literary, and other "works" produced by artists, whose interpretation is still constrained by reference to the artist's intentions, however open-ended. To call a book or product of mass art a "text" is to emphasize that *nothing* fixes its significance. Because the text is *iterable*, endlessly circulating into new contexts and used by new audiences, its meaning varies as different audiences interpret it in light of their aims in the context of its use. (If *what* gets repeated is the text, a text's *capacity for repetition* is its iterability.) As a feature that makes mass art possible, iterability simultaneously undermines shared conventions that will constrain a work's possible interpretations. Every response is as good as any other.

However, we should be suspicious of any line of reasoning that cannot rule out some interpretations as mistakes. Bob Marley's own recording of "Small Axe" cannot be about the Gulf War of 1991 or the way that cyberspace music distribution threatens large record companies. (Marley died in 1981.) Someone else might use the song to make such a commentary, much the way that American Armed Forces Radio used the Clash's "Rock the Casbah" to fire up American troops during the Gulf War. But taken as a communication from Bob Marley, Marley's recording says nothing about the Gulf War or music distribution on the Internet. While "Small Axe" might exemplify several different ideas and those ideas might apply to a wide range of situations, it hardly follows that every interpretation and response is as good as every other. Marley created something with open-ended meaning, not something infinitely plastic.

Rather different sorts of texts are at stake with recordings than with songs. As noted in Chapter 1, listeners know songs through particular instances. The song itself is a type, but any performance or recorded performance known by audiences will be a token of that type. But what gets repeated in new tokens is very different with performance than with mass art replication. Since two performances of the same song may have very little in common, repetition through performance is a much weaker mode of iterability than mass art replication. (Considered in all its richness, a performance is never iterable. Unlike the songs that are performed, performances themselves lack textuality.) Mass art involves a stronger form of iterability in which there is a very high degree of conformity across many tokens.

Let's begin with the weak iterability featured in live performance. In order to perform a song, whether "Happy Birthday" for grandmother's birthday or "Leader of the Pack" in a karaoke bar, there must be a *song* to perform. But musical activity cannot count as a performance of one song rather than another unless there are recognized conventions for deciding which features of the performance count as elements of that song—for distinguishing "Happy Birthday" from both "Happy Trails" and the Beatles' "Birthday." At the same time, each new performance differs in many, many ways from every other—part of what makes karaoke and cover versions so interesting. The relevant text will be present in (or absent from) any particular performance by virtue of certain identifiable patterns created within the richness of the performance.

Now consider the strong iterability that comes with a piece of recorded music. Strong iterability is only possible through the use of mass technologies. The presence of the text no longer depends on its being performed. Nor does it depend on audience recognition that a certain activity is similar enough to count as another new instance of the same text. Instead, the reappearance of "the same text" depends on the mechanical and technological processes that generate new instances. Whether a U2 fan lives in Ireland or India, mass technologies and mass distribution provide access to Bono's Charles Manson remark in the film, video, and album formats of *Rattle and Hum*. As with weak iterability, a text is cut free from the circumstances and context of its authorship. But unlike the weaker form of textuality, strong iterability invites the audience to regard any and every aspect of each instance as a relevant feature of that text.

Most fans will only encounter the Beatles' recording of "Birthday" on *The Beatles* (the "White Album," 1968). They will respond to it as part of a larger sequence of music, leading into "Yer Blues." Consider the sequence that closes that same album side, where "Helter Skelter" is sandwiched between John's "Sexy Sadie" and George's "Long Long Long." "Helter Skelter" comes off as incredibly dense and guitar heavy, with Paul McCartney's raw vocal shredding before our ears. It predates Nirvana's trick of accenting the chorus through a contrasting "quiet" verse, but the sequencing of *The Beatles* allows McCartney all the angst and power of a Nirvana chorus for four and half minutes. Presented as the opening track of *Rattle and Hum*, U2's live recording of "Helter Skelter" conveys something altogether different. Among other things, it tells us that U2 isn't the Beatles. In its originating live performance, U2's cover of "Helter Skelter" displays the song's weak iterability. Featured on *Rattle and Hum*, the track possesses strong iterability.

Although closely related, the distinction between strong and weak iterability does not correspond precisely with the earlier distinction between popular music and music made and distributed as mass art. Where the two distinctions have been recognized, there has been a strong presumption that each pair involves a fundamental conflict between the music's original, authentic mode and a subsequent, debasing mode.[6] One move is to equate rock with popular music and then to explore issues of meaning and identity by focusing on communities that are geographically *localized* and relatively self-contained. Such communities reveal relatively coherent local norms, and against this backdrop of a shared musical context the music expresses a relatively stable sense of identity. But in setting aside all the problems that arise from the relative poverty of shared musical contexts, much of what's interesting about popular music as mass art falls away.

There is much to recommend Barry Shank's detailed analysis of "the rock 'n' roll scene" in Austin, Texas. All the same, it typifies the tendency to reduce "popular musical practice" to a local scene of musicians playing mainly local gigs: "an aesthetic based in performance."[7] Shank's work is a study of popular art and weak iterability, not mass art and strong iterability. It is a foregone conclusion, then, that "the recording industry" will be positioned as an outside force constricting the activities of the local musicians, limiting their creativity and constraining their avenues for "the collective production of resistance."[8] Thus my copy of *Mud, Lies and Shame* (1988) by Austin's the Wild Seeds represents my complicity in the destruction of yet another local music scene.

A rather different slant emerges if we regard recordings as a core element of rock culture. Instead of assuming that the pleasures of commercial, recorded music inhibit participation in a collective identity that is both active and genuine, we begin to glimpse a more fluid, ephemeral community. This community is loosely organized around a series of influential recorded "texts." Individuals with very different backgrounds can participate in a common musical culture without having to agree to anything beyond those common influences, allowing bands as different as the Beatles, the Grateful Dead, the Who, and Los Lobos to issue their interpretations of Motown classics. They can respond to the same texts without agreeing on what they mean or what is valuable about them.

Finally, the distinction between strong and weak textuality has important implications for the concept of intertextuality. Meaning that arises in a culture of endlessly circulating texts is often discussed under the heading of intertextuality.[9] Roughly, intertextuality is a blanket term for the idea that a text communicates its meaning only when it is situated in dialogue with other texts. Intertextuality is often characterized as meaning that arises "between" texts: U2's reference to Charles Manson and the Beatles positions their performance as a repudiation of what Manson did, whereas Guns N' Roses' recording of a Charles Manson song on *The Spaghetti Incident* (1993) has precisely the opposite effect.

Coined by Julia Kristeva as a handle for the sum of tacit knowledge needed to derive meaning from a text, intertextuality begins in her observation that every new text is a transformation of other texts. The initial attraction of intertextuality was that it seemed to establish literature's unique literary quality. But meaning is meaning, and it was soon obvious that intertextuality holds for all signifying practices. From there it was a simple move to the conclusion that intertextuality is the key that unlocks a vast array of meanings and pleasures hidden away in relatively simple popular texts, from pop songs to teen magazines to professional wrestling matches.[10]

As developed in literary theory and cultural studies, the thesis of intertextuality is put forth as evidence that a text's actual history has no bearing on its meaning. For if the replication of texts puts each text into play with every other, the historical moment and cultural space that gave birth to that text loses any significance when interpreting it. But this argument is far less persuasive when we remind ourselves that strong iterability and weak iterability operate in rather different ways.

An oral or "folk" tradition continually obliterates its musical past. A mass art or "phonographic" culture has the opposite problem of being swamped with music that, once made, never goes away. With traditional art forms, including music, artist and audience participate in a common culture. So with most art there is a good chance that the initial audience will grasp an artist's intentions. (If most of Edouard Manet's contemporaries hated his paintings, we must be suspicious of any revisionist history that assumes his audience "misunderstood" his intentions. Their disgust suggests that they understood all too well. But Manet did not create texts in the same sense that mass artists create texts.) In passing along a song from the past, performers will alter and update the song so that it continues to speak to the audience. Weak iterability encourages the performer to recast the song to bring out its relevance in a specific context and a specific audience. In contrast, strong iterability simply delivers the same text, highlighting its increasingly random juxtaposition with all other texts.

The phonographically literate audience responds to all music against a swelling backdrop of commercial recordings. Mick Jagger had to send away to America to get a Muddy Waters album. Today, MCA Records (current owners of the Chess catalogue) releases a different "best of" repackaging of Muddy Waters every two or three years. New recordings by Paul McCartney, David Bowie, and Pink Floyd are launched into commercial and critical competition with their earlier work, which is continuously re-released in "anniversary edition" and "best of" repackages. Individuals labor to make music that will be renamed "product" by those distributing it; yet however much the musicians try to control the presentation and reception of their music, the mass market disrupts almost every effort to control the audience's reception of it.

At first glance the thesis of intertextuality has a certain appeal, if only because the basic idea is common sense. Whether a stop sign or the formula $E = mc^2$, every sign acquires its meaning from its location within a larger system of signs, affiliated with a set of conventions for their use. A person obeys a signpost, Wittgenstein notes, "only in so far as there exists a regular use of sign-posts, a custom."[11] However, intertextuality is supposed to go beyond the obvious truth that the spe-cific stop sign on the corner of my block commands drivers to stop because all the other red octagons marked "stop" are understood to com-mand exactly the same thing. The doctrine only takes on a certain urgency when we see it as a theoretical response to a long tradition of treating works of art as self-contained, unique entities: *l'art pour l'art* or "art for art's sake." (On the other hand, when intertextuality is taken to imply that there is never any reference to a world outside the play of texts, the difference between this theory and *l'art pour l'art* evaporates.)

The prevailing theory of intertextuality proposes that new meanings only arise because intertextuality enables texts to take a self-reflexive turn, playing with the very codes of meaning that we normally take for granted. Ethnic jokes and light-bulb jokes often have an intertextual dimension, since part of their very appeal is their explicit recycling of the conventions of the genre. This "general, anonymous intertextuality" is the sort that we find at work in most parody.[12] To be amused by the Rolling Stones song "Dear Doctor" (1968) or the film *Spinal Tap* (1984) demands little more than a general awareness of the basics of country music and heavy metal, respectively. Although each particular text arises from a history of specific influences, general intertextuality is supposed to account for complex significance even when the audience knows noth-ing of that history: if you know even a little bit about heavy metal, *Spinal Tap* is funny. But it also implies that there is no relevance to the dis-tinction between model and imitation. In other words, chains of influ-ence that convey a context for musical identity are rendered irrelevant. From the viewpoint of general intertextuality, an Eddie Van Halen gui-tar solo means basically the same thing as a Steve Vai guitar solo, and the Who's destruction of their instruments in live performance means the same as Nirvana's. General intertextuality thus warrants closer scrutiny.

Adam Raised a Cain: Specific Intertextualities

No Stairway to Heaven

—Sign in a music store pointed out to Wayne when he tries out a guitar in *Wayne's World*

It does a make a difference for much of the audience whether Eddie Van Halen or Steve Vai came first. It does make a difference which came first, Robert Palmer's videos for "Addicted to Love" (1986) and "Simply Irresistible" (1988) or Shania Twain's "Man! I Feel Like a Woman!" (1998). From the shallow stage setting with its blatantly fake "sunset" backdrop to her manipulation of the microphone stand to the way the robotic male backup "musicians" (that is, sex objects) sway to the music, Twain's video cleverly repeats and then inverts every cliché that Palmer exploits. Here are influences, connections, and allusions that create nuances of meaning that cannot be grasped simply through a general intertextuality: "as highly interested, active textual participants, fans create self-proclaimed interpretive communities *and define their activities in relation to specific texts.*"[13]

Such cases show that some aspects of a text's significance arise from recognition of *specific* intertextualities, demanding audience familiarity with a specific earlier text.[14] This holds true even when a text conveys some ideas through general intertextuality. Most viewers will take the opening sequence of the film *Austin Powers* (1997) to be a general spoof on the tribulations of celebrity: a secret agent whose "cover" identity is that of a fashion photographer, Powers must escape a horde of young girls chasing him. But the sequence becomes far richer if one recognizes that it is a very detailed parody of the opening segment of the Beatles film *A Hard Day's Night* (1964). The title and cover photograph of Soul Asylum's *Clam Dip and Other Delights* (1988) is simply odd if one has not seen the cover of *Whipped Cream and Other Delights* (1965) by Herb Alpert and the Tijuana Brass. Of course, this interplay between one text and a specific, earlier text is simply the familiar trick of textual allusion.

In practice, the interplay of texts is always, for each musician and member of the audience, interplay between specific texts. Within the rock community of the early 1970s, it seemed obvious that the Rolling Stones album title *Let It Bleed* was a playful inversion of the Beatles single "Let It Be." The Stones album actually came out about two months before "Let It Be," supporting Jagger's denial that any such allusion was intended. Yet it's always left to the *audience* to make the connections that generate an interpretation. With the two records competing in the stores and on the radio during the same general period, the similarity between *Let It Be* and *Let It Bleed* seemed too obvious to have been accidental. Even if coincidental, the contrast between the two was simply too delicious for the audience to ignore. (Perhaps sensing as much, Jagger pushed to have the song "Let It Bleed" released as a single.) At the other extreme, an allusion so obscure that no one makes the connection is no allusion at all; intertextual play with the code of a forgotten literary genre is a clever academic game, not a communicative gesture.

Mass art succeeds only when a mass audience finds meaning in it, and Keith Richards and Mick Jagger were not engaged in a generalized intertextual play when they first appropriated the conventions of the blues and then offered the music to pop audiences unfamiliar with such music. The musicians regarded themselves as a continuation of an existing musical tradition, and they wanted their audience to see them in that way. In one of the most striking instances, the Stones insisted that Howlin' Wolf appear on *Shindig* as a condition for their own appearance. Pop fans who watched the television broadcast to catch the group perform their current hit, "The Last Time," also saw the members of the Stones literally sitting at the feet of the blues legend as he performed.

Who Howlin' Wolf was, exactly, would have been something of a mystery to most *Shindig* viewers. Intertextuality presupposes that the conventions of the system can be taken for granted. But it is unclear what conventions are in place and at work in this case, where the Rolling Stones are positioned as part of the larger British invasion (at the time of the *Shindig* broadcast they were less popular than the Beatles, Herman's Hermits, or Gary Lewis and the Playboys). The Rolling Stones were positioned as little more than the bad boys of the Britpop invasion: popular dance music by and for white baby-boomers. At best, the average *Shindig* viewer would have grasped a series of surprising relationships in the coupling of the Stones and Howlin' Wolf: youth venerating age, pop deriving from blues, England imitating America, white respecting black. But the Rolling Stones had to go out of their way to make these connections for the audience. So television, with the immediacy of the visual, was exploited to confront the audience with a specific relationship that general intertexuality might never establish. Bonnie Raitt did much the same thing by singing duets with Sippie Wallace during a number of performances in the 1970s. In other cases the African American mentor is initially better known than the white novice. Teena Marie was signed by Motown records and produced by Rick James (1979), the Red Hot Chili Peppers brought funk genius George Clinton on board to produce their second album, *Freaky Styley* (1985), and

Eminem worked with Dr. Dre to avoid the negative stereotypes that general intertextuality assigns to white hip-hop.

Such examples also suggest the very real work that goes into cementing down the social facts that generate intertextuality. By necessity, little in the way of general intertexuality was present to enrich a Rolling Stones performance of "Little Red Rooster" or "I'm a King Bee" (leaving Jagger with little more to express than the reality of his own overt sexuality). They needed to communicate some rather specific connections in order to exemplify a more general situation for interpreting their activity. General intertextuality cannot be an essential characteristic of mass art. Most of the intertextuality of mass art is generated one text at a time.

These highly selective examples prove little about music until we note that specific intertextualities also arise on a purely musical level. Yet it obviously holds for musical structures as well as for verbal texts and visual messages, as when ELO's version of "Roll Over Beethoven" (1973) incorporates snatches of the opening theme of Beethoven's fifth symphony. But it even holds of a musical sound, apart from the specifics of melodies and chord progressions. R.E.M.'s "At My Most Beautiful" (1998) and most of the High Llamas' *Hawaii* (1996) pay unmistakable homage to Brian Wilson's arrangements on the Beach Boys' *Pet Sounds* (1966). More specifically, they recall *Pet Sounds'* distinctive wash of background vocal harmonies, lush but wordless, against piano, melodic bass punctuation, drum fills, and sleigh bells. (The songs "You Still Believe in Me" and "God Only Knows" are the clear precedents.) George Harrison's "When We Was Fab" (1987) derives much of its joke from its stunning simulation of the Beatles in full psychedelic bloom, circa *Magical Mystery Tour* (1967)—a feat that required Ringo Starr on board for the drums.

Any descriptive account of how meaning arises in rock must recognize that some rock music is received in light of specific earlier models. Earlier, I noted several cases where meaning is derived from an awareness of historical authorship. Yet any emphasis on texts and intertextuality must be a methodological recommendation rather than a description of how all meaning is produced.[15] But the real question about either account is its prescriptive force. That is, what reasons are there to suppose it is better if listeners emphasize general over specific intexuality, or to suppose the opposite? It does make a difference to the solo work that John Lennon was once a Beatle—the bitter "How Do You Sleep?" seems a puzzling diatribe unless one grasps that it is aimed at Paul. Lynyrd Skynrd's "Sweet Home Alabama" is a response to Neil Young's "Southern Man." The verse about "Mr. Young" connects to the verse about Watergate and George Wallace if one recognizes that "Southern Man" was a nasty swipe at the Southern voters who supported Richard Nixon. But should it matter to listeners when the song comes on the radio twenty-five years later? Can we make a case that listeners ought to look for specific intertextualities? Because doctrines of general intertextuality undercut any interpretation that considers the relevance of who made a musical text, and for what purpose, they remove active agency from the formation of identity through musical activity. Thus, we should be very careful about endorsing such recommendations in their strong forms.

There are four basic reasons to distinguish between general and specific intertextuality while rejecting the prescriptive value of the former. First, general codes cannot play any active role in producing meanings, for the codes and conventions invoked to account for a plurality of meanings are always mere abstractions from living practices. Any codes or rules require application and thus interpretation, but if the rules are themselves subject to interpretation, then we need a further code or set of rules, generating an ever-expanding set of codes and rules.[16] Second, a model of general intertextuality suggests that mass art paradigms are the ideas determining the reception of texts, but denies the importance of paradigms in the sense of exemplary cases. Again, this leaves us without a common ground for actively altering the codes and conventions governing interpretation. Third, in the absence of specific intertextualities it is not possible to accuse anyone of improper appropriation or racist exploitation in popular music, such as that of Muddy Waters by the Rolling Stones or of African American music in general by rock. For such accusations presuppose social and historical relationships that are ignored in general intertextuality, relationships that anchor the identity expressed by a work. General intertextuality cannot hold the audience responsible for failing to attend to a work's ties to historically situated musicians. (This topic will be explored in Part Two.) Fourth, in the absence of specific intertextualities there is no way to actively introduce subversive identities into rock. Once again, general intertextuality does not create the relationships presupposed by subversion. (This point will be explored in Part Three.)

To consider the first point in greater detail, we should not lose sight of the fact that texts are inanimate objects: ink on paper, paint on canvas, grooves in vinyl, or a digital stream of 1s and 0s. Texts are not puppies, frolicking together even when the humans are away; texts cannot engage in intertextual play in the absence of an audience. The audience provides the requisite self-reflexive turn by becoming explicitly aware of signifying practices employed in the construction of the text. Meanings arise as audiences make connections between one text and others. However, if the audience must do the work of deciding which connections are the relevant ones, then the text cannot itself position the audience. Recognition of the intertextuality of mass art challenges the belief that it invites merely passive consumption.

In place of general intertextuality and a profuse iterability that flattens every song and recording into an equally polysemic text, I recommend thinking about the organization of mass art in terms of *paradigms*. If general intertextuality cannot explain how a band like the Rolling Stones or the Sex Pistols can articulate some measure of their own identity, and if specific intertextualities often elude the mass audience, then paradigms hold promise as an intermediate case. Musicians cannot bind a single univocal meaning to the music they produce. Yet they can convey their intentions about the general context against which the audience is to position the music.

Re-Make/Re-Model: The Case of Cover Versions

There has been a time or two where a singer has interpreted my song in such a way that I was really let down, that I said, "That is so wrong, I hate this." . . . And those times it's probably just a misunderstanding; the person just didn't get it, you know? . . . They bring in things that are either true to the vision or not true to the vision.

—Carole King[17]

The most obvious examples of specific intertextuality are cover versions of other recordings. Cover versions illustrate the dual proposals that higher-level intentions are open-ended and that specific intertextuality provides a historical dimension to the experience of mass art music, highlighting issues of origins and authorial voice.

The open-ended quality of covers is reinforced by the legal norm that to record and release a song is to permit others to sing or record it. Once a songwriter publishes a song, other musicians have the right to sing and record that song without seeking the composer's permission. Releasing a recording of a song has the same effect. This blanket permission opens the door to further artistic interpretation. Direct permission is needed only if the cover version involves a significant revision of the basic song. Thus Danny and Dusty (Dan Stuart and Steve Wynn) had to get Bob Dylan's permission to add an extra verse to "Knockin' on Heaven's Door" for their album *The Lost Weekend* (1985). No special permission was necessary for Eric Clapton or Guns N' Roses to add a series of guitar solos to their versions of the same song, or for Clapton to recast it as a reggae tune.

Some "cover" versions are produced to fill a commercial void, as when TLC released a video for "No Scrubs"(1999) but no single, and so studio pros released a knock-off single for those who didn't want to buy the whole *Fanmail* album. More often, a remake is less a substitute than a distinctive interpretation of music popularized by an earlier recording. With most remakes, the performer is a new "speaker" who usurps the place of the historical author, generally by changing the emphasis of elements *within* the song. If we know both versions, we hear the gap between lower-level and higher-level intentions when cover versions offer distinct interpretations of songs. Cover versions thus remind us that different higher-level intentions—such as the music's overall emotional gesture—are consistent with a melody and a fixed set of words. Conversely, very different lower-level intentions can be used to preserve higher-level ones.

To succeed, most remakes will have to convey intentions to two rather different groups. The song will already be familiar to some of the audience. Others won't know the original. Those who don't know it may be drawn to a proven hit redone in a more congenial style. Most Dolly Parton fans aren't major Neil Young fans, so the 1999 *Trio II* version (Parton, Emmylou Harris, and Linda Ronstadt) of "Before the Gold

Rush" sold the song to a more conservative country audience that might not know Young's career. The addition of vocal harmonies wasn't the only change for the Nashville crowd: Young's "I felt like getting high" became "I felt like I could cry." Many remakes fall between the extremes of slavish imitation and stylistic overhaul, as when Ani DiFranco's version of the Dusty Springfield gem "Wishin' and Hopin' " was recorded to open the film *My Best Friend's Wedding* (1998). Although a less powerful singer, DiFranco's vocal closely shadows Springfield's original. Meanwhile, the musical accompaniment is similar but muted, stripped of its glossy 1960s pop production. Yet the song being covered was old enough that most of the audience for the remake had to be able to "get" the subversion without knowing the original. Here, intentions become complicated because the song is situated as a *DiFranco* performance. The irony of the performance is generated by audience beliefs about DiFranco's personal, "real" identity (overtly feminist, anti-corporate, and bisexual).

The most significant alterations tend to be musical and emotive rather than verbal. Johnny Cash's 1996 cover of Soundgarden's "Rusty Cage" (1991) finds a dignity and resignation in the lyric that Chris Cornell never managed. Graham Parker's 1977 remake of Ann Peebles's "I'm Gonna Tear Your Playhouse Down" (1973) substitutes venom in place of stubborn pride. Annie Lennox brings a steely anger to her 1995 version of the Clash's "Train in Vain." In the 1979 original, Mick Jones sounds bewildered by the situation and just on the verge of pleading. In the remake, Lennox has worked past the first flush of anguish and coldly accuses her lover. Part of the difference is Lennox's slower tempo and gospel styling; part of it is the Clash's busy arrangement in which the harmonica dogs and hems in Jones's vocal; part of it is the intimate quality of Lennox's voice. We are reminded that lyrics are just words and that inflection rather than syntax conveys many of our intentions.

There are other cases where a remake remains true to another artist's higher-level intentions by *changing* the music or lyric. Sometimes a songwriter's basic intention is best preserved by changing the lyric to reflect a change of gender, as when Shawn Colvin substitutes "he" for "she" in her 1994 remake of the Police's "Every Little Thing She Does Is Magic" (1981). Most listeners will take Colvin's voice to exemplify that of a heterosexual woman (not merely as Shawn Colvin speaking as Shawn Colvin). Most male listeners will place themselves as the "he" of this relationship. Most women will put themselves into Colvin's position and substitute a male love interest as the "he."[18] Are these gender reversals true to original intention? I believe that they are.

To summarize the point about open-ended intentions, elements of a lyric that seem to refer to concrete things and situations are merely exemplary. The historical author chooses specific places, objects, and people, but they function as placeholders for ideas more than as references to the individuals they mention. When Van Morrison seems to tell us details about his childhood and adolescence, the seemingly direct act of self-disclosure gives way to the indirect act of inviting the audience to make it relevant by engaging in imaginative substitution. But these intentions can be revised and supplemented by other performers covering the same song. Both musical alterations and the identity of the performer may suggest different exemplification. In other cases, revisions will be introduced to preserve a song's original (yet still open-ended) intentions.

4

You've Really Got a Hold on Me: Paradigms

Nothing Compares to You

After the Beatles, there were a lot of sub-Beatles, and after Nirvana, there were a lot of sub-Nirvanas.

—Smashing Pumpkins' Billy Corgan

We never heard jazz until punk came along, but when we did it sounded more like punk than rock to us. . . . But after the Minutemen, I froze the paradigm. I only knew one way to play.

—Minutemen bassist Mike Watt

The idea of paradigms and paradigm shifts has become so common throughout so many fields that we ought to begin by returning to its modern source. It comes from Thomas Kuhn's *The Structure of Scientific Revolutions,* in which Kuhn claims that paradigms perform an indispensable role in explaining how a scientific community comes into existence and then maintains itself over time. A scientific paradigm is the basis for creating agreement in an intellectual community divided by disagreement. Unfortunately, Kuhn's idea has usually been simplified into the idea that interpretive communities differ from one another by virtue of their distinct interpretive assumptions and strategies.[1]

Kuhn chose "paradigm" because it derives from the Greek term for "pattern." A paradigm is an intellectual achievement that each new entrant into a community must acknowledge as a condition for joining. Notable examples in the history of science are Newtonian mechanics, Darwin's theory of evolution, and Einstein's theory of relativity. Literary theorists have adopted Kuhnian jargon to explain the persistence of competing, incompatible "paradigms" of literary interpretation. Thus a paradigm is more or less equivalent to a set of shared assumptions that jointly define an intellectual tradition, creating obstacles to communicating with other traditions in the same general discipline. It is by appeal to this weakened sense of "paradigm" that Susan McClary dismisses musicology's resistance to new ideas about music: "we are in the throes of a paradigm shift ... between music theory and feminist criticism."[2]

However, this is *not* the sense in which I'm suggesting that paradigms are important to mass art. It trivializes too many of the interesting features of paradigms that Kuhn hoped to emphasize. Above all, it trivializes the idea that the paradigm comes first and most theorizing comes later, after its adoption as a model for community practice. As an object of common reference, the paradigm serves as a touchstone for practice. Yet even the community that acknowledges it to the point of taking it for granted will never agree on what it means. The community is united by the paradigm but not by their interpretation of it.[3]

If the notion of a paradigm seems imprecise, Kuhn himself deserves some of the blame. He freely admits that he is less than consistent about what a paradigm is. Sometimes he describes it as a worldview: "the entire constellation of beliefs, values, techniques and so on shared by members of a given community."[4] But when he is more careful, Kuhn makes it very clear that a paradigm is not a set of ideas and it is not to be equated with a scientific theory. A paradigm is an *exemplar* or "exemplary past achievement." It is a concrete problem-solution that a particular community "acknowledges for a time as supplying the foundation for its further practice."

Like a Supreme Court ruling, a paradigm is a concrete solution to a problem that a community wants to solve. As such, a paradigm is the starting point for tracing a sequence of events. A paradigm appears at a particular moment in time as something that guides subsequent thought, as a pattern for future activity. To invoke a paradigm is to introduce a fundamentally historical dimension into our thinking. At the same time, a paradigm's authority is accepted "without agreeing on, or even attempting to produce, a full *interpretation* or *rationalization* of it." Its application is open-ended. Initially, the Rolling Stones sought an identity by articulating a history in relation to specific African American paradigms. The Ramones unsuccessfully sought an identity in relation to the Beatles and 1960s pop—almost nobody made the connection. In the short run, the Raspberries and the Knack had better luck with the popular audience by emphasizing rather different elements of the same paradigm.

A paradigm is an exemplary case or body of work around which a community organizes its practices and beliefs. When this happens—and it may take some time for a community to agree that something is foundational for further practice—exemplars have a normative function within a community. Again, the Raspberries and the Knack are useful examples: both were judged to be relative lightweights in comparison to the Beatles, a fate that tends to befall anyone who dares to draw too heavily on central paradigms. Led Zeppelin suffered a similar (if not harsher) fate in the hands of critics who knew their African American sources, a topic that will get its due attention in Part Two. But to a popular audience coming of age after the Rolling Stones and the Yardbirds derived hard rock from the electric blues of African Americans, Led Zeppelin sounded like a progressive force in hard rock. Once Led Zeppelin emerged as a paradigm of hard rock, Led Zeppelin's blues sources were bracketed and ignored (if known at all) by those fans.

Clearly, then, a paradigm is neither a theory nor a set of beliefs nor an interpretive strategy. Rules and procedures are gradually abstracted from a paradigm as it continues to guide practices even across a range of new circumstances, until adherence to the resulting rules comes to seem fundamentally valuable.[5] Yet Kuhn notes that scientists can be united by a paradigm without sacrificing diversity. At the local level of small working groups, these rules are translated into practices that are often unique to the site of the research. At the level of practical activity, different teams of biologists may evoke Darwin as a shared paradigm without participating in precisely the same practices.

Artistic communities also form around paradigms. But Kuhn cautions that if we are to adapt his ideas to describe artistic communities, it will be exemplary artworks, *not styles*, that serve as paradigms.[6] Where a scientific community singles out one paradigm as a foundation for further research, artistic communities do not. Once Newtonian mechanics was accepted as a scientific paradigm, no other approach to mechanics counted as a rational basis for mechanics. "Unlike art," Kuhn observes, "science destroys its past." The artworld can admire multiple paradigms, representing different periods in art history, without risking incoherence: Picasso's success did not lead museums to put their Rembrandts into storage. When the Beatles came to America, they quickly placed five singles into the top five spots of the American pop charts, yet we would do well to remember that non-Beatles music filled out most of the rest of the charts.

Because mass art is directed to a widely dispersed audience, and because each member of that audience is bombarded with a constant array of competing products of mass art, its traditions can be expected to teem with competing paradigms. Musicians, in turn, will have to assemble their own understanding of the tradition from diverse influences. The Cowboy Junkies can pay homage to both Elvis Presley and the Velvet Underground on *The Trinity Session*. Each genre within rock, such as heavy metal or punk or progressive rock, will have its own body of paradigms known to some—but not all—of the fans and musicians. There may be no paradigms common to two genres, although the farther we go back in our narrative of influences, the more likely we are to find common roots. Thus, the Kinks are both an influence on heavy metal (their early, riff-driven explosions of distorted guitar) and progressive rock (their literate move into concept albums starting with *The Kinks Are the Village Green Preservation Society*).

Because paradigms are examples of practice and because the same example can suggest more than one practice, a stylistically unified body of work can inspire subsequent work in more than one style. Thus Matisse inspired both pop artists, such as Tom Wesselman and Roy Lichtenstein, and a wave of American abstract painters, such as Robert Motherwell, Frank Stella, and Richard Diebenkorn. To this extent, mass art resembles fine art. Led Zeppelin left behind a body of studio work that fits into both the progressive and heavy metal camps. Again, it must be emphasized that *the recordings* are the basic paradigms; the ideas and techniques that musicians derive from them, and the value fans invest in them, are features that arise only as they gain their status as paradigms. Thus, Led Zeppelin can serve as a paradigm of rock across a diverse mass audience who, if asked, might not agree on their meaning or on the nature of their accomplishment. There will be no inconsistency in finding both Tori Amos and Duran Duran covering Led Zeppelin songs on *Encomium: A Tribute to Led Zeppelin* (1995). Led Zeppelin was also the obvious musical source for the sound of Heart, one of the first successful hard rock groups fronted by women. Heart's *Dreamboat Annie* (1976) and *Little Queen* (1977) contain musical arrangements and dynamics that illustrate how a paradigm can be strip-mined for some of its features (heavy musical passages convey strength and power while acoustic passages convey spirituality and mysticism) but not others (the Wilson sisters avoid Led Zeppelin's preening masculinity).

Since a recording or an album or a set of recordings becomes a paradigm by serving as a common reference point for later music, a paradigm can easily overshadow its own influences. A mass audience can embrace a paradigm without embracing its history of influences and associations. Associations that are important for the music's initial audience may be irrelevant to the subsequent musicians who take it up and to why diverse audiences embrace it. The disco boom of the 1970s offers an interesting example of how a mass art paradigm can express new or even reversed higher-order intentions. As a mass art phenomenon, the film *Saturday Night Fever* (1977) and its multi-platinum soundtrack album formed the apex of disco:

> After *Saturday Night Fever*, it became impossible to ignore disco. Artists of all persuasions jumped on the disco bandwagon. Cher's "Take Me Home" on Casablanca reached number eight on the charts. Dolly Parton contributed "Baby I'm Burnin'." ... Even the Rolling Stones and Rod Stewart became disco converts. The Rolling Stones' "Miss You" sold 2 million copies, and Rod Stewart scored the best selling single of his career with "Do Ya Think I'm Sexy?" ... With such guaranteed hit-making artists as these on board, radio and television soon followed suit.[7]

Saturday Night Fever was disco's mainstream breakthrough, yet it created crucial associations for disco that erased two earlier associations. Prior to *Saturday Night Fever*, disco was associated with funk and it was regarded as black music. Early disco was also regarded as music for gay club-goers. Thanks to the Bee Gees' breakthrough hits on *Saturday Night Fever*, a wide range of other white artists recorded disco and it gained a high media profile. Thanks to John Travolta's starring role in the film *Saturday Night Fever*, disco was certified as club music for heterosexuals and not just for gays. In fact, most of the mass audience who ignored disco prior to *Saturday Night Fever* probably remained ignorant of the music's original connection with a fan base in a specific gay subculture. Thanks to songs like "Stayin' Alive," the disco beat suddenly represented the Friday and Saturday night hedonism of the working class. For most consumers, disco's association with homosexuality was limited to the Village People.

As a result, it is questionable whether the strong backlash against disco represents a backlash against gays and lesbians. It has become something of a commonplace to interpret the backlash as a response to "disco's particular history."[8] The association may have remained strong in a few urban centers like Miami and New York City, but just as it is unlikely that the 30 million purchasers of the *Saturday Night Fever* soundtrack were expressing solidarity with African Americans and gays, it is equally unlikely that the millions who hated disco were racist and homophobic. It's not that the mainstream audience *misunderstood* disco. The lesson of *Saturday Night Fever* is that the prior significance of musical elements and styles can be overwritten with astonishing speed when a paradigm exemplar draws selectively from what preceded it.[9] At the same time, the audience is unified by its appreciation of the paradigm without being uniform in their interpretation of it.

As the range of available styles proliferates, we might expect fewer musicians or members of the mass audience to share common paradigms, so that an album like *Saturday Night Fever* would gradually lose status. We might assume that the audience for popular music is deaf to the past, caring only for the music of the present moment.[10] Ironically, in an industry driven by what's current or "hot," this has not been the clear result. Both musicians and record companies count on back catalogue as a reliable source of profits. People will continue to buy the paradigm work of U2 or the Rolling Stones, but their next record is always a financial gamble. In any given year, Pink Floyd's *Dark Side of the Moon* and "greatest hits" compilations by Bob Marley, Al Green, Aerosmith, and Bob Seger outsell new releases by many of the bands featured on the glossy covers of popular music publications. (*Billboard* segregates a recording into the Pop Catalog chart after two years.) Sales of "catalog albums" are excluded from consumer sales charts so that *The Billboard 200* and other rankings will not reveal that older music regularly outsells all but the most popular of current hits.

Rather obviously, mass art must be preserving some version of its own history if this older music continues to strike a chord in a mass audience. In my own case, hearing Michael Stipe sing the Velvet Underground's "Pale Blue Eyes" the first time I saw R.E.M. told me more about the band than anything I'd ever read about them in the rock press. Nearly twenty years down the road, a student who makes a living as a professional musician asked me to make him a tape of the Velvets' third album, *The Velvet Underground*—the one with "Pale Blue Eyes"—only to have him comment that he was shocked by the resemblance to R.E.M. Musically, specific intertextualities cut both ways.

At one point Johnny Rotten and Glen Matlock found themselves so divided about the musical direction of the Sex Pistols that their manager forced them to have a drink together to find a common basis for writing songs together. They found only one band that they could agree to imitate: "The Doors was the common ground," Rotten recalls, "a band that we, shockingly, both liked."[11] The Doors continue to turn up as an unlikely influence, with "Light My Fire" serving as the basis for Lauryn Hill's hip-hop track "Superstar" (1998). The Doors, it turns out, are not the only common influence on both Johnny Rotten and Lauryn Hill. *The Miseducation of Lauryn Hill* (1998) resonates with the "classic" reggae style that emerged from Jamaica in the early to mid-1970s under the direction of producer Lee Perry (giving us both dub reggae and Bob Marley's mature style). But Lee Perry also serves as an important source for Rotten's first work after the breakup of the Sex Pistols, with Public Image's *Public Image Ltd.* (1978) and *Metal Box* (1979).

In order for a specific song, album, or body of music to serve as a paradigm for a disparate community of listeners, mass art must itself contain mechanisms by which musicians alert us to the identity of their sources. Given the artworld's tendency to preserve and thus multiply paradigms, the community will cease to function as a community if no works are accepted as singular accomplishments, surviving the test of time. If we understand avant-garde art as governed by an artistic impulse that continuously rejects established paradigms, so that it is unified only by its continuous rejection of the status quo, then mass art can only tolerate a limited avant-garde.[12]

On one level, popular music can serve some of its functions—as a commodity, as an inducement to dance—without paradigms. The rhythms of popular music have an appeal that has nothing in particular to do with specific *meanings*. The *expressive* dimension of most songs depends on harmonic movement and melody far more than on the lyrics, so the emotional core of most songs is comprehensible to almost anyone with basic understanding of Western musical patterns. One needn't grasp the Rastafarian iconography of Bob Marley's "Redemption Song" to feel its yearning, just as one needn't know anything about Kingston politics to feel the tension in the opening to "Concrete Jungle" (1973). There is a richer level to be discovered by those making the proper connections that will suggest an original authorial intention in Marley's songs,[13] but the music can connect with a mass audience in the absence of any such interpretation. A Bob Marley song still fits neatly between a Rolling Stones song and a Pink Floyd track on "classic rock" radio, just as it was meant to do in the radio context of its day.

Can't Turn You Loose:
Paradigms as Reference Points

This sounds like karaoke.

—My wife hears the Wallflowers' cover version of David Bowie's "Heroes" for the first time

If nothing ever emerges as a paradigm for a mass audience, there will be no stylistic reference points that are well known by most musicians and most of the mass audience. Distribution to remote sites makes new music physically accessible, and the more easily grasped structures of the music (melody, basic pulse and rhythm) make it accessible across cultures. But how do these basic features of music become cognitively accessible in a way that relates to the identity of the listener? A social group that recognizes *no* musical paradigms will be one in which new works fail to announce a differentiated identity. So a version of its own history must be built into mass art if there is to be genuine accessibility to the higher level intentions of new music. As I have already suggested, one of the most effective ways that rock carries out this function is through cover versions.[14] Or, as Greil Marcus once put it, every cover version "becomes an opportunity to join the Grand Continuum of Rock 'n' Roll History." But within that larger continuum there are different opportunities. The Rolling Stones positioned themselves differently than the Beatles. The Sex Pistols positioned themselves differently than the Clash.

Chrissie Hynde, leader of the Pretenders, was initially pegged as a punk, but that was the heyday of branding any aggressive newcomer in black leather as punk. (Although she was an insider in the London punk scene of 1976–77, the Pretenders were decidedly post-punk.) Like Patti Smith and Joan Jett at roughly the same time, Hynde showed that a woman could front a band without offering herself as an overt sex object. Again like Patti Smith and Joan Jett, Hynde was less interested in a musical revolution than in being taken seriously as a new voice in the rock tradition. Not unlike the Rolling Stones and their regular cover versions of their influences, Hynde has released her own versions of songs by Bob Dylan, Jimi Hendrix, the Kinks, Sonny and Cher, and Merillee Rush. While the Clash proudly announced "no Elvis, Beatles, or the Rolling Stones in 1977" (set to a riff borrowed from the Kinks), Hynde was proud to let the audience know that her roots were firmly in the 1960s. The Clash, in contrast, wanted the audience to turn to outsider musics, like reggae and hip-hop, as new paradigms for the shape of music to come. So their first British LP, *The Clash* (1977), carries only one cover: Junior Murvin's 1976 reggae hit, "Police and Thieves." The American release of the same album plays it safe by offering a backwards-looking reference in a cover version of "I Fought the Law." A galloping rockabilly song, its aggression was tempered with nostalgia even when it was new, in 1966. (The musical arrangement of Buddy Holly's "Peggy Sue" is the actual paradigm for Bobby Fuller's "I Fought the Law.") The song's placement on *The Clash* reassured Americans that

British punk had a strong foundation in traditional rock and roll, a history that most British fans already understood.

However, cover versions are merely one way among several to convey history and to show allegiance to specific paradigms. Hynde's strongest public nod is to Jimi Hendrix. Consider the *Packed!* album (1990), which features one of her several covers of Hendrix songs. The back cover sports a photograph of a room, evidently in a recording studio, and on the floor beside a chair is the American edition of the first Hendrix album, *Are You Experienced?* (1967). By way of that album cover, Hendrix is the only "person" in the room (even if, strictly speaking, he's not alone on the cover). Why choose this photograph, if not to highlight Hynde's debt to Hendrix? Perhaps the Hendrix album just happened to be in the studio when the photograph was taken; if so, it is interesting to know that she still listens to his albums. Perhaps it was carefully placed for maximum effect in the photograph, reminding us that her debt to Hendrix is via recordings. Another very subtle use of album art to acknowledge influence and establish intertextuality appears on the front cover of the Rolling Stones' "Get Yer Ya-Ya's Out!" (1970). It is difficult to make it out on the CD booklet photograph, but the front jacket of the vinyl release clearly illustrates a line from Bob Dylan's *Blonde on Blonde:* "binoculars hang from the head of the mule." Here we have a case that relies on no general code at all. Its intertextuality is quite specific.

Despite tens of thousands of new releases each year, rock has consistently embraced a limited number of new paradigms at any given time. On the one hand, new paradigms arise through consumer acceptance. Whatever one may think of Alanis Morissette, her sales made it difficult to respond to almost any new female artist in the late 1990s without considering similarities to, and differences from, *Jagged Little Pill* and its videos. On the other hand, musicians with unspectacular sales can become paradigms through their influence on other artists, whose popularity or further influence keeps the earlier source alive as a stylistic reference point. During Lou Reed's first visit to Czechoslovakia following the collapse of the Soviet Bloc, he was amazed at the ability of a group of middle-aged Czechs to provide backup on a spontaneous set of Velvet Underground material.[15] The Velvets never sold albums on the scale of Alanis Morissette, yet their influence is undeniable.

Consider the Sex Pistols, who sold far fewer units than many of their second and third generation imitators. Greil Marcus quotes the Replacements' Paul Westerberg as saying that the Pistols derailed him from his attempts to imitate the Allman Brothers Band. He had been diligently learning the slide solos off *At Fillmore East* (1971). He switched paradigms. "It was the first taste of rock & roll excitement I ever got.... the Sex Pistols came along and said, 'You don't need nothin'. Just play it.'"[16] But when did Westerberg ever see the Sex Pistols? I don't believe their brief United States tour ever reached Minnesota. The answer, of course, is that he never saw them. Just as Westerberg knew the Allmans from a recording, he interpreted the message "Just play it" from a recording. The irony is that *Fillmore East* was a live recording, while the seeming spontaneity of the Sex Pistols depended on Chris Thomas's production expertise in constructing each Pistols track from numerous sessions and overdubs.

Because Westerberg's reaction was not an anomaly, the Sex Pistols' music became a rock paradigm, in Kuhn's primary sense of the term: a clear central case copied by other artists in their practices and looked to as a point of comparison by audiences. The first step was that large numbers of people saw it as an exemplary model for future activities. But *what* it dictated to others depended on their particular circumstances; the crucial next step was that it served as an open-ended call to action, receiving ongoing interpretation. Westerberg's interpretation was that instrumental virtuosity matters less than the D.I.Y. (Do-It-Yourself) aesthetic of getting out there and making up your own music. Shortly before his suicide, Kurt Cobain praised the same record for its fine *production* values rather than for the D.I.Y. message that attracted Westerberg.

We have perfectly good reasons to regard the Sex Pistols as a rock paradigm, and not just as another short-lived punk band among the hundreds that flourished from 1975 to 1978. For *many* musicians of that period and of later periods bear their influence, and *many* fans have rethought what rock means as a consequence of hearing them. Yet there has never been (and, I suspect, there will never be) agreement about *what* the example dictates about future practice. The Sex Pistols occupy a defining moment in rock's history because their mass art serves as a convergence point, figuring in the narratives of large numbers of other rock musicians. However wonderful their music, the recordings made by Anne Richmond Boston and the Swimming Pool Q's do not figure to a similar degree as influences. Their work does not, at present, count as a rock paradigm. However, because of their music's status as mass art, there remains a remote possibility of attaining that status, as happened with Alex Chilton and Big Star.

There is also, in the life of each fan and musician, a set of personal favorites that might be called personal paradigms. "'Highway 61 Revisited,' 'Blonde on Blonde,' 'Electric Ladyland'—I waited for those records, pored over them," recalls Patti Smith. "It was inspiring, and it helped me though all those difficult adolescent times when you feel like a jerk and isolated."[17] Criticism rooted in personal taste can have a certain charm, as in Joe Carducci's *Rock and the Pop Narcotic* and anything by Lester Bangs, but unabashed fanaticism does tend to leave one preaching to the choir. Only those interested in the same personal paradigms will feel the force of the arguments. Worse, one risks elevating prejudices into a set of rules, leading to such blind spots as Lester Bangs's belief that there is not a single progressive rock band worth hearing.[18] Bangs had a clear enough idea of progressive rock, based on paradigm examples like Emerson, Lake, and Palmer, even if he didn't subscribe to them under his personal paradigm.

Although my arguments never exclude marginal or less mainstream figures when there is something interesting to be gained by thinking about them, I have taken some pains to take account of musicians and bands that fans and critics generally count as central to rock. By theorizing about central paradigms, we sidestep the questionable assumption that the marginal is more illuminating than the mainstream.[19] It would be odd to theorize about classical music by concentrating on Hans Leo Hassler, William Billings, Clara Schumann, Jean Jacques Rousseau, and Johann Gottfried Walther, while never mentioning Bach, Beethoven, Mozart, Hadyn, Wagner, and all the others who are recognized by last name alone. There is no qualitative assumption at work here, just as there is no qualitative assumption at work in choosing the Sex Pistols, the Rolling Stones, and the Velvet Underground as central cases for discussion if one is discussing racism and sexism in popular culture. One can hardly grasp what's at stake here without reference to a canon of paradigms as exemplary cases.

All of this is consistent with Kuhn's original proposal about the operation of paradigms. In proposing that paradigms unify scientific communities, Kuhn explicitly denied that fixed *theories* are the starting point for scientific research. He also doubted that any fixed scientific *values* could justify why one paradigm was chosen over another. Recognizing a plurality of values embraced by science, such as accuracy and scope, Kuhn concluded that different communities would embrace the same paradigm while emphasizing or weighing these values differently in the face of changing circumstances. In other words, scientific communities lack any neutral or "objective" procedure for applying these values. As a result, communities that have no common paradigms tend to talk past one another, as if they live in different worlds.[20] The paradigm is the common ground, even as its meaning and value is constantly renegotiated.

To summarize my position, the general accessibility of mass art demands wide recognition of some works as paradigms. There is no need to postulate a basic semiotic code uniting them all. There is no need for universal recognition of the works that function as paradigms, nor is there any need to postulate a shared musical language. It is quite enough that some listeners share a general consensus about which artists and works are most significant as models for future practice, while another group of listeners does the same with other musicians and music. Yet even then, there is no need for listeners who admire the same musicians and music to agree on the full significance of that paradigm. A large number of very different works will count as paradigms, allowing the possibility of some shared paradigms for any two groups of listeners whose tastes appear fundamentally distinct. Yet these shared paradigms will be weighted differently in value by different subcultures and individuals within the larger whole.

If I am correct about the importance of paradigms in mass art, then the interpretation of mass art texts will be constrained by reference to other texts while nonetheless remaining open-ended. As a result, mass art texts will be compatible with a variety of interpretations, with different interpretations valid for different audiences.[21] Some elements of meaning and identity remain open-ended even for the best-informed listeners. However, a number of recent theorists have tended to emphasize readings of some rock paradigms as though specific meanings and constructions of identity were somehow inherent in the texts. As usual, the Rolling Stones are a case in point. Both their appropriations of African American music and the masculinity of their music have been attacked as ideological defects. Ranging over many examples besides the Stones, the remainder of this book examines these issues in detail.

PART II

Issues of Appropriation

**There we were, stirring Dixieland and surf music, rockabilly
and R&B, pseudojazz and honky-tonk country and western
into a big gumbo. We had no idea we were breaking down
barriers and cross-fertilizing genres. In those days, the
definitions were not so firmly fixed.**

—Rock critic Robert Palmer recalls his apprenticeship as a horn player in
   Arkansas juke joints in the 1950s

5

All You've Got to Do Is Pick It Up

Their work songs returned to the most primitive "holler," part sung, part cried. . . . The melismatic distortions of pitch sound more Eastern than European, transplanting into American English the pitch-inflections of the ancient African language.
—Wilfrid Mellers on "Negro music"

The songs are all around us. It's just a matter of whether you're there to receive them. . . . Music is everywhere; all you've got to do is pick it up. It's just like being a receiver.
—Keith Richards

Four Tales of Musical Appropriation
Tale One: Folk Roots

Today, most rock fans who know about Leadbelly (Huddie Ledbetter) learned of him from the closing number of Nirvana's *Unplugged in New York* (1994). Kurt Cobain introduces the final song, "Where Did You Sleep Last Night," as "written by my favorite performer," Leadbelly. After some banter about an opportunity to buy Leadbelly's guitar for half a million dollars, the group launches into a bleak, plodding, and deliberate rendition of a traditional work song that several country and bluegrass artists have copyrighted as "In the Pines." There are some chilling moments where the addition of cello recalls John Cale's contribution to some Velvet Underground classics, but Cobain is working in unfamiliar musical territory and doesn't know how to use vocal subtleties to communicate emotion. He insists on signaling anguish by unleashing his throatiest vocal mannerisms in the last verse.

Cobain sings the chorus as featured in versions by the Louvin Brothers (1952), Bill Monroe and the Blue Grass Boys (1954), and Roscoe Holcomb (1964). However, both the Louvin Brothers and Monroe alternate that chorus with verses lifted from a related song, "The Longest Train." Associated with Kentucky coal miners but also documented by folklorists in Alabama and North Carolina, the oldest variants of "In the Pines" render Leadbelly's (and thus Cobain's) "my girl, my girl" as "black girl, black girl." In contrast, white country artists like Monroe, Holcomb, and the Louvins use "little girl, little girl." The race issue would likely have made Cobain uncomfortable had he known of it, and was simply not an option for white country artists covering the song. But blackness can connote other things. With no hint of irony, the Carter Family's "Coal Miner's Blues" (1938) featured the chorus "These blues are so blue, they are the coal black blues."

Cobain's choice of "In the Pines" was certainly the most audacious selection of the several covers chosen for *Unplugged in New York*, but Nirvana was hardly the first white group to pick up the mantle of Leadbelly. In 1950, Pete Seeger and the other Weavers helped spark the "folk" revival of the 1950s and 1960s by taking "Goodnight, Irene" to the very top of the pop charts. Leadbelly had copyrighted the song as his original composition in 1936, but he died a few months before the Weavers struck gold with it. He had called it "Irene." Although Seeger and the other three Weavers would soon face blacklisting in the Red Scare of McCarthyism, they also faced bitter attacks from elements of the left. A typical Weavers' concert included such songs as the Negro spiritual "All My Trials," Leadbelly's "Midnight Special," and the South African song "Wimoweh," all functioning as coded protests against oppression. Yet the Weavers were immediately taken to task as oppressors as an editorial in *Sing Out!* asked, "Can an All-White Group Sing Songs From Negro Culture?"

Thanks to performers like Pete Seeger and Burl Ives, such songs were swiftly entrenched in the American mainstream. Ten years after the Weavers opened up the folk scene, no one cared that Bob Dylan covered both Anglo folk songs and African American blues on his first two albums; with Dylan, progressives only took exception at the *pop* move to electric instruments. In the second grade, I was taught several of the "folk" songs popularized by the Weavers, although I didn't know that they were responsible. Some of my peers in suburban California, the members of Creedence Clearwater Revival and the Beach Boys, paid fond tribute to their own sense of the American tradition by recording Leadbelly's "Cotton Fields" (1969 and 1970, respectively). After that, no one would ever regard Kurt Cobain's use of Leadbelly as a "blackening" of grunge. Yet in the days before Elvis Presley, there were clear views of what was white and what was not.

The idea that the Weavers were not entitled to sing Leadbelly songs might seem rather quaint were it not for the way that hip-hop has reintroduced questions about racial interaction in popular music. But if the Weavers found themselves challenged by the white intelligentsia, today the most vocal challenge is from the black hip-hop community. Facing hostility for signing and producing white rapper Eminem (a.k.a. Slim Shady), Dr. Dre faced "awkward" questions: "It's like seeing a black guy doing country & western."[1]

While Eminem confesses that he knows nothing about the historical basis of racism in America, he is unusually perceptive about the ironies of his own situation. On the one hand, he knows that most hip-hop fans, white *and* black, are "living a fantasy life of rebellion." On the other hand, he subscribes to the prevailing myth that music itself knows no color line: "Music, in general, is supposed to be universal. . . . Sometimes I feel like rap music is almost the key to stopping racism."[2] Then again, he knows that listeners aren't color blind: facing a hostile reception whenever he practiced his rapping skills in black clubs, Eminem found that, like the Beastie Boys a decade before, hip-hop credibility demanded acceptance by African Americans. Hence the need for a patron like Dr. Dre, producer of N.W.A.'s *Straight Outta Compton* (1988), an album that serves as a linchpin in the argument that rap is black music for black Americans.

But was there ever an African American culture that wasn't already the result of miscegenation and hybridization? Folklorists now believe that Leadbelly "wrote" the song "Goodnight, Irene" by reworking some verses of a Southern "folk" song that he'd learned from his uncle, Terrell Ledbetter, which was itself a modification of a commercial waltz written by Gussie Lord Davis for minstrel shows touring the South in the 1880s. The chorus remained more or less intact through all its variations.[3] Its most morbid lines, touching on both drug use and suicide, were struck from the Weavers' radio-friendly arrangement. Yet such subject matter was perfectly ordinary fare in the subculture of country music, and the suicide threat was left intact for Red Foley and Ernest Tubb's cover version of "Goodnight, Irene." It competed directly with the Weavers' version in 1950, making its way into the top ten on the pop charts and taking the number one spot on the country and western chart. The same verse also appeared in the Louvin Brothers' rearrangement of the same tune, "Let Her Go, God Bless Her" (1956)—the Louvins made the song their own by giving entirely new words to the chorus.

In other words, a good deal of what Leadbelly "wrote" was taken over intact from material that crossed back and forth between whites and blacks. In these respects, Leadbelly was firmly in the African American tradition of the songster rather than the blues singer. As Francis Davis notes, the repertoire of the songster "was more or less identical to that of the period's rural white performers."[4] Furry Lewis, a coarse singer but a guitar virtuoso, kept "Let Me Call You Sweetheart" in his performing repertoire for six decades. Like another songster, Mississippi John Hurt, Lewis was likely to follow his version of the traditional black tale of Stagolee with a song about white railroad engineer Casey Jones. (Lloyd Price appropriated a different variant of "Stack-o-Lee" for his 1958 rock and roll hit, "Stagger Lee." The Clash got their ska arrangement of it, "Wrong 'Em, Boyo," from a Jamaican release by the Rulers.[5]) Another staple of Hurt's repertoire was the hymn "Nearer My God to Thee," one of the last songs played by the musicians on the *Titanic* as she sank into the North Atlantic in 1912.

As with many African American singers of that era, Mississippi John Hurt's early recordings obscured his true identity as a songster. Hurt was already in his thirties when the success of Blind Lemon Jefferson's

"Long, Lonesome Blues" (1926) created a voracious demand for country blues.[6] White talent scouts auditioned hundreds of rural performers, footing the bill to bring the best of them to recording studios in northern cities. The recommendation of a white fiddler who sometimes employed Hurt as an accompanist at square dances secured him an audition in Memphis with the OKeh Record Company. A test recording confirmed Hurt's talent, and he was soon off to New York for a full recording session in 1928. OKeh's advertising boasted of its roster of "real race artists." For nearly a decade this had meant the sophisticated "Classic" blues of singers such as Mamie Smith, Ma Rainey, and Bessie Smith. Ironically, OKeh had started the blues boom with Mamie Smith's 1920 recording of "Crazy Blues" and then let Bessie Smith go to Columbia Records because she sounded "too rough." But the audience now wanted the seemingly more authentic sound of the rural blues. The recording industry was always ready to offer the paying customer whatever was wanted, so the country blues uncharacteristically dominated Hurt's OKeh sessions.

The same pattern was repeated with Leadbelly in 1935. His first commercial recording session (as opposed to archival recordings of folklorist John Lomax) consisted almost entirely of standard blues tunes, some of them learned directly from Blind Lemon Jefferson when Leadbelly was Jefferson's partner and traveling companion. It has come to light that even Robert Johnson, archetypal Delta bluesman, was a songster. Johnson's contemporary, Johnny Shines, recalls Johnson's fondness for Bing Crosby and Jimmie Rodgers records: "And the country singer—Jimmie Rodgers—me and Robert used to play a hell of a lot of his tunes, man. Ragtime, pop tunes, waltz numbers, polkas—shoot, a polka hound, man. Robert just picked songs out of the air. . . . Hillbilly, blues, and all the rest."[7] So much for Dr. Dre's belief that a black musician doesn't play country music.

Six 78 rpm discs featuring John Hurt were released before the Wall Street crash of 1929 and the ensuing Great Depression devastated the market for recorded music. Hardest hit was the "race" market that accounted for nearly 20 percent of record sales. New talent was still recorded (Robert Johnson was not recorded until 1936), but labels had no incentive to stick with marginal sellers. OKeh lost interest in Hurt and he returned to physical labor to support his family. He did not even own a guitar when a white folklorist, Tom Hoskins, tracked him down in 1963. Yet blues fanciers had come to place considerable value on Hurt's music, including "Avalon Blues," in which the singer announces "Avalon's my home town." Hoskins had no trouble locating Hurt once he realized that Hurt meant Avalon, Mississippi; because Hurt's style was not the stereotypical Delta sound of Tommy Johnson or Charley Patton, collectors had assumed that he hailed from Avalon, Georgia. (It was not an altogether fanciful guess, for Hurt's delicate guitar style shares similarities with the intricate finger work and "ragtime" counter-rhythms of Georgia natives Blind Blake and Blind Willie McTell.) Rising to stardom within the folk circuit, Hurt liked to lead his white audiences in a sing-along of a tune written by one of Hurt's contemporaries in the Mississippi Delta. The song was Jimmie Davis's "You Are My Sunshine," the massive country hit of 1940. Big Joe Williams, popularizer of the blues "Baby, Please Don't Go," cited the same song as his all-time favorite.[8] Cultural barriers may have separated blacks and whites in the Mississippi of 1940, but the two cultures were never self-contained and their cultural boundaries were not impenetrable walls.[9]

Reflecting on such practices, enthomusicologist Charles Keil suspects that the classic Mississippi Delta blues style did not derive directly from the African American field hollers of the late nineteenth century, as is generally supposed. Blues music as we know it arose when the loose meter of the field holler was tamed by the standardized meters of the dance floor and as basic African melodies were yoked to—and made "strange" by—the European harmonies of the guitar and piano. "I don't dispute the possibility that a rural Mississippi blues style may have existed before the first white recordings," writes Keil, but white minstrel singers constitute the entire legacy of early recordings called "blues." For instance, the first sheet music copyrighted as a "blues" was Hart Wand's "Memphis Blues" of 1912; Wand, a semi-professional musician, was white. (Both black and white minstrel show performers already employed the term in uncopyrighted songs. Some of Robert Johnson's lyrics can be heard in "blues" recordings by white minstrel acts that date from this period.)

When Blind Lemon Jefferson was first recorded, he may well have been imitating what he heard on those early recordings, adapting a white stereotype and turning it into a black identity. Blues may have arisen "as a white idea about blacks" that infiltrated the African American community in its recorded, mass-mediated form. If there were twelve-bar blues with flattened thirds and sevenths and a I-IV-V-IV-I chord progression in the Delta prior to World War I, white interest in the form transformed it into something more than an occasional oddity. "Eventually," concludes Keil, "we may come to see 1928 to 1968 as a golden age of African American blues bracketed by white blues epochs."[10]

Tale Two: Cosmopolitanism

In 1957, a sixteen-year-old Paul Simon was singing doo-wop with his pal Art Garfunkel. Doo-wop and *a capella* rhythm and blues were all over his native New York; they were literally to be heard on street corners. The music was as familiar to Simon and Garfunkel as the music of their synagogue. Fascinated by Elvis Presley, Simon set himself apart by imitating Presley's hairstyle and dress. Elvis attracted Simon through his sheer *otherness:* "There was nobody named Elvis anywhere in the vicinity of Queens that I knew of."[11] But Simon was shy and did not feel confident about public performance without Garfunkel. The duo adopted the stage name of Tom and Jerry and imitated the Everly Brothers, whose "Bye Bye Love" was high on the charts. Tom and Jerry were invited to appear on Dick Clark's *American Bandstand* when their single "Hey Schoolgirl" reached number 54 in *Billboard*. Although Jerry Lee Lewis was on the same program, Simon had the nerve to adopt a Southern accent when Dick Clark interviewed them. Simon even claimed to be from Macon, Georgia (Little Richard's hometown).

Paul Simon's love affair with the music of "the other" was only beginning. Tom and Jerry had no further hits, but Simon and Garfunkel changed with the times and re-emerged in 1963 as a pair of Bleecker Street folkies. Prominent among their immediate sources was Bob Dylan, a Minnesotan who had invented his own biography to authenticate his borrowings from black Southern sources. Simon also soaked up British folk music during two lengthy trips to England in 1964 and

1965, a tradition reflected in Simon and Garfunkel's recordings of "Scarborough Fair" and "Anji." The duo's concerts and final album, *Bridge Over Troubled Water* (1970), included a tribute to the Everly Brothers in the form of a live rendition of "Bye Bye Love." By then, Simon and Garfunkel's more daring harmonies were patterned on a more obscure source, the recording *Music of Bulgaria* (1965), part of the Nonesuch International Series.

Bridge Over Troubled Water netted five Grammy Awards and was the biggest selling album of the early 1970s, its success ensured by "The Boxer" and the title track. The song "Bridge Over Troubled Water" was directly inspired by Simon's fascination with a line using that key phrase in the Swan Silvertones' arrangement of "Oh Mary Don't You Weep," a Gospel music classic. Aretha Franklin, no stranger to Gospel, reached number six on the "pop" charts and number one on the "soul" charts with her cover version of "Bridge." Simon, in turn, recorded half of *There Goes Rhymin' Simon* (1973) with the core backing musicians used by Franklin from 1967 to 1971, and in the very facility—FAME Studios, in Muscle Shoals, Alabama—where she recorded her breakthrough hit, "I Never Loved a Man (the Way That I Loved You)." As if to complete the circle, the Swan Silvertones accompany Simon on that album.

Little has been made of the fact that the *Bridge Over Troubled Water* album featured Simon's first use of the specific approach to "world music" that would gain so much attention with *Graceland* (1986). Long before the days of digital sampling, Simon took the instrumental track for "El Condor Pasa" (a Peruvian folk melody) directly from a commercial recording by the Peruvian group Los Incas. Simon wrote original words and contributed his vocal part.[12] He employed a similar technique for his first solo album, *Paul Simon* (1972). In that case, he traveled to Kingston, Jamaica, to record with reggae musicians for a backing track that became "Mother and Child Reunion." (The words and vocals were done later. The title was taken from a menu in a Chinese restaurant in New York: chicken with eggs). At the time, Simon complained that American music was "provincial."[13]

Simon's practices only sparked negative response after he visited South Africa in February 1985, then under the grip of the forced segregation of apartheid. The resulting *Graceland* album was built on basic tracks recorded with "township" musicians at Johannesburg's Pinki Jazz Clinic and Ovation Studio; they "knew how to make the sound naturally."[14] Many observers criticized Simon on the grounds that his visit violated the 1980 United Nations cultural boycott of South Africa. However, in 1987 the United Nations Anti-Apartheid Committee ruled that, lacking public performances there, Simon did not violate the boycott. The committee then extended the boycott to include cultural events beyond performing. A number of Simon's critics were not satisfied and continued to question his right to "own" and profit from the music produced in South Africa.[15] "Visually and aurally," the accusation runs, "Simon appears as the white master who exerts a benign rule over his black subjects."[16]

Tale Three: Exoticism

In the 1990s, intermittent interest in world music suddenly flowered in a fresh infatuation with the music of India. Within a fairly short period, Indian instrumentation sweetened releases by Def Leppard, Sam Phillips, Beck, Screaming Trees, the Butthole Surfers, Kula Shaker, Aerosmith, Sheryl Crow, Travis, the Mavericks, and Splashdown. Many mainstream fans got their first small taste of it from Madonna's performance of "Ray of Light" on the broadcast for the 1998 MTV Video awards; prominently sporting henna body art on her hands, wrists, and face, Madonna unveiled a new arrangement that drew on the sounds of India. A few months later, Beck brought a trio of Indian instruments along for his January 1999 performance of "Nobody's Fault but My Own" on *Saturday Night Live*.

Some of these musicians are signaling their personal interest in Indian culture and music. Others seem to have roots no deeper than the raga-rock of the mid-1960s—an offshoot of psychedelic rock that appropriated Indian instruments and sounds.[17] Notable examples of this minor trend include the presence of the sitar, an exotic twenty-one stringed instrument, on the Rolling Stones' "Paint It, Black" (1966), the Incredible String Band's "The Mad Hatter's Song" (1967), and the Box Tops' "Cry Like a Baby"(1968). (One of my personal favorites is the ersatz sitar tone featured on Joe South's 1969 swamp-rock classic, "Games People Play.") Truer to the spirit of the source were the

raga-influenced guitar improvisations of "East-West" by the Paul Butterfield Blues Band (1966).

The most serious exponent of the east-west hybrid was Beatle guitarist George Harrison. "One night at a London dinner party, George
was introduced to Ravi Shankar, India's best-known sitar virtuoso, who
was then little known by the Western world. Shankar invited George
to come to India to study with him."[18] Harrison took up Shankar's invitation, and the Beatles first featured sitar on "Norwegian Wood" (1965).
Three decades later, the British band Cornershop responded with their
own recording of "Norwegian Wood," sitar intact but with the lyrics rendered in Punjabi by the British-born Pakistani Tjinder Singh.

As Harrison continued to study sitar, he built "Love You To" (1966)
and "Within You Without You" (1967) around more authentic-sounding
groupings of Indian instruments. "Love You To" featured Anil Bhag-
wat's improvised tabla, while "Within You Without You" employed a
quartet of Indian instruments. Harrison actually released the first solo
album by any of the Beatles; most of his soundtrack album, *Wonder-
wall* (1968), was recorded in Bombay, India, using local musicians.
(Three decades later the album lent its name to the American breakthrough single by Oasis.) An unused track from the Bombay sessions
became "The Inner Light," Harrison's first composition to appear on
a Beatles single—as the flip side of "Lady Madonna." The lyrics were
lifted almost directly from a translation of the Chinese classic, Lao
Tzu's *Tao Te Ching*. Although he soon realized that he would never
become a great sitar player, Harrison's commitment to the instrument
was no flash in the pan. Harrison worked with Ravi Shankar on a documentary film and soundtrack recording, *Raga* (1971), and Harrison
made sure that Shankar opened the two benefit concerts for the famine
victims of Bangladesh in August, 1971, affording him considerable
prominence on the subsequent album and documentary film. Shankar
also served as the opening act for Harrison's 1974 tour, promoting the
Dark Horse album. In 1997, Harrison both produced and contributed
instrumentation for Shankar's *Chants of India*. Ravi Shankar also played
a major role in the American version of raga-rock, but it had nothing
to do with the Beatles. This time, it was entirely through the medium
of recordings.

In Los Angeles in early 1964, producer Jim Dickson was gathering together the quintet that became the Byrds. Enticed by the offer of free cheeseburgers, the trio of David Crosby, Jim McGuinn, and Gene Clark practiced regularly at Dickson's World Pacific Studios, best known for jazz. Developing their signature harmonies and instrumentation, they added Chris Hillman, who had recorded bluegrass for Dickson, and then drummer Michael Clarke. Dickson found financial backing to purchase instruments and then, almost accidentally, got their demo recordings noticed by jazz great Miles Davis. Within days, Davis got them an audition with Columbia Records, who signed them. Their time at World Pacific gave the Byrds access to recordings of Ravi Shankar. Shankar worked at the studio when he toured the United States, releasing music through World Pacific Records. (Hardly a purist, Shankar played with jazz flutist Paul Horn on one World Pacific release.) David Crosby took some World Pacific recordings home with him. Driving from show to show in a rented motor home in the wake of their first hits, the Byrds were regularly subjected to Crosby's musical tastes. "I was trying to program my partners," relates Crosby, who kept putting Shankar and then John Coltrane's *African Brass* into the tape player.[19] As a result, the single "Eight Miles High" (1965) combines the music of both.

Gene Clark's graceful melody could easily support an arrangement dominated by the group's lush harmonies, in the mode of Byrds ballads like "John Riley" or "Wild Mountain Thyme." But the classic recording of "Eight Miles High" is best remembered for its complex instrumental interplay of bass, drums, and guitar. Derived from a four-note motif used to open Coltrane's "India," McGuinn's soaring riff is an electric guitar adaptation of the sound of the sitar. McGuinn's chaotic solo is his take on Coltrane's free improvisations. Sitar lines were also conspicuous in McGuinn's two guitar solos for "Why," first released as the flip side of the "Eight Miles High" single. Having lost the Byrds to Columbia Records, World Pacific tried to cash in by releasing an instrumental version of "Eight Miles High" on the Folkswingers' *Raga Rock* (1966), with a real sitar in place of McGuinn's twelve-string.

For the Byrds' final great single with Crosby, "So You Want to Be a Rock 'n' Roll Star" (1967), the group moved away from raga-rock to work with South African trumpet player Hugh Masakela. As before, Jim Dickson's World Pacific was the catalyst. Dickson organized a benefit concert in Los Angeles for a civil rights group—the bill also featured Masakela, the Doors, and Buffalo Springfield. Impressed by Masakela, the Byrds invited him to contribute trumpet to the "Rock 'n' Roll Star" single. They shared a stage again at the Monterey International Pop Festival in 1967, when Masakela joined them at the end of their set to recreate his horn part on that song. In an interesting twist, Masakela came to Paul Simon's defense in the wake of the *Graceland* controversy, eventually touring the world with Simon in 1987. At Masakela's urging, Simon added another politically active exile from South Africa to the tour, Miriam Makeba (once married to Masakela).

Tale Four: Plastic Soul

Most rock styles are identified with specific places. Nirvana and Pearl Jam made grunge synonymous with Seattle. Rockabilly is identified with Memphis, and the Summer of Love with San Francisco. The outlaw country movement was pure Austin, Texas.

In 1974, the spotlight was on Philadelphia, particularly Sigma Sound studio and its house producers, Kenny Gamble and Leon Huff. Working with a stable studio band built around Earl Young's drumming, Gamble and Huff were among the first black producers to follow the pattern of the Beatles: unlimited studio time was available to work on the basic grooves and then to sweeten each track with multiple overdubs. There would be some overlap between the Philly sound and the disco hits of the second half of the 1970s, but the sound of Philadelphia dominated the airwaves between 1972 (the O'Jays' "Backstabbers" and Billy Paul's "Mrs. Jones") and 1976 (the Spinners' "The Rubberband Man"). The apotheosis of their production may well be the theme song they contributed to television's *Soul Train:* "TSOP (The Sound of Philadelphia)," which hit the top spot of both the pop and R&B charts in 1974. A funky beat battles a sweeping string arrangement, gradually augmented by nightclub horns and a touch of swirling church organ. The song's message was a simple invitation: "People all over the world! People all over the world!"

Although Gamble and Huff continued to produce top-ten hits throughout the 1970s, the music came to sound increasingly "soft" in the face of Eurodisco.[20] But while Gamble and Huff were still at their commercial and creative peak, David Bowie's *Diamond Dogs* tour arrived in Philadelphia for two nights at the Tower Theater. Recording the shows for the superfluous *David Live* (1974), Bowie decided to cut some demo tracks and booked time at Sigma. Delighted with the studio and the local musicians, Bowie returned for eight days in August and cut nine usable tracks.

As Davie Jones with the King Bees and then as vocalist for the Manish Boys, Bowie had been an unsuccessful participant in the first British invasion. It was an "invasion" in which commercial forms of blues were interpreted, recommercialized, and resold to their country of origin. Except for Bowie's contributions on saxophone, his early efforts were strongly influenced by the Rolling Stones, the Who, and the Yardbirds. There was little direct influence of African American music on Bowie's first half-dozen solo albums. *Pin-ups* (1973), on which Bowie recreated his "favourites from the 1964–67 period of London," contained only the music of white British and Australian groups.

Because Bowie had established himself as one of the most theatrical and British of British rock stars, many fans experienced quite a shock when the "Young Americans" single (1975) was so obviously derivative of *current* black styles. Working for the first time with former James Brown sideman Carlos Alomar, Bowie created the *Young Americans* album, which featured smooth vocal arrangements in the style of Gamble and Huff—largely thanks to the arranging and singing of Alomar's friend Luther Vandross. In short, Bowie took the Philly sound and fronted it with a white voice. He jump-started his floundering career with two hit singles, the title track and "Fame." Based loosely on the bass pattern from Shirley and Company's "Shame Shame Shame" (1975) and a guitar riff from James Brown, "Fame" was one of two tracks recorded with John Lennon in January (after the Sigma sessions). "I'm really knocked out that people actually dance to my records," said Bowie afterwards, "but let's be honest . . . 'Young Americans' is the definitive plastic soul record."[21] Nonetheless, "Fame" led to his appearance on *Soul Train*, a program that almost never featured white performers.

Thank You for Talkin' to Me Africa: Musical Appropriation

Musical content moves from one culture to another; we know this well even from non-Western cultures.

—Bruno Nettl[22]

Basically, every rock 'n' roller is a hybrid of some very diverse influences, and we were no exception.

—Phil Everly[23]

Appropriation is basically a fancy label for certain types of borrowing. A jumble of practices are bunched together under the concept, the common element being the way "appropriation" serves as a synonym for "'use." When literary theorists talk about a child's "appropriation" of *The Cat in the Hat*, they mean that she read it. That very broad sense of the term, dating back at least to Edmund Burke's writings in the eighteenth century, is not the focus here. My focus is the special case of artists from one culture adopting the artistic forms of another culture, as in Paul Simon's appropriation of African music and David Bowie's appropriation of Philly soul. Appropriation is contrasted with the use of cultural products that are traditional parts of one's own culture (i.e., enculturation).

While popular musicians often "pick up" the musical elements of other cultures, such practices are culturally, politically, and morally complex. In discussing such issues, I hope to suggest that they are even more complex than typically thought. Here, I borrow an insight from the arguments of Michelle Moody-Adams, who argues that prevailing positions in social and cultural anthropology assume that cultures are internally integrated wholes and that each culture is fundamentally a set of self-contained and discrete practices and beliefs.[24] The same assumptions infest discussions of appropriation in cultural studies, folklore studies, and ethnomusicology. But these assumptions are highly questionable.

As a first approximation, it is important to think of appropriation as a borrowing of cultural rather than material resources. The Navajo Indians of the American Southwest are famous for their so-called "sand painting," which is more aptly described as drypainting. (Powdered pigments are arranged on a bed of sand on the hogan floor during ritual chants, then destroyed at the end of the ceremony.) But the Navajo people adopted the practice from the neighboring Pueblo Indians. In the terms just summarized, the modern Navajo who undertakes mastery of drypainting is not appropriating the practice, for its cultural significance has become second nature. Only the generation that introduced the practice appropriated it. Similarly, the techniques of Navajo blanket weaving were appropriated from the Peublo Indians, while their tools for carding wool are copies of Spanish ones.

Some borrowings are perfectly harmless. ("Hey, Joe, borrow me your jumper cables so I can get this car started," is the sort of request that one commonly hears in Minnesota.) Others are clearly subject to censure, such as the girl who takes off with Bob Seeger's American Express card in "Sunspot Baby." Yet there is surprisingly little debate about the morality of *cultural* appropriation and where it fits into the range of borrowings. It is often asserted, with minimal argument, that appropriation is fine unless one belongs to a dominant cultural group. No one, so far as I can tell, has ever criticized the Navajo people for appropriating drypainting and weaving techniques. No one sees any problem in African Americans in New York's South Bronx creating hip-hop music by borrowing Jamaican DJ practices and Puerto Rican syncopation from recent immigrants. Yet many cultural theorists and persons of color believe that appropriations by white Europeans and Americans from other cultures are automatically exploitative and fundamentally wrong.[25] (Indeed, many recent writers treat "appropriation" as synonymous with "wrongful cultural appropriation.") Since rock would not exist without appropriation, this is a deeply troubling charge against rock. While they are not the same things, mainstream rock is heavily indebted to the blues, so appropriation of the blues is an important test case for consideration.[26]

Yet what, precisely, is supposed to be so wrong with appropriation? It is not simply a question of actual economic exploitation: George Harrison's sitar licks on "Norwegian Wood" seem immune from the charge that Harrison, then a pop musician of low cultural status, took advantage of Ravi Shankar, an Indian "classical" musician. Since we are talking about George Harrison's and Paul Simon's *musical borrowings*, the accusation of media imperialism is not a complaint that American values are being imposed on India or black South Africans. It is a very different charge from the complaint that lyrics and video images which position the non-Western "other" as a resource for exploitation thereby degrade and denigrate them. That charge parallels the complaint that rock's typical representations of women are objectionable because they defame and degrade women (addressed in my later discussion of rock's gender problems).

Many theorists locate the problem in the *symbolic* exploitation communicated by these borrowings, as the individuals symbolically represent the larger cultures to which each belongs. Timothy Taylor devotes a recent book to the argument that appropriation is a cultural practice through which colonialist ideology sneaks back into the postcolonial world. While he recognizes that Paul Simon was motivated by a genuine love of South African music, Taylor contends that Simon's behavior constitutes a wrongful practice of domination. Yet Taylor devotes almost no space to the theoretical question of how appropriation's recapitulation of "the old subordinating structures of colonialism" actually *harms* anyone in this new, purely symbolic form.[27] While Taylor's criticisms are often on target when directed at the marketing of world music, it is simply unclear how ideology ever gets encoded into the music in a way that would reach most listeners.

Perhaps it is supposed to be obvious how *Graceland*'s music advances colonialist ideology. At the very least, it seems to require three assumptions. First, it assumes that rock musicians have attained enough status to count as intellectuals and members of the dominant sphere of culture. Second, that as such they count as representatives of the dominant culture when appropriating from others. Thus Simon's—or Harrison's, or Bowie's—individual behavior is a display of domination. Third, that their display of domination in creating the music spills over into the meaning of the music, so that the audience is exposed to their displays of domination.

Appropriation is assimilated to another situation that often arises in the interaction of formerly distinct cultures. As John Travolta's character relates in the film *Pulp Fiction* (1994), the arrival of McDonald's

"Quarter Pounder" in Paris was complicated by French reliance on the metric system. McDonald's renamed it the Burger Royale. ("Burger" had already been appropriated from American English.) Yet it would be unusual to regard *McDonald's* as having been appropriated by the French. McDonald's seems to have done something *to* the French. While they now have something they did not have before (much the way fans of world music have new sounds to hear), they are dominated rather than dominating in this exchange. For the McDonald's Corporation controls the spread of its product while existing apart from the cultures it infiltrates. This pattern is variously described as cultural imposition, "swamping," or homogenization. Where the United States is the offender, it is simply Americanization. Concern over such practices is not confined to the bureaucrats at France's Ministry of Culture charged with protecting French culture from corrupting influences.

Many cultural theorists lump appropriation and Americanization together as cultural imperialism, of which *media imperialism* is a major element.[28] Media imperialism is usually considered a problem when aggressive capitalist economies (or, more precisely, their representatives) benefit from their presence in another culture, particularly a non-Western culture, commercially exploiting what was (until then) noncommercial. As David Bowie puts it, "To be in Java or somewhere on the day a McDonald's opens is really depressing."[29] McDonald's outlets are now found in more than one hundred countries. Or consider the Japanese craze for singing Merle Haggard and Frank Sinatra tunes in karaoke bars. These "borrowings" are between two of the world's most aggressive capitalist economies. Japanese karaoke adapts American commercial products for local needs. But this cultural transfer begins to look like cultural imperialism if it is found to *replace* "native" practices; if, for instance, the practice of visiting karaoke bars is a major factor in the decline of the traditional geisha system, with the sound of honky tonk replacing the sound of the three-stringed *samisen*.

Cultural imperialism also arises within culturally plural societies, like the United States, where a dominant group constantly threatens the cultural cohesion and continuity of other, dominated groups. On these grounds, when the Navajo copied Pueblo drypainting and blanket weaving, it was not cultural imperialism. But it was a case of cultural imperialism when white Americans first convinced a few Navajo ceremonial chanters to recreate their drypaint designs with "wet" paints on cotton cloth for commercial sale, around 1903–05. The introduction of commerce continually threatens to undermine the traditional significance of the rituals associated with drypainting. In a parallel manner, no problem arises if Mississippi John Hurt wants to sing "You Are My Sunshine" (although even that is sometimes called into question). But warning alarms sound when whites appropriate African American music.

We have, therefore, two rather different modes of media imperialism, appropriation and Americanization. One involves the "theft" of cultural materials, while the other involves the imposition of one culture on another. Both occur with popular music. The common element is that processes of commodification and mass art mediate the activity. This element of cultural interaction is the obvious place to search for a common wrong in the range of cases I have identified.

Money Changes Everything: Co-optation

Most Americans have a taste for shit. That's why they like [John] Mayall and ignore Robert Johnson. They like distortions of the real thing.
—Johnny Otis[30]

Charles Keil is as clear as anyone is when it comes to articulating the central concerns about media imperialism in popular music. The author of important studies of Chicago blues, polka music, and the indigenous music of the Tiv tribe of Nigeria, Keil is philosophically opposed to any commercial mediation of music.

Keil's main case against cultural crossovers and cross-fertilizations is that "exploitation" inevitably follows with any appropriation of traditional, *collective* musical forms. "All the traditions get screwed over. . . . How many more decades do we have to see before we can tell the next layer of exploited third-world musicians not to buy the dream?"[31] Here, Keil is specifically bemoaning the "world beat" phenomenon, which he likens to Leonard Chess's exploitation of Muddy Waters. Keil recognizes that Waters did not regard himself as exploited, working for Chess for three decades on no contract beyond a handshake. But Keil believes that the arrangement "smacks of the old plantation and paternalism."[32] Like Deep Throat's clue to the journalists digging into the Watergate scandal, Keil's mantra is to follow the money.

Keil is not just criticizing the exploitation of individual musicians (Muddy Waters by Leonard Chess or the South African session players by Paul Simon). His further target is the cultural imperialism that typically accompanies the expansion of capitalism, producing a "consumer culture" that displaces existing cultures.[33] Here, Keil's position dovetails with that of Amiri Baraka (LeRoi Jones). Borrowing from a blues lyric by Sonny Boy Williamson, Keil calls it "fattening frogs for snakes," while Baraka calls it "the Great Music Robbery."[34] Musical appropriation by capitalist cultures supposedly wrongs the originating culture, not just the individual musicians who are personally exploited. Indeed, their indictment of such appropriation would stand even if it could be shown that no individual was exploited in the process; nothing really stands or falls on the question of whether Leonard Chess exploited Muddy Waters. If Leonard Chess is a villain, it is because he wronged the African American community.

As with the aesthetics of R. G. Collingwood, Keil recommends the ideal of face-to-face interaction between musicians and audience. For Keil, this position also favors live recordings of music for the way they preserve audience-artist interaction. (Keil admits that recordings have been of some benefit in the creation of some musical communities, but he still regards direct artist-audience interaction as the norm against which everything else is to be measured.) In the overlap of Keil and Collingwood, we see that ethnomusicology and philosophical aesthetics can be comrades in arms. However, I think that their common position leaves something to be desired.

A key element of this position is a principled objection to copyright laws. Here Keil echoes Collingwood, complaining that the modern system of legal copyright is ruining music. Both call for a communal system that does not assign ownership of musical materials to individuals. The power of music comes from *participation*. As Keil puts it, people "have to be satisfied in their localities and to feel intense local involvement, participation, and deep identification."[35] In particular, local involvement means direct interaction between musicians and audience, ensuring that the needs of the audience are genuinely satisfied. Although their vocabulary is quite different, both Keil and Collingwood are interested in the way that art plays a role in the emotional life of the community. A great singer is, literally, "the voice of your people." The successful musician's style is always a function of the community in which it developed, and in this rather limited sense Keil allows that "everyone's music belongs to everybody else."[36] Any musical idea should be available for anyone else's use, without charge (through illegal sampling and bootlegging, if that's what it takes in a capitalist system). If a black rapper gets rich from a record, Keil opines, the bulk of the money belongs back in the 'hood.

Commercial appropriation of oral traditions—whether "folk" (Muddy Waters leaves the plantation and heads to Chicago; Ravi Shankar gets an American recording contract) or some other "collective" musical culture (Hugh Masakela's work with the Byrds)—results in music that is *commodified*. In this system, music does not emerge into the light of day unless it fits into all the hoops of modern contracts and copyright law. It goes without saying that these steps determine the distribution of all profits generated by the commodities that are thereby created. This flies in the face of the lesson that Keil draws from his studies of Native Americans and the Tiv: music is a "natural" component of the social world. It is not, in its original and natural form, a commodity. "The only people who profit from copyright are the huge, ever-growing companies and an ever-smaller cluster of superstars. Everybody else is getting screwed by it."[37]

As in the work of so many theorists of popular music, power relations embedded in class relations are thought to be the dominant force in shaping the music and its meaning. The appropriation of music is thought to be particularly evil and pernicious for commodifying what is not, in its original form, a commodity. However, if one is not already committed to the ideal of a classless society, the commodification of a social enterprise is not obviously a loss. But I am just pessimistic enough to think that access to recorded music and other mass art will continue to demand acceptance of music's commodity status for some time to come.

Communal Property and Commodity Culture

If Adam and Eve were naked before the fall, let's all get naked!
—Charles Keil[38]

Muddy Waters was like a king. You never treated Muddy Waters with disrespect. . . . He came to Chicago, just like my father, and what's an immigrant's big dream? To make money.
—Marshall Chess, son of Leonard Chess[39]

I want to suggest that objections to the commercial side of mass art mask another, deeper objection to the appropriation and commodification of music. The deeper objection is that appropriation through commodification violates the integrity of an internally integrated whole. Mass art drives out genuine popular culture, so that a self-contained and coherent way of life is no longer self-contained. Integrated cultures are destabilized.

Modern musicology's search for "natural" music continues a trend in Western aesthetics that can be traced back at least to the sixteenth century. In 1562, the Council of Trent of the Roman Catholic Church called for liturgical music that would be functional, that is, intelligible to the congregation. It would avoid the impurities of musical showmanship of secular styles. The forerunner of opera appeared in Florence within two decades, the result of a conscious attempt to return to the synthesis of music and drama found in ancient Greek theater. Similarly, Keil believes that *modern*, Western music is debased in comparison with natural, noncommercial modes of music, which should be revived. His conviction that debauched musical practices are replacing healthy ones reverses typical charges of cultural imperialism, which worry that the dominant culture destroys "weaker" ones. In this, Keil recalls the analysis of Peter Burger.[40] Both are carrying forward a theme of Jean Jacques Rousseau: "All the true models of taste are in nature." In situations where the arts are subsumed under business relations, taste is debased. We turn to "beauty which has its source in whim subject to caprice and to authority and is no longer anything other than what pleases those who lead us."[41] What is natural and communal is debased when it becomes business.

Consider an analogy. The need for food is natural, if anything is, and in virtually every "primitive" society, eating is a communal event with clearly prescribed rituals. But it hardly follows that restaurants should be banned, or even that chain restaurants are immoral. To take an even simpler case: drinking water, juice, and fermented beverages is more "natural" than drinking soda pop. Commercial soft drinks manifest the same commodification that upsets Keil in the case of music; a few corporations get rich as Coke and Pepsi replace more "natural" choices in our daily lives. As a few monolithic corporations come to dominate an area, our choices diminish: I like to drink cream soda, but it cannot be purchased at my local supermarket. Even coffee was an intensely social drink when it first caught on in Europe in the seventeenth century, giving rise to the European cultural staple of the coffeehouse. (Bach's "Coffee Cantata," BWV 211, of 1734, features a hilarious domestic drama in which a father and daughter argue over her addiction to coffee.) But in many American cities the local coffee shop competes with the omnipresent Starbucks corporation. In one small town near San Francisco, local residents recently fought a new Starbucks by distributing bumper stickers that read "Friends don't let friends visit Starbucks." Surely the coffee at a local coffee shop is no closer to "nature" than that brewed by an international firm. Both are removed from what's found "in nature" and the degree of commercialization involved does not make our pleasure in one or the other less natural.

More importantly, what if remaining the same is not what a substantial number of people in those cultures choose for themselves? If Westerners are disturbed to find people in the Third World drinking Diet Coke, watching *Baywatch*, and hustling to get a recording contract, perhaps it is the Western observer who has the problem in thinking that native cultures should remain static, "natural" communities or should only embrace changes that conform to our ethnocentric perspective about other societies. This question will be taken up in more detail in the next section.

A second problem with some accounts of cultural imperialism is that they are deeply paternalistic. Joseph Shabalala, leader of Ladysmith Black Mambazo, responded to the charge that Paul Simon had no business in South Africa: "Those who criticize Paul Simon and say that he did wrong to come and do this thing, they themselves are now ashamed, because so many people have said this is good—especially my group. It was my chance, this was a good opportunity to disclose our music all over the world, because many people didn't know this kind of music. . . . I say that what Paul Simon did for us is good."[42] Keil responds that Shabalala should "be content" with less, on the grounds that "nobody needs that extra margin of greatness and stardom anymore." Stardom simply feeds the system of "wicked exploitation."[43] Others complain that Simon's collaboration with Ladysmith Black Mambazo benefited the forces of apartheid more than it benefited the oppressed majority in South Africa. But such arguments assume that one is a better judge of the true interests of the people in question than they are themselves. While we can see that musicians from oral traditions will be "screwed" by their participation with multinational corporations or as the pawns of the government, those individuals are in no position to decide this for themselves. In other words, we should not allow them to benefit someone else by becoming musical "tokens." We must not allow them to abandon their traditions, language, and rituals in order to Westernize or to become fodder for white Western musicians. Of course, this claim to know better is precisely what constitutes paternalism.

As noted by Keil's sometimes collaborator, Steven Feld, there is also a disharmony in Keil's belief that it is fine for him to make a living *writing* about traditions (without turning over his royalties to the people he writes about), but wrong for others to market *recordings* of the same traditions. Keil seems to absolve himself on the grounds that his motives are pure, and he feels free to condemn Bob Dylan, Frank Zappa, and Sting because their political activism is found wanting.[44]

It may be the nature of ethnomusicology to emphasize some similarities at the expense of others. The Tiv are just not very comparable to Muddy Waters and Ladysmith Black Mambazo, who were already professional musicians in a commodity culture when they began to work with white producers. Muddy Waters grew up in a cultural space where it was common to learn blues from commercial recordings. When Eric Clapton adapted Robert Johnson's "Cross Road Blues" (1936) as Cream's "Crossroads" (1968), he was following Johnson's lead, for Johnson had based the song on another recording, Charley Patton's "Down the Dirt Road Blues" (1929).[45] Arthur "Big Boy" Crudup's "That's All Right, Now, Mama" (1947) was supposedly "stolen" by Elvis Presley as his first single, "That's All Right" (1954). Asked his thoughts on Presley's behavior, Crudup reported that he had received regular royalty statements. He also noted that black singers such as B. B. King and Elmore James had been less than forthright about getting royalties to Crudup when they recorded his songs. Asked if he had any animosity toward Elvis, he said, "No. . . . They're all right with me," suggesting that he made no distinction between black or white covers of his songs.[46]

Money matters aside, Baraka thinks that Muddy Waters has the right to emulate Robert Johnson and Charley Patton because Waters is an African American. Eric Clapton has no right to do so, because he is not. But this argument treats the blues as the intellectual property of African American culture.[47] Baraka's case for this, however, is that *individual* members of the black community are the chief stylistic innovators in the blues tradition, and that the achievements of these *individuals* are denied in the process by which Clapton's "Crossroads" replaces Johnson's "Cross Road Blues." Just as Elvis is remembered while Crudup is forgotten, Clapton's "competence" comes to overshadow Johnson's "genius."[48]

Of course, this argument against appropriation cuts both ways, for attributing it to Robert Johnson's genius undercuts any claim that "Cross Road Blues" is a collective achievement. Such arguments presuppose a notion of intellectual property in which *individuals* have rights regarding the products of their creative work. Thus, the blues cannot belong to the African American *community*. There is no clear way to derive communal ownership claims from the intellectual property rights of individuals within that community. On the other hand, it is not altogether clear that Baraka *wants* to invoke an English legal concept that was first recognized in 1710.[49]

Suppose we grant the assumption that the blues tradition did *not* treat music as property (a commodity) in its original, African American culture. What happens when Muddy Waters brings a country tune to Chicago in 1943, rewrites a few words, and records it in 1948, claiming authorship?[50] It is not clear how his action of copyrighting the song constitutes theft (i.e., wrongful loss of property). To draw on the foundational assumptions of property rights, consider John Locke's discussion of how *communal* ownership (the state of nature) gives way to *personal* property. It was Locke, after all, who codified modern attitudes about property in the phrase "life, liberty, and the pursuit of property" (amended to "the pursuit of happiness" in its famous American appropriation). In Locke's *Second Treatise of Government,* one acquires property rights in certain "goods," transforming the communal into one's own, by "mixing" one's labor with it. In short, by modifying it. The community is not wronged as long "there is enough, and as good, left in common for others." One of the more noxious by-products of this idea is the implication that migratory peoples do not own their homelands if they do not "improve" them, again suggesting that modern property rights are not the model for thinking about some traditional cultures.

No one faults Muddy Waters's behavior in making a commodity out of a "folk" source. Although Waters's motives were blatantly commercial, he never deprived the community of anything. Problems supposedly arise when the dominant ("slave-master") culture undertakes "co-optation" and "commercial dilution" of the music, *replacing* authentic African American expression with similar but *inferior* music.[51] Similar charges surface with respect to white rappers such as the Beastie Boys: "Not only does pop put Black art under siege but the natural function of culture and the way it perpetuates itself are all undergoing an obvious, shameless, systematic perversion."[52] The charge is that when Eric Clapton, Bonnie Raitt, Stevie Ray Vaughan, and Paul Butterfield appropriate blues styles, or when the Beastie Boys and Eminem appropriate hip-hop, their commercial imitations merely skim the surfaces of the style. Whatever it is that they're selling to white audiences, it is not what the best African American artists sell to African American audiences. However, in Locke's terms, whites have mixed their labor with it— after all, Baraka harps on the fact that whites *change* the music when they appropriate it. They do not, despite Keith Richards's words, "pick it up." It is *not* "just like being a receiver." Hence those engaged in appropriation have some right to claim ownership of the music they perform.

Baraka's argument also contains the complaint that white blues music lacks another sort of authenticity; "white blues" is *inappropriately* derived from the black sources, leading to a music that does not pre-serve the deep realms of meaning that make it so expressive within an African American context. Yet, considered on a case-by-case basis, some whites seem to have been properly initiated into the blues community. There is, for instance, Dr. John (Malcolm "Mac" Rebennack), who learned New Orleans piano from its acknowledged master, Professor Longhair (Henry "Roy" Byrd). As "Dr. John, the Night Tripper," Rebennack scored two major hits in 1973 with "Right Place, Wrong Time" and "Such a Night," on which he worked with the Meters and Allen Toussaint.[53] We can similarly point to Paul Butterfield, who grew up listening to Chicago blues music on the radio. Butterfield perfected his harmonica style by sitting in with Muddy Waters and Little Walter. Or consider Mike Bloomfield, who came to national attention as one of two lead guitarists in Paul Butterfield's integrated blues band of the 1960s. Bloomfield perfected his playing sitting in with Howlin' Wolf and Big Joe Williams. Blues harmonica virtuoso Charlie Musselwhite fol-lowed a similar path through the Chicago blues scene. More recently, B. B. King has toured with white blues-guitar prodigy Kenny Wayne Shepherd, who describes King as his mentor. Do we therefore regard Shepherd as more authentic than, say, Jonny Lang, merely because Lang learned to play blues guitar in Fargo, North Dakota, mainly by listening to records?

But a case-by-case approach does not really deal with the charge that *most* of the blues played by whites is inauthentic and as such poses a threat to African American culture. Having found little merit in the other common complaints against appropriation, I will now turn to the criticism that the cultural dilution that comes with media imperialism amounts to cultural genocide.

6

Don't Play That Song

Autonomy, Dilution, and Cultural Genocide

Let's put it bluntly: how can a pampered, milk-faced, middle-class kid who has never had a hole in his shoe sing the blues that belong to some beat-up old black who lived his life in poverty and misery?

—Albert Goldman

White appropriation attempts to erase the culture it plunders—a metaphor for the submission that dominant groups will upon others.

—Armond White

Charges of wrongful appropriation tend to be expressed as accusations that a musical activity is inauthentic. Those accusations dovetail into concerns about commodification. These links can be read as a symptom of a deeper concern. They can be read as a proposal that appropriation of African and African American music undermines the *autonomy* of black culture. In Baraka's words, "after each new wave of black innovation . . . there was a commercial co-optation of the original music and *an attempt to replace it with corporate dilution.*"[1] The "original" music is replaced with diluted music: rhythm and blues gives way to rock and roll as Muddy Waters gives way to Eric Clapton and the Jon Spencer Blues Explosion.

This is not the charge that whites have robbed African Americans of their property. It is the harsher accusation that appropriation contributes to cultural genocide, threatening the very existence of African American culture. Although Baraka simply calls it "genocide," it is not, for the individuals survive their loss. Even if the changes result in a world in which individuals lose their present culture, so they are no longer members of an identifiable African American community, Tiv community, or Ojibwe community, everyone involved will still have a cultural identity of *some* sort. Yet there is an important sense in which an involuntary loss of cultural identity represents a loss of self, a loss of personhood that is akin to genocide. The analogy with genocide hinges on the thesis that, were it not for the nonreciprocal behavior of the cultural imperialist, the "dominated" culture *would not have changed*. Hence the cultural change is imposed and can be understood as a wrongful "killing" of a culture (rather than a legitimate transformation).

The concern is that when the acoustic patterns of African American music permeate the dominant white culture and become part of that culture, those sounds also come to embody the values and ideas of the dominant culture. African Americans constitute a distinct American subculture, and most do not embrace the ideas and values projected into the music by the dominant culture. So the music will no longer embody the ideas and values of the black community. Baraka argues that this is precisely what happened to early jazz, which became "swing" when whites appropriated it.[2] However, we will make little progress in coming to grips with this criticism unless we get a better sense of its underlying assumptions. Doing so involves clarifying the notions of culture and cultural identity.

Let us begin with "culture." The idea has been refined considerably by Western intellectuals since the German term *Kultur* gave way to *Cultur* in the philosophies of Herder, Kant, and Hegel. It received its recognizably modern formulation in 1871, in E. B. Taylor's *Primitive Culture*. As it is now understood, it refers to the ideas, values, and associated behavioral patterns expected of members of an ongoing, self-identified group. These expectations are transmitted to new members of the social collective through the use of symbols, by modes of organizing behaviors, and through their embodiments in artifacts. As this suggests, the cultural is tightly connected with the social. Culture is distinguished from other aspects of the surrounding social terrain in terms of its constituting a system of *symbolic forms* through which people "communicate, perpetuate, and develop their knowledge about and attitudes toward life."[3]

Today, most cultures embrace a range of overlapping subcultures. Many of these subcultures are aligned with distinctions among social classes. Many of these subcultures have ethnic origins, by which I mean that the members are primarily identified as belonging by virtue of their common ancestry. At a risk of stating the obvious, ethnicity should not be confused with biological or "racial" identity. For those who recognize that there is no biological reality that justifies the racial distinctions we commonly impose upon individuals, racial classification must give way to ethnicity: thus "race music" gives way to "African American music," acknowledging that the category involves cultural identification linked to geographic origins. While one can choose to join a nonethnic subculture, one cannot elect one's own ethnicity. At best, an individual can choose to embrace or deny it. Thus the Sex Pistols' Johnny Rotten and the Pogues' Shane MacGowan belonged to the punk subculture by self-identification, while both belonged to London's Irish community by virtue of ethnicity.

Examining general issues of cultural imperialism, John Tomlinson makes a number of observations that may be useful in refining our thinking about appropriation. Tomlinson takes pains to remind us of two facts.[4] The first is that cultural identity is a matter of large numbers of people making the same choices with respect to practices, values, and shared meanings. There are no cultures over and above the cultural practices of communities. The second is that cultures are not static. Every culture has a historical, diachronic dimension. It is important to recognize the implications for cultural traditions that have an ethnic dimension. As with any culture that persists for very long, a particular ethnicity is a historical product. Ethnicity *develops* when cultural patterns are altered to meet the changing needs and circumstances of the community.

Unfortunately, cultures are often treated synchronically, as located at a specific place and "frozen" at a specific time. Many Japanese and

European visitors to the American West want to see cowboys and all the other trappings of the "old West" as represented in Hollywood films. But cultures exist diachronically, constantly changing and developing. Cultures are, quite literally, always in the process of becoming themselves: "This process comprises a ceaseless becoming, persisting, and passing away of symbolic forms."[5] This is not to say that everyone *in* the culture supports the changes; in "Are There Any More Real Cowboys?" (1985), Neil Young laments both the modern cowboy "snorting cocaine" and the spread of housing developments that put the cowboy out of business. Ironically, those who try to preserve an ethnic tradition are sometimes responsible for changing it. Muddy Waters self-consciously sought to play the *Mississippi* blues of Son House and Robert Johnson after he reached Chicago: "people like Wolf and myself," explained Waters, "we're doing the stuff like we did way years ago down in Mississippi."[6] But in amplifying the Mississippi blues for the Chicago club scene and then recording that variation, Waters altered the course of the very tradition he hoped to preserve.[7]

It is particularly tempting to regard culture as static (synchronic) when we consider its material aspects. The physical embodiments of a culture are all too easily equated with the culture. Typical artifacts often become emblems of the culture: the Coke bottle tossed from an airplane that initiates events in *The Gods Must Be Crazy* (1980), or the Fender guitar and black leather jacket that adorn Bruce Springsteen on the cover of *Born to Run* (1975). Yet the meanings of these artifacts are neither inherent nor automatically grasped. The fact that an artifact crosses cultural boundaries cannot determine how it is interpreted after relocation.[8] To gaze at the walls of an ancient Egyptian tomb is not to know the meaning of the hieroglyphs. So although Germans may love to watch *Baywatch* and Russians love *Dynasty* reruns, it hardly follows that they passively consume American ideology in the process. It is a matter of what they collectively make of it. Some cultures build their own pop culture on a backbone of imported goods, remaking popular culture in their own image. During most of the 1990s, for instance, Japan comprised about 20 percent of the world market for recorded music, yet 70 percent of those recordings were of Japanese pop musicians (amounting to some $5 billion in annual sales).

Even if one does not automatically dismiss commodified music, there is no denying that such music invites cultural strife. Key features of commodification—the transportation of the music between cultures, independent of any authentic initiation into the music for those hearing it and, eventually, copying it—fuel worries over media imperialism. The unequal power relation between different cultures may encourage homogenization or "cultural grayout," with a potential loss of cultural identity for the culture with less power.[9] This also seems to be the point of Baraka's cryptic suggestions about the evils of "diluted" music when they are separated from issues of economic exploitation.

As Baraka puts it, black self-determination begins with self-definition. African American culture "is defined by its opposition (contradiction) to the dominant culture." According to Baraka, "Its most advanced (even its healthiest) existence is in some fashion predicated on resistance. . . . that the culture of the oppressed exists at its most essential is a proof that people have survived and have not been liquidated by imperialism, its cultural aggression and genocide."[10] Because African Americans have remained virtual slaves, have not been allowed to "melt" in the American melting pot, and "have never been admitted" into the dominant culture, Baraka insists that black identity must be oppositional to that of the dominant culture. Music, as a key component of black culture, cannot remain oppositional if it is the music of most whites. Through white appropriation, the music takes on "values and [an] aesthetic . . . antithetical to the values and aesthetic of the artists themselves, as well as to the essentially black mass audience for whom the works were created."[11] Hence white appropriation and "dilution" is a form of cultural imperialism that constantly frustrates African American attempts at self-definition. Black music will not resonate with oppositional messages if white, dominant culture resonates with those same sounds. Intended or not, appropriation is a mechanism of cultural genocide.

Baraka's appeal to self-determination following self-definition suggests that he is talking about African American culture's loss of cultural autonomy. Since Baraka provides so little theoretical background about what this means to him, let us adopt John Tomlinson's analysis. For Tomlinson, what's wrong with one culture "swamping" another is that the "swamped" culture is prevented from developing along its own lines. The right to cultural self-determination (i.e., cultural autonomy) only makes sense in contrast to cultural heteronomy, "manipulation or control" of the culture by members of a different culture.[12]

However, only *actions* are autonomous or heteronomous. Where there is no choice (because there is no "agent"), there is neither heteronomy nor autonomy. Thus, many events occur that cannot be counted as actions; an earthquake alters many houses in the neighborhood, but the shaking of the ground cannot be traced to anyone's actions. In other cases we may have an agent who does something, yet there is no action. To count as an action, an agent's behavior must be purposeful and intentional, *reflecting the possibility of choice*. An involuntary sneeze is not an action.

So when a brick falls off a building during an earthquake and hits someone on the head, it makes no sense to ask whether the brick displayed autonomy. When an adult throws a brick at someone's head, we have an action and may very well inquire into the person's soundness of mind in order to determine if the act was autonomous. To determine this, we must examine the situation holistically: we do not ask whether the person's arm acted autonomously, even if the arm hurled the brick. We inquire about the person. Similarly, if we are concerned about cultural imperialism as a violation of autonomy, we might approach the culture or subculture *holistically:* like a person, a culture is not just the sum of its parts.

Tomlinson warns about the resulting difficulty of extending the notion of autonomy to cultures. Cultures just aren't the sort of things that are free or not free to act; even taken in a holistic sense, cultures aren't *agents*.[13] Cultures are contexts in which people live—contexts in which and from which people meaningfully choose. As before, we want to be careful not to confuse a culture with a society. Political institutions, like other social institutions, are thought to "act" autonomously. It is tempting to simplistically equate cultures with political entities such as nation-states. But since most modern nation-states are culturally diverse, it is clear that a category mistake is made in assigning autonomy to a culture along social or political lines. Political autonomy is not cultural autonomy.

The only plausible sense in which cultures "act" autonomously is that *representatives of the culture*, such as key agents controlling education and the arts, do so. Key individuals may make choices on behalf of the culture. Most members of the culture may embrace those choices. But the culture, in the holistic sense of the totality of collective practices, does not "make a choice." Moreover, the culture often changes *despite* choices sanctioned by prominent cultural representatives. Rock and roll became an American institution despite attempts to kill it by many key cultural agents. Vicious anti-rock campaigns were waged by ASCAP, the country's main implement for registering and licensing music, and by *Billboard*, the influential trade magazine of the music industry.[14] Prominent African American voices were equally damning. *The Cleveland Call and Post*, a black newspaper, damned Alan Freed's radio program for its attempt to "exploit the Negro teensters" with rhythm and blues music of "bum taste" and "low morality."[15]

Tomlinson rightly emphasizes that the autonomy principle directs us to examine actions of agents, not the outcomes for the culture. Any appeal to cultural autonomy leaves us "quite indifferent to the *outcomes* of cultural practices and processes." Cultural autonomy is violated when the agents who are the "gatekeepers" or representatives of the culture or ethnic community are displaced by the activities of outsiders, and as a consequence, indigenous cultural patterns and artifacts give way to cultural imports. As long as agents from a different culture do not control the process of change, "the autonomy principle is entirely satisfied." Even if all music comes to sound like Western rock, "defenders of autonomy could not grumble, so long as this homogeneity was the outcome of autonomous choice."[16] Appropriation and assimilation are common instruments of cultural change, and we must not attack them simply because we want other cultures to remain the same. As long as Joseph Shabalala and the other musicians are not coerced into working with Paul Simon, and as long as Muddy Waters is not coerced into working for Leonard Chess or playing music with Eric Clapton, the Band, Johnny Winter, and the Rolling Stones, the cultural homogeneity that might follow from such choices is not a matter for assigning blame.

Shakin' All Over

And then there was Johnny Kidd. Totally unlike any other English singer, Kidd was like some transplanted American maniac, steeped in rhythm & blues, snarling and swaggering as if no one had ever told him it wasn't proper for a British singer to be so crude.

—Greg Shaw, Editor, *Who Put the Bomp*[17]

Let us consider one example in greater detail. On standard accounts, rockabilly music was one of the five or so original styles of rock and roll. Pinpointing its cultural soil with some accuracy, Charlie Gillett called it "Memphis country rock."[18] It was Southern, it was white, and it originally emerged from Sun Studio, a small storefront operation at 706 Union Avenue, Memphis, Tennessee. It was codified in a very short period, 1954 through 1957, on the recordings of Elvis Presley, Carl Perkins, Warren Smith, Johnny Cash, Sonny Burgess, and a number of other young Southern whites.

But rockabilly attracted a broader audience. In the East Bay suburbs of San Francisco, the adolescent John Fogerty was studying the sound that he later romanticized as the "Big Train (From Memphis)."[19] (More than a decade later, Fogerty scored his first hit with Creedence Clearwater Revival's cover version of Dale Hawkins's "Susie Q.") Canada produced "the greasiest rockabilly of all, a leering, slobbering, second-generation singer," Ronnie Hawkins.[20] Buddy Holly crafted his version of the music on the plains of West Texas.

Rockabilly's emergence illustrates culture's historical or diachronic dimension. Rockabilly did not exist in 1953. In 1956 it was a well-defined musical form throughout much of the South. Its embrace by non-Southern whites is, in contrast, a cultural relocation. Yet there is little concern that this represents cultural imperialism or a violation of cultural autonomy. To some degree, rockabilly's rapid spread may have been due to the reception of its *meanings,* which tended to remain the same even after cultural relocation. You could dance to it, of course, but there was also its semiotic side. Both the individual songs and the genre itself seemed to have been understood as embodying basically the same values that it had for its originators: "Rockabilly was a celebration and a way out of the insidious social system that had risen in the South since Reconstruction to contain the so-called white trash. There was a menacing air of violence about it, and of impulsiveness. . . . Rockabilly was the young white Southerner's every Saturday-night blowout."[21]

This attitude received its most perfect embodiment in Carl Perkins's "Dixie Fried" (1956). His tale of a backwoods juke joint and its party out of control adopts a casual, matter of fact approach to violence, machismo, and inebriated hell raising. The music's raunchy, twitching swagger is perfectly suited to the emotions and stories exemplified in the lyrics, inviting every dissatisfied kid who felt left behind by the postwar economic boom. Since the broader audience voluntarily embraced the music, rockabilly musicians and Southern record labels did not impose alien ideas or values on working-class white fans in Canada or California. There is no obvious violation of autonomy in their appropriation of it.

Issues of cultural imperialism are thrown into sharper relief by the fact it soon had *British* fans. Thanks to Radio Luxembourg and the "media imperialism" of record retailing, rockabilly became the unofficial music of England's Teddy Boys. Also known as "Teds," they were named for the Edwardian clothing style they adopted around 1953: "bright peacock-blue or deep scarlet suits with velvet-collared jackets that ran down to their knees, and thick, crepe-soled shoes."[22] The Teds used the music to assert carnal rebellion to the older generation and class pride to their peers. Dick Hebdige describes them as "uncompromisingly proletarian and xenophobic . . . defiantly obtrusive." If the music *initially* meant America to them (an America filtered through Hollywood movies), its African American roots were obscured in the Atlantic crossing, and Teddy Boys "figured prominently in the 1958 race riots."[23] Within a short period, 1950s rock was "their" music, in a way that 1960s rhythm and blues or soul was not.

The Teddy Boys *voluntarily* appropriated rockabilly and other early rock and roll—even doing so in the face of strong social disapproval. Despite the racism of many Teds, they were as open to Chuck Berry as to Carl Perkins. Both singers were important influences on the Beatles, several of whom went through a phase as Teddy Boys. There was no organized plan by American record companies to "conquer"

British taste; Leonard Chess was not thinking about the market in Liverpool when he recorded Chuck Berry, even if Chuck Berry was pleased when the Beatles endorsed his music and spurred sales in 1964.[24]

The Teds had a surprising persistence, passing on their musical tastes and attitudes to subsequent waves of similarly situated British youth. As a result, 1950s rock 'n' roll remained in steady circulation in England. Bill Haley's 1954 recording of "Rock Around the Clock" was a top-twenty hit there in 1968. The music remained in print, licensed for local consumption on labels like Charly Records at a time when multinational labels only cared about new product. A strong revival took place between 1972 and 1974, feeding into early punk; Joe Strummer's 101'ers played some rockabilly. Strummer was only returning to his roots when the Clash featured Vince Taylor and the Playboys' "Brand New Cadillac" on *London's Calling* (1979). Although the basics of the music remained fixed, the meanings gradually changed. On Hebdige's interpretation, the 1970s Teds were "differently positioned in relation to their parent culture and other youth cultures." By enduring into a third decade, these later Teds seemed *traditional:* "an authentic, albeit dubious part of British heritage."[25] It made perfect sense to his English audience when Sid Vicious covered Eddie Cochran's 1958 hit, "C'mon Everybody."

In other words, the sound of rockabilly music became a part of British culture. Ted self-identification was at peak intensity in the early 1960s, as the dress styles and musical tastes of the mods arose as an alternative for working-class males. Growing up in Liverpool rather than London, the Beatles developed a more catholic taste and embraced rhythm and blues styles that London Teds detested. It is not entirely a joke when, in the "interview" sequence of *A Hard Day's Night,* a reporter asks Ringo whether he's a mod or a rocker (a 1960s Teddy Boy). "I'm a mocker," he replies.

Should white Americans be bothered that the Teddy Boys appropriated early rock and roll and then, through the Beatles and other performers, recycled it commercially in the early 1960s? Not really. It preserves autonomy, both of the British fans who created their own rock and roll scene and then of the Americans who bought the recycled music. Cultural autonomy requires a certain level of respect for the process by which the participants in a culture define and create themselves, and thereby their culture. It does *not* imply that a culture must remain static or that its cultural patterns must not overlap with those of other cultures. If the Teddy Boys decided for themselves that American rockabilly fit their cultural needs, the mere fact of its American origins does not count against the autonomy of the Ted subculture in developing their own subculture. (Autonomy is not isolationism, however xenophobic the Teds may have been.) If British youth don't care to sing Gilbert and Sullivan anymore, nobody wrongs English culture.

By the same logic, complaints like those of Baraka and Keil lose much of their sting. When British youths like George Harrison imitated Sun rockabilly while others copied the sounds they heard on imported Chess recordings, and when Westerners record non-Western music and repackage it as world beat or world music, it is still up to members of the originating culture to decide what musical tradition to follow. It remains open to *the participants* on both sides of the exchange to decide what *their* music will be.[26] Just as rock co-exists with bluegrass, country, church music, and a range of other popular forms in Arkansas or Oregon, *Graceland* and *Planet Drum* can co-exist alongside more "natural" musics in Africa. In the absence of a plausible case that large numbers of African Americans have fewer choices as a result of cultural appropriation, or that the members of Ladysmith Black Mambazo have fewer choices as a result of working with Paul Simon and signing with Warner Bros., any resulting musical homogenization does not deserve the label of cultural genocide. It would be "genocide" only if each culture is fixed and immutable in its cultural forms.

We may see dangers in cultural homogenization, but cultural diversity is not an end in itself. Two cultures currently predominate in South Dakota (Anglo and Native American), but South Dakota has no particular reason to seek diversification—there is no reason to suppose it would be a better place simply for having ten, twenty, or thirty distinct cultures within its borders. Respecting the processes of cultural autonomy (by *not* being paternalistic) will not always preserve cultural diversity.

Baraka's argument now looks less like a principled moral critique and more like a bid by an influential member of a culture to redirect a cultural shift of which he disapproves. Similarly, Keil may resist musical homogenization because it runs counter to his interests as an ethno-musicologist, and he may resist commercialization because it runs counter to his own preferences for "natural" musical communities. But neither of these legitimate criticisms has any moral force against the interaction of Paul Simon and Joseph Shabalala or of Muddy Waters and the Chess brothers.

We Are Family: Collective Rights and Collective Change

In a world where we're becoming more and more connected with things like, for example, the Internet . . . we need to recognize the specialties of small groups. They have a right to be what they are.

—Björk[27]

I thinks to myself how these white kids was sitting down and thinking and playing the blues that my black kids was bypassing. That was a hell of a thing, man, to think about.

—Muddy Waters[28]

Another dimension can be read into Baraka's emphasis on self-definition as a prerequisite for black autonomy. Perhaps there is an important difference between the appropriation of music from geographically remote cultures and the interactions of dominant and nondominant cultures within a culturally plural society. Perhaps the model for preserving cultural autonomy in the former case should not be extended to the latter. Whether or not Paul Simon did anything wrong in adapting the Everly Brothers, Peruvian folk songs, and Soweto township jive, we may have a very different situation when he appropriates African American gospel music or when David Bowie appears on *Soul Train* and resells James Brown riffs to African Americans. It is time to address the problem of "swamping."

Liberal theorist Will Kymlicka has developed a theory of "minority rights" or "collective rights" that is sensitive to just such issues. Focusing on culturally plural societies and the threat of cultural homogenization, Kymlicka articulates the conditions under which such homogenization would demonstrate a lack of respect for a minority ethnic community, particularly an aboriginal people. The heart of his argument is that in a culturally plural society, the dominant group will "get for free what the aboriginal people have to pay for: secure cultural membership."[29] Thus white Americans hear the sounds of "their" music everywhere and anywhere, becoming musically literate in it without effort or expense.

To personalize the example, as a child I made no effort to internalize the conventions of rock music, yet when I became interested in music in my teen years I already knew hundreds, if not thousands, of rock songs. An Ojibwe (Chippewa) child on a reservation in northern Minnesota, bombarded by the television and radio programming of the dominant culture, will have only occasional exposure to traditional Ojibwe songs and drumming. It will require considerable effort on the part of the child's family to ensure that he or she will find the tribe's music as "natural" as rock or hip-hop music. Ojibwe culture is at risk even if their own preference is to maintain it, through no fault of the Ojibwe people.

In practice, it can be very difficult to distinguish homogenization that comes from "swamping" by another culture from loss that comes about due to choices *within* the community. It is equally important to note that native, aboriginal, and other oppressed communities do not deserve special rights simply because they have, as a community, made a different choice. (For if that were so, *any* subculture might demand special rights after having become a subculture precisely by making different choices.) African Americans have no special "rights" to blues if the blues fell out of favor when new styles like Motown, soul, and funk supplanted the blues tradition within the African American community. Nor does an ethnic community deserve special rights simply because it makes choices that will be difficult or expensive to carry out (for then again, any subculture might demand special rights upon introducing a new, exotic cultural practice; Teddy Boys might decide to start eating lobster at every meal). The mere presence of special practices within a threatened community cannot justify special rights. Instead, any special rights must exist *to remove inequalities in the context of choice which arise before people even make their choices.*[30]

Cultural options always arise against an existing "context of choice," and one's cultural heritage is the most basic such context. We can only make meaningful decisions about our future by measuring our choices against our culture: "it's only through having a rich and secure cultural structure that people can become aware . . . of the options available to them, and intelligently examine their value."[31] *Forcing* Ojibwe children to attend school in English, systematically depriving them of their native language, is to heteronomously deprive them of one of the community's most significant tools for making choices in life. An accommodation must be made to preserve "native" use of that language if the Ojibwe people so desire. Similarly, my own state of Minnesota bans smoking inside public buildings but makes an exception for ceremonial use of tobacco by tribal members.[32]

In the case of the Teddy Boys, rockabilly suited their needs for its American flavor and its sharp, noisy contrast to the English "pop" charts of the 1950s. This choice made sense against the "secure" backdrop of the British class system; by British standards, the music was aggressive and defiant. The same music could have little value for African American teens living at the same time on Chicago's South Side; compared with the music of Muddy Waters and Howlin' Wolf playing in Chicago's clubs, Carl Perkins was the tepid sound of Southern white trash. However, if the tepid white imitation swamps the airwaves, African Americans may no longer have comparable access to their own music, and it will no longer figure in their context of choice for the musical dimension of the culture.[33] Thus, blacks had a legitimate complaint against MTV in the initial years when there was a virtual boycott of music by blacks on that station. But this admission deprives African Americans of grounds for complaint after MTV put hip-hop videos into heavy rotation and white teens embraced hip-hop music and culture. Only an extraordinarily static view of culture can find fault with MTV for being excessively "white" in 1981 and 1982 (thus swamping African American culture) and then again for making hip-hop too accessible to whites in the 1990s (thus diluting hip-hop's African American identity).

The payoff of Kymlicka's analysis is that whenever two cultures interact, special protections must be granted to the culture that is likely to face the loss of its culture *in spite of* the choices of its membership.

(MTV programmed more types of music because of, not in spite of, pressure by African Americans. Michael Jackson's "Beat It" video was the turning point.) This approach does not make the mistake of treating cultures as agents. It recognizes that respect for the individuals within the threatened culture requires respectful treatment—including special protections—of the cultural context from which they choose. When fear of the media imperialism of the United States leads Canada to restrict the amount of non-Canadian music on its airwaves, and France to limit the amount of American programming on French television, then the United States has no grounds for demanding unrestricted access to these markets. If the Ojibwe tribe decides to limit access to tribal ceremonies held on the reservation, to forbid the sale of tribal land to nonmembers, and to bring orphaned Ojibwe children back to the reservation rather than allow them to be placed in non-Ojibwe foster homes, then whites have no grounds to complain.

Kymlicka cautions that the context of choice must not be equated with the cultural practices or *character* historically associated with a community, such as religion or political organization. In short, he is quite sensitive to the difference between diachronic and synchronic analyses of culture that Tomlinson highlighted. Kymlicka strongly emphasizes the diachronic quality of culture; French Canadian culture "was radically transformed in the 1960s," yet French Canadians were not threatened in their cultural identity, for *they* had changed their own cultural practices. If French Canadians were less apt to be practicing Roman Catholics or to support parochial schools, it was not because Mormon missionaries flooded Montreal from the United States, shut down the churches and schools, and forced them to change. The cultural community, francophone Canada, continued. It is this sense of culture— "a viable community of individuals with a shared heritage (language, heritage, etc.)," free to be *and become* very different because of their own choices—that deserves protection though any special collective rights.[34]

Consequently, if the members of a subculture *seek* some degree of assimilation or choose to copy the dominant culture, there is no collective right to maintain the status quo. If some Navajo want to share their drypaint designs with whites, if some French Canadians want to become Mormons, or if some African Americans want to work with white record producers and sell records that will be copied by whites, then the community has no special right to prevent these actions simply to maintain the unity of the community or the continuance of its historical practices. Because cultural protection is motivated by respect for autonomy, it cannot be secured by *preventing* members of threatened cultures from assimilating into the dominant culture if they so wish. Upholding collective rights out of respect for autonomous choice does not justify refusing individuals the choice of cultural "emigration."[35]

Nor do collective rights prevent the dominant culture from imitating the threatened culture; enlarging the cultural space they occupy does not diminish cultural resources like language and music. If Muddy Waters helps Paul Butterfield learn to play blues and the patrons of the club don't walk out in protest, if Vanilla Ice raps in dance clubs in black neighborhoods of Dallas and the patrons cheer him on, or if David Bowie appears on *Soul Train* and most black viewers stay tuned, then Baraka has no high ground from which to object to the choices made by other African Americans. Since Muddy Waters became a musician in a cultural space in which it was well understood that recordings were a basis for learning to play the music of others, he was in no position to be surprised when the Rolling Stones played "Mannish Boy" and "I Can't Be Satisfied." Following Kymlicka, a culture is wronged only if it faces the loss of its cultural traditions *in spite of* the choices of its membership. The historical evidence just doesn't satisfy the best available criteria for saying that the dominant culture's appropriation of African American music amounts to cultural genocide.

Critics of free appropriation appear to be more concerned with preserving cultural *purity* and with maintaining cultural *differences* than with respecting cultural change that comes about through autonomous choices. Such critics also seem a tad hasty when making assumptions about the direction of causality. Given that all cultures change, and change rapidly in modern, industrial societies, it is nearly impossible to isolate the causes from the effects when two cultures interact in complex ways. (Recall the complex genealogy of Leadbelly's "Goodnight, Irene.") As Ray Charles explained, "along came Elvis Presley, and the white kids had a hero. . . but Black musicians started to get a little play, too. When the English boys came on the scene, they admitted where they got their inspiration and that caused even more interest in the real blues. I'm glad to see these youngsters doing our music. It enhances the guys who originated it."[36]

After scandalizing many African Americans by putting their "church" music onto the rhythm and blues chart, Charles scored one of his biggest hits with "Lonely Avenue" (1956), written by white songwriter Jerome "Doc" Pomus. Ahmet Ertegun, a Turkish immigrant, oversaw production. When Charles hit the number-one position on both the rhythm and blues and pop charts in 1962 by covering country music standards, he revealed that he'd listened regularly to the *Grand Ole Opry* since childhood.[37] Charles also reported how much he loved the playing of white swing players Artie Shaw and Benny Goodman.[38] Despite these influences, the music of Ray Charles is regarded as a paradigm of black popular music.

What sense can we make of the charge that as a black musical form attracts whites, white culture dilutes African American culture? If African Americans are alienated from white culture and are therefore engaged in a resistive project of self-definition, why do they care about inept white imitations of their music? The presence of *inept* forgeries of Matisse does not disrupt the market for original works by Matisse; only *excellent* forgeries have that power. (On the other hand, how inept was Benny Goodman if he attracted black players like Charlie Christian and fans like Ray Charles?) We should deplore the racism inherent in the practice of cutting into the profits of black musicians and independent labels by falsifying publishing and by promoting white "cover" versions of black hits, or the exclusion of black faces in the early days of MTV. But how is African American culture threatened when whites buy Vanilla Ice records? In other words, there is an important difference between the complaint that African Americans are routinely underpaid and squeezed out of the competition for dollars in the music industry, and the complaint that white imitations of African American music homogenize the culture. Furthermore, if the economic issue were largely about access to the money of white consumers, there would be no such issue without some homogenization of the musical culture.

Or does the bulk of the mass audience tend to accept the music only after the fact, as it ceases to be a fresh form for African Americans?

Urban audiences seemed to be moving toward funkier, harder edged sounds at about the time that David Bowie "discovered" the Philly sound. Shortly after Charles Keil studied B. B. King and Bobby Bland for *Urban Blues* in the 1960s, the audience for the blues "passed from the black community to white bohemia," including Chicago's South Side clubs at the heart of Keil's study.[39] Aware that musical culture is subject to change, Keil based his book on the assumption that cultural change "is usually measured, if at all, in generations and centuries."[40] Yet he seems to have been studying blues at just the time that black taste was shifting from the guitar-driven, urban blues of the 1950s to the more polished sound and look of Motown and the funkier rhythms of Memphis soul. "Young Negro kids now . . . they just turn away from the old blues," complained Muddy Waters as he watched his audience shift from black to white. "It's not the music of today; it's the music of yesterday."[41]

On any given weekend night that Muddy Waters performed in Chicago in the early 1960s, he played to an audience of seventy or eighty. If more young black men had shown up asking to sit in with the band to play harmonica, perhaps he would not have invited Paul Butterfield onto the stage. Waters formally integrated the Chicago blues in 1967 when he added a white harp player, Paul Oscher, as a regular member of his touring band. Other white players soon followed. Waters felt he had no choice: "There ain't enough of my peoples trying to get interested in playing the blues and that's what really keeps me kind of worried about it."[42] Waters, of course, was not the only blues player to confront his own community's lapse of cultural memory. In the late 1960s, B. B. King was gratified to receive an enthusiastic reception from white audiences at blues festivals and rock venues like the Fillmore Auditorium. But back home in Memphis, King's appearances at black clubs aroused almost no audience response. The indifference of African Americans "hurt him so badly that he has gone offstage and cried."[43]

Because African Americans were actively engaged in the reinvention of their own culture, new styles of black music emerged in each decade of the twentieth century. Nelson George claims that the "black audience's consumerism and restlessness burns out and abandons styles" more quickly than in the dominant white culture.[44] (Perhaps some of these changes were defensive responses to white appropriation, perhaps not.[45]) As a consequence, Muddy Waters's context of choice was very different in the early 1960s, when Paul Butterfield asked to sit in, than it had been in 1943, when Waters arrived in Chicago. In 1943 he could help create a new music. Twenty years later he was looking for a way to keep it going, and whites may have offered him hope. But we must never suppose that, were it not for the cultural imperialism of whites, African Americans would occupy a static context of choice.

Because he believed that they did not constitute "contemporary blues," Keil was not interested in spending any time in Memphis at Stax Records, interviewing Otis Redding. Keil was positively disdainful of the idea of visiting Motown, "the so-called Detroit sound engineered by Barry Gordy," in order to interview Gordy or Marvin Gaye or Diana Ross.[46] Consequently, Keil's seminal project of validating black urban culture downplayed the choices that many blacks were making for themselves. Rather than driving black musicians away from their own music, as Baraka supposes, white appropriation may be precisely what keeps "dead" cultural forms alive when African Americans shift to newer forms. While this process changes both the sound and the cultural meanings of black music, it does not follow that racist "corporate owners" of the music business and "critical establishment" are the main culprits in the process by which music gets watered down.[47] The same radio waves that brought the blues to Paul Butterfield brought the Grand Ole Opry to Ray Charles. Few cultures can remain uncontaminated without total geographic isolation. The Soviet Union made a valiant effort to avoid swamping by American popular culture and values; even then, Frank Zappa albums and Velvet Underground albums made their way behind the Iron Curtain to inspire dissident artists throughout Eastern Europe.[48]

By a rather indirect route we have now worked our way back to the topic of intertextuality. There are no "natural" or fixed affinities among texts: there are only cultural norms implicit in patterns of practice. The identity of a style or even piece of music depends on its derivation from other styles and pieces of music, and thus so does the cultural identity that musicians and audiences assert by embracing them. But practices evolve or even change with astonishing speed, so that previously incompatible styles are brought together as complementary rather than antagonistic. A living culture is a very messy thing, so messy that any distinction between pure and polluted cultural forms reflects little more than the tastes of the theorist who makes the distinction. But taste, it's said, merely classifies the classifier. What's being classified here is often the behavior of audiences rather than the music itself, and so the agency of the audience demands further attention.

1

Message in the Music

I used to beat on a five-gallon can when I was a kid, kerosene you know, beat on the bottom of it and sing. "I don't want no woman to chollyham my bone." I'd beat on that can and sing that all day long. I still don't know what that means.

—Muddy Waters

It would be silly to deny that the *activities* of certain musicians and record companies are exploitive and even colonialist. It simply doesn't follow that their *music* is similarly tainted. Playing the Beethoven violin concerto on a stolen Stradivarius won't make the music into an expression of theft. So how can the incorporation of "stolen" rhythms into a Peter Gabriel track like "Come Talk to Me" (1992) result in music that expresses postcolonial hegemony?[1] That accusation places too much emphasis on musicians—the Paul Simons and Peter Gabriels—as intellectuals whose behavior dominates and wrongs another culture. But what accounts for the transfer of meaning from source to audience?

I want to explore the position that a piece of music cannot be described as colonialist or disrespectful or hegemonic unless listeners can discover appropriate characteristics in the music. (I assume that we are talking about listeners with basic understanding of the music rather than naive listeners.) A melancholy composer may or may not produce a piece of melancholy music, just as a highly religious composer may or may not produce religious music. We don't normally assume that John Lennon's efforts to amass wealth and to relocate to the United States in the early 1970s inform the progressive political message of songs like "Imagine" and "Working Class Hero." Lennon's personal life did not reflect the values of a man pursuing a future without class distinctions and without national borders, yet "Working Class Hero" and "Imagine" brilliantly express higher ideals that Lennon himself did not always pursue.

In short, the source of a piece of music is relevant to interpreting it without being the only relevant factor. John Lennon worked with a relatively narrow range of musical resources, yet he managed to produce combinations of words and music that could not be predicted in advance. Some of Lennon's songs express progressive political views ("Woman Is the Nigger of the World," "Happy Xmas [War Is Over]"), while others express extremely traditional views about personal relationships ("Jealous Guy," "Grow Old With Me"). The fact that a song is by John Lennon does not determine the identity that it will convey.

Similarly, the place and time of a song's composition is relevant without being conclusive. The fact that a song was written at the height of the war in Vietnam does not make it a song about the war. The Byrds' "Draft Morning" (1968) and Creedence Clearwater Revival's "Fortunate Son" (1969) are about the war, but their album mates "Down on the Corner" and "Dolphin's Smile" are not. Nothing about the political activities of David Crosby or John Fogerty are relevant to the presence or absence of the anti-draft messages of "Draft Morning" and "Fortunate Son."

The same points apply if we want to say that Peter Gabriel's "Come Talk to Me" perpetuates hegemony and Western dominance. Knowledge about Gabriel's creative process in producing "Come Talk to Me" does not, by itself, provide the music with a colonialist identity. At best, the fact that Gabriel places his music and voice over African drumming supplies a reason to listen for such messages in the music, just as the fact that a specific album was made in 1968 or 1969 is a reason to listen for statements about the war in Vietnam.[2] Suddenly, a slight and whimsical Simon and Garfunkel song like "Punky's Dilemma" (1968) can suggest unexpected implications.

If there is a colonialist identity in "Come Talk to Me" or *Graceland*, it has to be available to listeners with basic musical understanding. It is legitimate to raise questions about the mass audience's practices of reception. Ultimately, the wrongfulness of wrongful musical appropriation hinges on a relatively subtle consequence of the appropriation of cultural forms, particularly music. Texts and styles are appropriated, but their originating culture is not. The objects for interpretation are radically recontextualized. But if meaningful music gives way to the mere object, then how is a *culture* deprived or violated? After all, the text's *cultural* dimension is left behind, untouched and undiminished. Strictly speaking, the music is untouched. What's needed, then, is a clear statement of what's so wrong with turning one culture's music into another culture's "texts." We have yet to find a definite reason to think that there is something blameworthy about this transformation, for it seems to arise naturally as a byproduct of the basic processes of mass art. It's less a matter of what musicians do with the music than of what the audience does—and fails to do—with the music. The key question for appropriation is how the audience listens and how much the audience understands.

But this argument will only make sense after we rehearse some points about the meaning of music, leading to complications for any attempt to invoke a universal standard that will condemn all appropriation.

What We Hear in the Sounds

You will never understand this music.

—Persian music teacher's warning to ethnomusicologist Bruno Nettl[3]

Let's begin with the basic point that a string of sounds can be heard with comprehension or without comprehension. Without comprehension, there is noise. With it, there is music.[4] In the visual arts we say that there is no such thing as an innocent eye; in music, there is no innocent ear. Perception is infused with cognition.

We only hear music when we understand what we're hearing. Yet Stephen Davies reminds us that musical understanding cannot be a merely intellectual appreciation. Understanding must be integrated into the very process of listening:

> To hear music as such is to hear it in terms of the principles of order that give it its identity as the music it is. It is to experience the music, *in hearing it,* as sound organized in accordance with the conventions of style or category applying to it. The relevant conventions differ (to some extent) from one type of music to another and are established by, and within, the music-making practice of the given culture or sub-culture. . . . If the music never comes naturally to the ear, it probably is not heard as the music it is.[5]

Consider an amusing anecdote. Leonard Bernstein tells of taking the musical director of a troupe of Indian musicians and dancers to a performance of Mozart's G Minor Symphony (No. 40; K. 550). His guest promptly fell asleep. When Bernstein queried the man during intermission, his guest explained that Mozart put him to sleep. "It's baby music—it's for little children. . . . The melodies are dumb, the rhythms are ordinary and square." Bernstein tried to redirect his attention to the music's harmonic adventure, but to no avail.[6] His guest did not know how to regard that dimension of the sound as musically important.

Bernstein's story illustrates that we only recognize and properly value musical qualities if trained to do so, where the most basic form of training is growing up in a culture where those qualities are the basis of musical composition. In short, all listening to music has a complex interpretative element, influenced by one's previous exposure to music. Three pitched sounds played simultaneously may be heard as just that, three pitched sounds. But understood in light of the appropriate concepts, they may be understood as a triad forming a consonant or dissonant chord. Within the system of diatonic harmony, expectations are generated by the introduction of a harmonic pattern and musical interest is generated by harmonic exploration, culminating in the anticipated return to the tonic. If Bernstein's guest did not appreciate Mozart because he heard melodies but none of the music's harmonic adventure (a failing that is not uncommon among modern Western listeners), he is hardly to blame. In light of his training, he could only hear "baby music."

In August 1971, George Harrison organized two concerts at Madison Square Garden to raise money for the United Nations Children's Fund for refugee children of Bangladesh. The concerts opened with a sitar and sarod duet featuring improvisation by Ravi Shankar and Ali Akbar Khan. On the album assembled from the shows, *The Concert for Bangladesh* (1971), Ravi Shankar is introduced and admonishes the crowd to refrain from smoking and to listen respectfully. His words are followed by about thirty seconds of sound from the four instruments on stage. The audience applauds with considerable enthusiasm. Ravi Shankar tells them that he hopes they enjoy the music as much as they've enjoyed the tuning.

These anecdotes illustrate how learned expectations are essential to perception of musical qualities in a stream of sounds. Because Bernstein's companion did not regard its diatonic dimension as an organizing element, the music proved unrewarding. But he was not a "naive" or "passive" listener in absolute terms; he was naive relative to the musical values of this type of music. Cross-cultural exposure seems to be the only type of music listening where an adult's listening can be characterized as naive.[7] The listener from India found organization to the degree that he was prepared to find it, but the style of music involved a further principle of organization that was lost on him. Where Western rock fans had no idea of the organization of Indian music, they enthusiastically accepted random noise as music. To put a common name on the two examples, each illustrates a lack of musical competence. This situation will arise whenever music is commodified through recording and then radically relocated.

Now consider the situation when rockabilly first reached England, or when a Jewish kid in Hibbing, Minnesota, first heard Little Richard on the radio in 1954, or when Paul Simon listened to the bootleg tape of the Boyoyo Boys in 1985, or when white kids in Idaho saw their first rap video on MTV. Does anyone really think that in hearing the sounds, they hear *in it* what is heard by members of the culture in which it originated? Most music is more than mere patterning of sound. It is also a matter of embodying meanings in sound. As with other systems of human communication, music has meaning through its roles in the ongoing life of a society. The significance of an artist's design, notes anthropologist Clifford Geertz, "is always a local matter. . . . Art and the equipment to grasp it are made in the same shop."[8] No musical form or song is ever arbitrary *within* its original cultural space. It is made arbitrary by being wrenched from that space. Designs and styles may make their way from one culture to another, but designs are not a culture. Extracted from its cultural space, a design is a text, not a work.

Martian Music

Rock's musical and lyrical practices, while often taken from other traditions and cultural formations, are almost always received as if they were already part of rock's conventionality.

—Lawrence Grossberg[9]

The sad truth is that responding to music does not always involve appreciating it as the music that it is. A listener who does not listen against a background of relevant stylistic conventions cannot really be said to hear a piece of music for the piece that it is: "she does not appreciate the music qua music, though the music causes her enjoyment."[10] Music may yield pleasure despite one's ignorance of the appropriate conventions, but the pleasure would be quite accidental, like the pleasure that a blind person might derive from the smell of a painting by Monet.

But it's also the case that basic musical understanding and appreciation involves the interplay of two rather different sorts of background information. We must grasp principles of musical organization, and we must grasp the musical expressiveness that arises through decisions about musical organization (and, with songs, we have the third element of the literal meaning of any lyrics). Although there's considerable dispute about how expressiveness can be perceived in music, there is something approaching universal agreement that music's expressiveness is a byproduct of its perceivable organization. Since both aspects of musical identity are governed by mutable, arbitrary conventions, it is clear that a listener must come to grasp purely musical conventions before the music's expressive character can emerge.[11] Once those operations become second nature, listeners can take the next step, relating musical works to the time and place of their origin in order to appreciate them as immensely complex statements—hearing Jimi Hendrix's distorted, mangled performance of "The Star Spangled Banner" at Woodstock, for instance, as a commentary on the state of the union in 1969. Yet it remains the case that structure is primary to the experience, and an audience may come to understand and enjoy the musical and expressive qualities of a style of music far in advance of appreciating its full implications.

Brian Eno's formative exposure to rock and roll was doo-wop, just as it was for Paul Simon. Although Simon experienced doo-wop as "local" and Southern rhythm and blues music as exotic, all of it was exotic to Eno. Nonetheless, doo-wop was available in the shops of his native Suffolk thanks to the local presence of two huge U.S. airforce bases. Eno's sister began to buy the American hits, and around 1958 he became fascinated by the music. What seemed "native" to Paul Simon, back in Queens, struck the young Eno as "magical," as "Martian music" from outer space: "I had never heard music like this, and one of the reasons it was beautiful was because it came without a context."[12] Granted, 1950s rock and roll was not completely alien in its harmonic structure. But it was different enough from other music he'd heard that he felt free to make of it anything he wished. Years later he recreated something of the experience with his 1975 cover of the Tokens' "The Lion Sleeps Tonight (Wimoweh)"—itself a remake of a remake of a remake, since the Tokens were reworking the Weavers' arrangement of a tune recorded by a South African Zulu ensemble, the Evening Birds.[13] As Eno listened to the song in 1961, he occupied a thoroughly decontextualized frame for apprehending appropriated music. With many of his own cryptic songs, Eno captures that experience of a world of missing connections.

Because popular audiences so seldom discuss what they take the music to mean, it's easy to assume that different audiences "read" it in more or less the same way. Discussing Aretha Franklin's immense popularity, Charles Keil and Steven Feld are struck by the fact that her popularity has had limited effect on white dealings with black America. Reflecting on the popularity of black music with white audiences, Feld wonders, "Do we know anything about *how* white people listened to this music? What did it reinforce? . . . *What* crossed over? How blackened did we get from listening to all that?"[14] But why suppose that any "blackening" must take place in order for the new audience to embrace this music with basic understanding? Whites could groove to soul music or grasp both the pain and the joy of the blues without grasping that both reflect an American form of a larger African diaspora. Cultural relocation always obscures the music's more complex meanings, and my hunch is that this loss is routinely disguised by the generally unrecognized tendency to substitute different meanings for the original meaning.

Literature offers an interesting example of loss and then change of meaning in Walter M. Miller Jr.'s novel *A Canticle for Liebowitz*. Many centuries after a nuclear catastrophe in the late twentieth century, a monk comes across a scrap of writing by the founder of their order, I. E. Liebowitz. Learned monks recognize "pound pastrami," "six bagels," and "Form 1040" as examples of some sort of English, but they have no idea about their meanings. The phrases are simply meaningless to readers in a culture lacking deli food and the Internal Revenue Service. The scrap of paper ceases to be literally meaningful. Its sole significance is its causal history; it is significant as a relic of Liebowitz, but not as a list of items to bring home. Its new significance rests on its function within the monastic culture now surrounding it, ironically investing it with an import that it did not originally possess. However, in what sense do the monks have something belonging to another culture? They only have a piece of paper with sloppy penmanship, stripped of its original significance. However much they may treasure the object itself, their uses of it are independent of its cultural source.[15]

The irony of Liebowitz's note about deli food and tax forms only arises for "bilingual" readers who understand it in light of both monastic culture and the cold war. But how many whites really understand the "political" elements that they deleted from the blues? Did working-class heterosexuals who responded so enthusiastically to *Saturday Night Fever* (1977), Donna Summer, and the Bee Gees really understand disco's origins in a gay club milieu? Did disco's detractors? Meanings are not inherent and responses are not innate; we only hear what's "in" the music because we know what to listen for in the music.[16]

Proceeding as if texts retain their original meanings after recontextualization—as if everyone knows the same things about the music's origins—undercuts the whole point of noting that whites and African Americans, or gays and straights, employ different "values and aesthetic" in listening to the same songs and recordings. After all, different audiences employ different values and aesthetic categories because those audiences have very different uses and associations for different musical styles. So we must remain on guard against the easy trap of believing in any necessary or direct connection between meaning and genealogy. Only knowledgeable listeners can keep the connection alive.

Those who do not know about the connection will not hear what that music originally expressed. Unless the sounds are given new meanings, they can never function as more than noise or as aural wallpaper.

At the same time, the fact that relocated blues forms no longer convey the attitude, meaning, and values of African American culture does not demonstrate that uninformed listeners must find the experience devoid of meaning. Recall that the scrap of paper with the strange words from Liebowitz resists easy incorporation, and remains meaningless—yet behavior directed toward the relic is meaningful. Such behavior is always informed by its own cultural parameters, and it becomes the basis for new meanings grounded in a different way of life. The monks have a use for the relic that makes sense from their perspective. Eno's claim that he heard doo-wop "without a context" is not quite accurate; he loved the music because its strangeness was a product of *his* listening context.

For a visual example, consider the large tattoo of a praying mantis that adorns Perry Farrell's right shoulder. Shortly before he founded the seminal alternative band Jane's Addiction, Farrell underwent repeated tattooing, body piercing, and scarification. He began to wear dreadlocks. Reading *National Geographic* inspired him to adopt most of these "tribal" signifiers; he wanted something that "took a lot of guts" in order to distinguish himself from the poseurs or "weekend punks" coming into the Los Angeles club scene. Although Farrell is fuzzy about the specifics, he believes that the praying mantis is worshipped in India. But since he's not in India, he feels free to construct a "personal mythology" about what his tattoos and body modifications mean.[17]

Perry Farrell has appropriated symbols and practices from a range of cultures, but he has not appropriated their culture. On the contrary, he seems to have chosen them largely as a sign of his commitment to an alternative lifestyle, and for the opportunities they provide him to project his own meanings onto his cultural pastiche. Farrell's tattoo serves to signal his hipness in dealing with "otherness," and to signal his own otherness within the dominant culture. But if that symbolic activity takes place in the United States, how does it wrong anyone in India? Pushing too hard on cultural difference will always subvert the charge that appropriation is destructive or that it does violence to others in "stealing" their cultural images and sounds.[18]

It subverts the critique by generating one of the classic puzzles regarding relativism. There is a fundamental discord between insisting that different cultures are so independent that they are incommensurable, each inscrutable to the other, and then insisting that no culture should ever exploit the cultural resources of another.[19] In shifting from anthropological observation to the moral high ground, we must wonder whose standard is to do the work of condemning appropriation. From whose moral perspective do we judge those cultural practices? Do we embrace relativism and apply the standards of those engaged in the appropriation?

However much we are tempted by relativism, it won't help to appeal to the standards of African Americans or Hindus in India to critique the behavior of Mick Jagger or Madonna. While bell hooks may rebuke Madonna, it can't be on the grounds that each culture's practices must be evaluated from their own perspective. After all, we cannot suppose that Madonna is subject to bell hooks's censure if the pair do not share common values grounded in a shared culture. Worse, if domination and exploitation are the norm when "Western" meets "Other," then again there is no ground for complaint: if Western ideology is colonialist, then Jagger and Madonna are to be applauded, not criticized, for they are successful representatives of their own culture—that is, unless we rid ourselves of the model of distinct cultures with distinct values and recognize a more complex model of cultures as weakly integrated collections of practices, beliefs, and values, any of which may take on a radically different character when relocated to a different cultural context.

If some musical appropriations are wrongful and some are not (if, say, the Tokens were wrong in recording "The Lion Sleeps Tonight" but Eno did nothing wrong in adapting it from them), then any difference must lie in how the music is used in its new cultural context. Mass media encourage the transportation of signifiers and styles to audiences who lack the cultural bearings to get at the works attached to the texts. As George Lipsitz demonstrates throughout *Dangerous Crossroads*, every cultural crossover invites misunderstandings. But crossovers also invite understanding, *or at least they do so for those recognizing that the significance of whatever is appropriated does not magically accompany its consumption.* The barriers between incommensurable cultural systems are not easy to overcome. At the same time, the barriers are not insurmountable: the world's population is increasingly bilingual. The most important thing about the Brian Eno and Liebowitz examples is that they imply that there are greater and lesser degrees of comprehension. Surely this conclusion extends to the purely *musical* aspect of songs.

All or Nothing?

The blues ... serve naturally as projective tests; white liberals, black militants, and others of varying pigmentation and persuasion hear in the blues essentially what they want to hear, find in the blues ethos what they expect to find.

—Charles Keil[20]

There's a big difference between why white kids are listening to hip-hop and why black kids are making it.

—Jimmy Iovine, founder of Interscope Records[21]

If unprepared listeners cannot hear how organization and meaning are embodied in the onward flow of sound, there is a very real sense in which they cannot be said to have heard the music. They will misperceive it. When musicians imitate another culture's music, there is a very real sense in which it must be a different music (however similar it may sound), for they will imbue it with a different significance. But then we cannot claim that a culture has been "ripped off." A thing is not stolen if it is not taken. The more we emphasize the arbitrary link between meaning and its material embodiment, the more compelling the argument.

A major obstacle to appreciating this argument is the simplistic belief that whenever we *respond* to a piece of music, we *understand* it. Baraka sometimes argues as if the blues automatically retain certain meanings—such as the experience of living as a "slave"—and these meanings are preserved and carried with the music into the new cultural space. Racist whites cannot handle these meanings and subsequently dilute and falsify the music.[22] A similar story is told to account for the widespread hostility to disco music in the 1970s. Because disco was *initially* identified with an urban gay subculture, it still possessed a gay sensibility, so mainstream opposition to disco is really a homophobic backlash.[23] But this story wrongly invests texts with a magical ability to retain meanings apart from their originating cultural context.

In light of these points, recall Baraka's complex indictment of white appropriation of African American music. Baraka complains that white musicians "dilute" the music by bringing it within the scope of their inappropriate cultural background. But he also complains that white listeners and white music critics cannot listen "objectively" because their "values and aesthetic [are] antithetical to the values and aesthetic of the artists ... as well as to the essentially black mass audience for whom the works were created."[24] Think of Jack Skellington, the Pumpkin King of Halloween Town, unable to understand and replicate Christmas Town in the film *The Nightmare Before Christmas* (1993). The inhabitants of each town know only their own holiday, but the values of Halloween are so antithetical to those of Christmas that Skellington makes a mockery of the Christmas spirit of generosity with his earnest attempts to copy what he's discovered.

This argument comes very close to the position that I endorsed in the previous section. Unfortunately, Baraka assumes that the "essentially black mass audience" counts as a unified culture. However, there's no reason to believe that it is. Surely Taj Mahal was in the same boat as Eric Clapton when reggae first made its way from Jamaica to the mainland. Mahal's 1974 cover versions of the Slickers' "Johnny Too Bad" (1972) and Bob Marley's "Slave Driver" (1973) involve no less cultural appropriation than Eric Clapton's more famous cover of Bob Marley's "I Shot the Sheriff" (1973). Taj Mahal justifies excursions into reggae on the grounds that his stepfather was Jamaican, so he heard a lot of earlier Caribbean music on records. Yet Mahal's more general appeal to his grasp of "the African diaspora" gives him no special claim to the music.[25] One cannot get at higher-level intentions except through lower-level ones, and here his advantage stems from having a mother who was a gospel singer and a father who was a jazz musician.

To his credit, one of Baraka's arguments recognizes that there is no automatic process by which the original meanings of a cultural product will be preserved when it is viewed from the perspective of the other. As a result, white appropriation "dilutes" the music by making it into a mere style "behind which there is no serious commitment to expression or emotional profundity." It is "music" without "attitude." In its most diluted form, it is quite meaningless.[26] Music gives way to pure text. But we are again left wondering how pure text destroys the meaningful, culturally embedded musical style that it imitates.

The puzzle we face can be stated with greater precision. How can we condemn an audience that listens to appropriated music from a state of ignorance, unable to hear it as the music that it is? Surely there is no great wrong in being curious enough about unfamiliar music that one wants to listen to it or wants to imitate it if one finds it appealing. At the same time, we can hardly make sense of the idea that an audience would *regularly* listen to music in a state of ignorance and miscomprehension. Why would an audience respond with pleasure to music when ignorant of essential information needed to hear it as organized and significant? The audience would have to assign the music a significance that differs markedly from what the music expresses within its community of origin. But at this point the original music has dropped out of the equation.

Assumptions about cultural incommensurability seem to be at the heart of many complaints about appropriation. Such assumptions certainly inform two of Baraka's arguments, his complaint about the "dilution" of the music and his complaint that racist whites cannot handle the messages in the music that they appropriate. The two cultures are described as being so different in their ideas and values that there is no common, objective yardstick for comparing their cultural achievements. (The two cultures are so different that dilution is inevitable, or so different that the messages embedded in the music must be rejected.) From this starting point, it is easy to fall into the conclusion that ethnocentric perspectives can never be overcome and so musical appropriation must always be regarded with extreme suspicion.

In actuality, three rather distinct outcomes are possible when music is appropriated, even in a situation of cultural incommensurability. There is incomprehension, there is full comprehension, and there is the interesting position that falls somewhere between those two extremes. These three responses to appropriated music are the focus of my next chapter.

Speaking in Tongues

Three Ways of Knowing

This one old guy, Sleepy John Estes, would come out on stage, blind and infirm and barely able to walk, and you'd think, "This is the music business? Look what it's done to this guy." But then I would say to myself, "Yeah, but it sounds good, it feels good, and I like it."

—Ry Cooder

The three ways that another culture's music can "cross over" are hybridization, immersion, and aestheticism. Of the three, only aestheticism, the doctrine that art should be valued for itself alone and not for any purpose it may serve, will regularly support the charge of wrongful appropriation.[1]

First, another culture's musical instruments and compositions can serve as raw material from which a new, hybrid form emerges. Introducing the Clash's version of Junior Murvin's "Police and Thieves" one night, Joe Strummer told the crowd "This is punk *and* reggae.... There's a difference between a rip-off and bringing some of our culture to *another* culture."[2] The problem, of course, is how to distinguish a rip-off from hybridization. The Jamaicans encountered by Joe Strummer in London were immigrants, and it was not as if Strummer's knowledge of reggae reflected genuine contact with Jamaican culture. T. S. Eliot was surprisingly prophetic:

"The [immigrant] culture which develops on the new soil must ... be bafflingly alike and different from the parent culture: it will be complicated sometimes by whatever relations are established with some native race and further by immigration from other than the original source. In this way, peculiar types of culture-sympathy and culture-clash appear."[3]

The Police and the Clash were both agents of culture-sympathy. With the passage of time, the Police sound more like agents of hybrid music than do UB40's relatively authentic cover versions of classic reggae hits. But there's no reason to suppose that hybridization simply involves bringing one culture to bear upon another culture. Cultural purity is hard to find: the Clash and the Police merged punk and reggae, but reggae was deeply influenced by recordings of New Orleans R&B. In similar fashion, the hip-hop element of the rap-metal hybrid of bands like Limp Bizkit was originally a New York City hybrid of Jamaican DJ rapping and South Bronx verbal rapping.

Second, music can cross over to an audience that makes a sincere effort at cultural immersion, working to understand the originating culture on its own terms and actively seeking to reduce ethnocentrism. George Harrison displayed a genuine and long-standing commitment to understanding Indian music in relation to Hindu thought. Here, musicians are initially in the same position as any other listener, approaching "foreign" music in ignorance. In this respect there is nothing unique about hip-hop, reggae, or world music. Harrison had to make a similar commitment and transition as a British teenager in the 1950s in order to perform the rockabilly style that was his initial impetus to learn the guitar. "Elvis had an incredible impact on me," he recalls, "because I'd never heard anything like it."[4]

In the initial stages of appropriation, immersion looks a lot like aestheticism. "The classic learning curve with world music," notes Peter Gabriel, "is you start off thinking anything strange is good. Then you realize there's good and bad and later wonder 'Why would I like *that*?'"[5] Assuming that these value judgements are really one's own and not mere reflections of what's become fashionable, the listener who can ground value distinctions in the music itself will have moved beyond aestheticism.

What ultimately distinguishes immersion from aestheticism is the desire and effort—on the part of either musician or listener—to reach a point where the structural and expressive riches of the music come naturally. In the extreme case, to borrow a metaphor of colonialism, the outsider "goes native." In the most advanced cases, the outsider becomes a participant. Johnny Otis, famous for "Willie and the Hand Jive" (1958), was white (his parents were Greek immigrants). Yet his wife was black and Otis himself was accepted as black in the African American circles of Los Angeles; he was a frequent presence (as writer, producer, or bandleader) on the "race" charts of the 1950s; he was responsible for important recordings by such vocalists as Etta James and Big Mama Thornton. Even as he popularized rhythm and blues to a larger audience, Otis voiced contempt for whites who responded to white appropriations of African American music (other than his own, that is).[6]

Perhaps the question is whether stoned hippies listening to Ravi Shankar and kids at the high school hop doing the hand jive brought *enough* knowledge to the experience. Most of them probably brought no more to it than most adolescents bring to any other passing fad. But then again, some get hooked and dig deeper into it. Among my friends there is a southern Quaker who's made several trips to India and devoted many years to a serious study of Indian singing; we refrain from playing Western popular music when he visits us because he finds it too disturbing in comparison with Indian music. Within my immediate family is a sibling whose preservation of rare 78s helped the Memphis Archives to re-release the early jazz of black bandleader James Reese Europe. Arguments against appropriation may simply put too much emphasis on the many who make a more limited investment. After all, it's not as if everyone in England makes a personal investment in Shakespeare or everyone in France can quote Mallarmé and Rimbaud. No culture demands that. Why should popular art be so very different?

Third, there is aestheticism. Just as reproductions of paintings by Monet and van Gogh adorn dormitories where the students would never bother to learn art history, music is often embraced by an audience that makes little or no effort to understand its context of production. Cultural products are consumed as style without substance. In some measure, the problem stems from the common myth that music is a universal language. Think here of world music anthologies that juxtapose recordings of music of diverse cultures, and new age labels that sell the music of "other" spiritual traditions as a background for meditation—as if music were a narcotic that does its spiritual work simply through ingestion. Aestheticism is common in music videos: Porno for Pyro's "Tahitian Moon" (1996) alternates footage of traditional Tahitian dance with footage of Perry Farrell miming the song while dressed in an imitation of traditional Tahitian garb. There is no sense of engagement with Tahitian culture, and no perspective from which to understand it. There is nothing beyond exoticism for the sake of novelty.

Of these three approaches, hybridization is surely the most common in the realm of mass art. It includes most white blues, Britain's Teddy Boys, the rapping of the Tom Tom Club and the Beastie Boys, British "house" music, and Paul Simon's *Graceland*. All are better understood as hybrid forms than as direct but "inept" theft. Cultural immersion is the most desirable from the perspective of respecting cultural diversity, provided there is sufficient immersion to meet the material on its own terms. The third approach, aestheticism, is the most objectionable.

Of the three, only hybridization is likely to sustain enough interest to create a mainstream audience base. Few people immerse themselves in a radically different culture—American college students on spring break in Mexico don't count—and at the other extreme there are probably relatively few who regularly listen to the music of other cultures for the sake of its exoticism.

Understood as hybrid music, even relatively "diluted" music may not be such a bad thing. It may offer an indispensable bridge or transition across the obstacles to musical understanding that are so intuitively circumvented within the music's originating culture. While Vanilla Ice is now regarded as a joke, "Ice Ice Baby" (1990) was the first rap song to reach number one on the popular charts, exposing white America to a style of music that had, until then, been subcultural in its appeal. Millions bought *To the Extreme* and its major hip-hop competition at the time, M. C. Hammer's *Please Hammer Don't Hurt 'Em* (1990. Surely their success played some role in preparing the ears of middle-class record buyers for the explosion of "authentic" rappers who stormed the sales charts in the 1990s. Without a middle ground in David Bowie's "Fame," Aretha Franklin's cover of "Bridge Over Troubled Water," and films like *Saturday Night Fever*, the gulf between cultures and subcultures can appear so dauntingly wide that there is little incentive for attempting to understand others on their own terms.

Furthermore, music is a public aspect of culture by which the members of a culture *themselves* come to know their own culture. So coming to know another culture through its music is one of our best strategies for subverting incommensurability. The Rolling Stones and Beastie Boys may have started from a position of aestheticism, as listeners attracted to music they did not understand, but the Rolling Stones ended up as personal friends of Muddy Waters, sharing the stage with him on many occasions. Thanks to white fans, the music of Robert Johnson is now more widely available and has higher status than it had when Johnson was alive. Thanks to a living tradition of blues, we continue to have a genuine opportunity for emotional—not merely intellectual—engagement with a range of African American experience that would otherwise be lost to us. Because the Beastie Boys built up a body of work that showed they were serious about a hybrid of rap and rock, their Tibetan Freedom Concerts and other efforts at publicizing China's mistreatment of Tibet come across as sincere efforts to advance the cause of the underdog and not as American hegemony. At the same time, featuring Tibetan music on a musical program dominated by rock and hip-hop is to invite audience misperception and aestheticism.

Communication at the Crossroads

Primitivism is rarely better the second time around.

—Robert Christgau[7]

If rock audiences are so attracted to "exotic" forms despite their incommensurable expressive values, surely the loss of musical meaning is compounded by its reinterpretation. The process of musical reinterpretation has an unexpected implication: the music now means whatever it means in relation to the culture adopting it, not the culture from which it's appropriated. An additional twist in this debate is that there are usually two distinct sites of reinterpretation: that of the musician and that of the audience. One of the most common situations with hybrid music is that of *musicians* engaging in immersion or hybridization for an *audience* practicing aestheticism.

Hybrid musics emerge when musicians appropriate by imitating selected elements of a foreign style.[8] When the Byrds incorporated elements of John Coltrane and Ravi Shankar into "Eight Miles High," a song about a trans-Atlantic airline trip (double-coded as a drug song), it was not merely empty style. While their song has relatively little to do with India or Coltrane, it is a highly original psychedelic achievement that conveys the disorientation of a sudden cultural relocation. Despite a ban by radio networks concerned that it was somehow about drugs, "Eight Miles High" was the first genuinely psychedelic track to break into the top twenty, eventually reaching number fourteen on the American pop charts.

In the context of 1966 top-forty radio, the track's musical rush and subsequent atonal guitar freak-outs functioned whether or not one understood its musical sources: even today, the two guitar breaks refuse to conform to our expectations. But that does not imply that the elements derived from Coltrane and Ravi Shankar are irrelevant. The guitar breaks function as they do because they're organized, but organized in patterns that are completely at odds with the basic song. (That is, they express disorientation by adopting a mode of organization that is dissonant and chaotic relative to the more standard verses and chorus that start the song.) Listen to Roxy Music's 1980 remake of "Eight Miles High," which rearranges the song as a smooth soul ballad. Roxy Music delivers the song without any hint of nostalgia or irony. But without the musical cocktail of the Byrds' arrangement, the Roxy Music arrangement sacrifices the mood swings and the visceral power that make the original so extraordinary.

However, such hybrids can only emerge when musicians have at least a basic grasp of the musical organization of the appropriated style. For surely the ability to *reproduce* a piece of music or to *produce* a new piece in a specific style is our primary evidence that an individual understands that piece or style.[9] Indeed, it is virtually impossible for *musicians* to engage in mere aestheticism when appropriating music, because the ability to generate music in a recognizable style requires a working understanding of its organizing principles. While the visual and literary arts can represent "foreign" cultures in ways that have no correspondence to those cultures, building up a false account of it, music cannot. Music itself represents nothing, so music that calls to mind another culture's music does so by entering into that style, by entering (at least partially) into that culture.[10]

The Byrds had to learn the basics of both jazz and Indian music in order to craft original songs that were simultaneously pop songs and hybrids. In this respect, the main difference between hybrid music and cultural immersion is often a mere matter of degree of immersion. Yet some hybrids reveal a profound immersion in several distinct musics: witness the fusion of country music and R&B that dominates the Flying Burrito Brothers' *The Gilded Palace of Sin* (1969) or the marriage of hip-hop and Motown of Lauryn Hill's "Doo Wop (That Thing)" (1998). But if the musicians who create hybrid music must have made an investment in another way of thinking and creating music, enough to grasp some musical basics and to reflect them in musical behavior, then their efforts cannot be dismissed as mere aestheticism. This takes much of the force out of George Lipsitz's condemnation of appropriations that fail to "accurately represent the aesthetic, political, and social context giving determinate shape to the music in its area of origin."[11] How could any hybrid music accurately represent these originating contexts? It cannot be a hybrid except by *deviating* from these sources.

Further complications arise when we remind ourselves that musical understanding can take place on several levels. Understanding can be confined to musical organization, but most of the time it involves a grasp of musical organization as rich with emotional expression.[12] Or it can move beyond basic understanding to a more enhanced understanding, at which point the music exhibits a wide range of higher-level intentions, including social and political commentary. Many of Polly Jean Harvey's best songs are infused with a brash, unsettling carnality. An enhanced understanding recognizes that they form a running commentary on expectations about women and femininity. But at this point our interpretation moves well beyond basic musical understanding.

At the very least, the Byrds possessed a basic musical understanding of the styles they worked into their original compositions. What they lacked, perhaps, was a firm grasp of the social and political implications of their musical choices. But surely the same is true of many, if not most, of the musicians working in whatever we want to count as their "natural" musical idiom! No musician knows in advance of audience response how many different people will embrace that music. Recently a student of mine who is Native American stopped by to chat. Looking at the various postcards stuck to my office door, he incredulously asked if I really listened to Joy Division. As a matter of coincidence, I assured him, I'd been listening to Joy Division just the day before. Ian Curtis had no way of knowing that he'd help to articulate the identity of two very different people, of different ethnic identities and a generation removed from one another. When Norman Whitfield and Barrett Strong co-wrote "War" in 1970, they had no way of knowing that it would resonate again in 1986, when Bruce Springsteen used it as a bitter slam at the Reagan administration's policies in Nicaragua.

Let us now shift to the perspective of the audience for appropriated music. Suppose that, as listeners, we know enough about the elements combined in a musical hybrid to possess basic musical understanding of each element: we cannot be accused of aestheticism. Suppose we want to move beyond basic musical understanding in order to make claims about its moral or political messages. We want to make claims about the music's higher-level intentions involving social and political issues. Yet even these intentions are future-directed and open-ended. At best, they place limits on what counts as a sensible interpretation. They cannot predetermine its total range of application. So appreciation beyond basic musical understanding demands active interpretation from the audience to secure its continuing relevance.[13] Armchair textual analysis cannot establish that a new use of an established musical style or piece of music is problematical until we know what the new use signifies. Is it resistive? Reactionary? Misogynist? Feminist? Racist?

Any interpretation that moves beyond recognition of musical expressiveness requires two bodies of knowledge. There is historical knowledge that will allow the listener to discern its relationship to earlier music upon which it draws. Such knowledge plays an indispensable role in clarifying the musical organization of a particular piece.[14] But there is also knowledge about other music emerging from roughly the same cultural site at roughly the same time: one needs to understand that Cream and the Band were musical contemporaries to hear the ensemble work of the Band's *Music From Big Pink* (1968) as a repudiation of the grandstanding of the power trio format, so that their competing formats suggested competing models for social organization in the late 1960s. The upshot of these points about basic and enhanced musical understanding is that higher-level intentions emerge only in relation to a relatively sophisticated knowledge base. But part of the point of possessing this knowledge is so that one can hear Cream's "Crossroad" as the musical hybrid that it is, occupying a very different position in musical and social history than Robert Johnson's "Cross Road Blues."

Cream's music is neither a theft nor a dilution of Robert Johnson's music. Cream's musical interpretation is also a social reinterpretation. To borrow the terminology of Judith Butler, all speech has the potential for "resignification" when it breaks free of its prior social context. Any redeployment, "improper use," or repetition that lacks "prior authorization" allows for a "reformulation" of meaning. So all misappropriation holds political promise.[15] The sin of inauthenticity, supposedly committed whenever whites sing the blues, may be the blessing of unanticipated communication.

This resignification is illustrated by the history of another hybrid, Stephen Foster's "Oh! Susannah." It has been suggested that the song is racist for the way that it draws on major elements of the nineteenth-century minstrel tradition. The song is certainly a strange hybrid. Although the music is a polka, its lyrics use minstrelsy conventions to mock, ridicule, and stereotype African Americans.[16] Yet the Byrds did not revive the minstrel tradition by performing "Oh! Susannah" on *Turn! Turn! Turn!* (1965), nor did James Taylor by performing it on *Sweet Baby James* (1970). Their versions are not *about* African Americans, even if that was true of Foster's original lyric (in verses the Byrds and Taylor do not sing). Foster's song addresses racial issues, but neither the Byrds nor James Taylor are simply replicating Foster's intentions. His song offers them a text with weak iterability, and they have selectively adapted it to produce two new cultural artifacts: a recording by Taylor and a recording by the Byrds. Foster's original meanings have been overwritten, as is so easily done when a weakly iterable text is fleshed out in a strongly iterable text of mass art.

This overwriting is particularly evident in the Byrds' version, where McGuinn's twelve-string electric guitar mimics the banjo of "with a banjo on my knee" without sacrificing its unmistakable electric Rickenbacker tone. Only a very naive listener will fail to recognize the hybrid quality that comes from combining nineteenth- and twentieth-century elements. The Byrds' message is that the pleasure of music is first and foremost a foregrounding of sound: the song lies in the music. Their decision to simply repeat nonsensical couplets like "it rained so hard / the weather it was dry" mocks folk-rock's reputation for political relevance, their own included, as if expressly illustrating the point that if the music gives us pleasure, we'll put up with almost any piece of nonsense.

Theorists have been quicker to recognize the resignification in such activity when the medium is a visual art than for popular music. The most interesting fine art example of this sort of activity is a pair of artworks by Marcel Duchamp: *L.H.O.O.Q.* and, years later, *L.H.O.O.Q. Shaved*. They are nothing much to look at, so far as visual art goes. In fact, *L.H.O.O.Q. Shaved* looks exactly like a postcard reproduction of Leonardo da Vinci's *Mona Lisa*. As well it should, for Duchamp created *L.H.O.O.Q.* by taking a postcard reproduction of the Mona Lisa, drawing facial hair on it, and adding those letters to the bottom. (Just as reading 'C.D.B.' produces the phrase "see the bee" in English, *L.H.O.O.Q.* provides a mild sexual innuendo in French.) *L.H.O.O.Q. Shaved* came later; it is a postcard reproduction of the *Mona Lisa* with nothing added but a title. While visually simple, its complex joke thus depends on two pieces of specific intertextuality. The point, of course, is that neither *L.H.O.O.Q.* nor *L.H.O.O.Q. Shaved* is simply a reproduction of the *Mona Lisa* once Duchamp transforms the basic "text." Stephen Foster may have given us the song "Oh! Susannah," but the song-as-performed-on-recordings by mass artists is something else altogether. On another level, Duchamp is a master of the self-reflexive intertextuality. His two works also suggest that these sorts of over-writings are business-as-usual in the artworld—he wants to call our attention to what artists are really doing whenever they "create" art.

The Byrds use "Oh! Susannah" to thumb their noses at the sanctimony of their peers in folk music. Their version is playful, joyful, and witty. (They were, perhaps, the first postmodern rock band.) But, as suggested earlier, these qualities are only apparent against the backdrop of the music's origins and in relation to their own situation. Their recording is a playful jibe at (white) folk appropriation, particularly those cases where an earnest young musician tries so very hard to be authentic and to get it right. Such music was hard to escape in the 1960s, as musicians like John Hammond Jr. and Tom Rush worked to erase themselves (that is, their "white" identities) and to let the music speak through them. But of course there was little use for that, since the blues recordings that the white singers were imitating were available to anyone who cared to hear the originals. Yet the early blues cover versions by Bob Dylan, the Rolling Stones, and the Paul Butterfield Blues Band remain compelling in a way that most of that music does not. Like the Beastie Boys with hip-hop, Dylan and Keith Richards and the white guys in the Butterfield group had gotten past the idea of being authentic by the time they made it to the studio, sparing us the embarrassment of those very lame blues tracks on the first Grateful Dead album. Skip James may have hated Cream's very inauthentic version of "I'm So Glad," but would Skip James have preferred hearing James Brown or the Fugees performing it? These performers would also impart a distinct identity to their interpretation, producing music that is also historically and socially removed from the music originally created by Skip James.

However, recorded music manifests both weak and strong iterability. The weak iterability of performance (not the strong iterability of mass art) explains why the Byrds' version of "Oh! Susannah" counts as a performance of a Stephen Foster song or why Cream's "Crossroads" counts as a performance of a Robert Johnson song. While the former counts as "Oh! Susannah" by repeating (and then toying with) a melody that is central to that particular piece, the musical activity that establishes that identity involves only a small part of what Foster wrote. All the same, their performance of the song locates them as participants in a shared musical culture, an accomplishment that demands at least some musical understanding of a culture to which they in many ways remained outsiders.

But since so much of the Byrds' or Cream's performance of these "traditional" songs reflects their own musical decisions, the particular songs are overwritten with values and implications that Foster and James would not recognize as their own. As with most musical performance, the source music is altered according to the musicians' goals, competence, understanding, and varied influences. Yet thanks to the strong iterability that comes with their mass art circulation, all of the Byrds' and Cream's relevant musical thinking remains available in each playing, unchanged by reinterpretation. The recordings democratically present all listeners with the same evidence about the musicians' higher-level intentions. Some listeners will understand. Many will not. The musicians must become participants in a certain set of cultural values in order to perform a style of music, whereas listeners can remain complete outsiders when listening.[17]

On balance, it does not appear that the wrong of wrongful appropriation can be equated with the fact that new expressive meanings arise in the process. The new meanings are a natural byproduct of weak iterability. The question, then, is whether any particular social or political values attach to the music simply because the musicians were base or negligent while creating it. We cannot conclude that a specific piece of hybrid music, such as Peter Gabriel's "Come Talk to Me," is an expression of colonialist ideology simply because we find an echo of colonialism in the musician's creative practices and privileged cultural position. Since no comparable transfer arises from other behaviors that musicians engage in when making music, only a basic understanding of the music and its higher-level intentions can tell us when musical appropriation results in music expressing colonialist attitudes.

We can now make some provisional conclusions. Performances of appropriated musical styles can never simply circulate styles and texts in a new context. Although musicians engaged in such appropriation must participate in the musical thinking of another musical culture or subculture, they will actively re-inscribe both musical styles and specific pieces of music. But music can travel between cultures and subcultures more directly, as mass art. In this case, strong iterability provides listeners with music that will be misperceived, for most listeners will not make the connections necessary to grasp its musical identity. When hybrid music is itself recorded and circulated as mass art, the strong iterability of those recordings allows the hybrid music to reach an audience with no background to appreciate it for the music that it is, again inviting misperception. Responsible listeners who appropriate music through strong iterability must engage in some transformation of identity, retraining their musical tastes so that their response will be adequate to the demands of the music.

Standards of what counts as wrongful appropriation will have to be applied with sensitivity to the music that actually gets made. Of course, that assumes that we can articulate some general standard. Assuming we can, we still face the burdensome task of having to consider each case on its own merits, to see how it fares in light of such standards. Which, in turn, generates the burdensome responsibility of bringing ourselves to the point of understanding enough about the specific piece of music to understand what it does or does not communicate.

So we have a rather perverse conclusion: an outsider's knowledge will not be sufficient to distinguish between acceptable and unacceptable musical appropriations. Only those who know enough about a hybrid to hear the music for what it really is will know what that music expresses. But to hear the hybrid for what it is, a responsible critic will have to practice the same immersion (however deep or shallow) that invites censure when practiced by Western musicians. Like the musician, the critic must possess basic musical understanding of at least two traditions. So there is a deep contradiction buried within the position that Western musicians should not create hybrid music while urging Western audiences to open their ears to the resistive messages of some world music. Anyone in a position to determine that the hybrid music of Ladysmith Black Mambazo or Djur Djura is politically progressive must have made some investment in such music, thereby joining the cultural milieu of musicians who are condemned for making a similar investment in the music of another culture.[18] Except, of course, that the musician must reach a basic musical understanding, while the listener can make inferences from the lyrics provided in the CD liner notes.

Free as a Bird: Exoticism Through Aestheticism

We approach music not as a natural object but as a human product imbued with a significance derived from the life and experiences of its creator (and its performers). Music, unlike willow trees and Saint Bernards, is redolent of the intentional context in which it is created and performed, and this, quite properly, affects the way we are inclined to experience its expressive aspects.

—Stephen Davies[19]

We have gradually roped off the ground where we can expect to dig out the wrongfulness of wrongful appropriation. It cannot rest in the garden-variety ignorance that is typical in the face of another culture's music. It cannot be reduced to a privileged musician's practice of finding new uses (and thus new meanings) for music appropriated from less privileged groups. Yet it must involve the intercourse of different cultures, and it must lie in the cultural practices of the musicians or audiences engaged in that appropriation.

Having already replied to relativism, I want to pursue the possibility of a standard for cultural interaction that is universal, at least in the sense that any cross-cultural communication presupposes it. Denying the radical incommensurability of cultures, such a standard denies that we are condemned to misunderstanding the communicative products of other cultures.

Even theorists whose basic principles seem opposed to it are tempted to embrace such a standard. Baraka, for example, strays from his own position of cultural incommensurability. He often makes evaluative judgments of white music and comparative judgments of white and black music. But such judgments lack "objectivity" under any assumption of incommensurability. For if there is genuine incommensurability, then Baraka cannot know what the blues represents when it is recontextualized. He can only suppose that all *decontextualization* (a step that precedes recontextualization) is wrong. But that would be a silly position to saddle him with. Furthermore, this is not the argument he actually makes; we've seen that much of his complaint centers on what the recontextualized blues have come to mean. Yet, to recontextualize the blues, members of another culture must have taken some pains to understand it; while their version of it may lack "authenticity," the resulting music can offer rich potential for expression. The error is to suppose that this expression must somehow be about the music's origins, that it must somehow express white attitudes about African Americans.

In many ways the appropriation of music is similar to the appropriation of food. Cuisine can carry cultural meanings: good champagne at an American wedding banquet means something rather different from cheap beer. The obvious disanalogy is that there are fewer specific meanings involved with food, and we do not approach most food with the expectation that it carries a message. In eating Chinese food or Thai food, we are not likely to *interpret* the stir-fry or the bowl of soup as a personal message from the cook to the diner. But food, like music, crosses over between cultures. Like music, food isn't automatically "translated" in this cultural crossover. Furthermore, it is the whole dish as served that has meaning within a cuisine, not isolated ingredients. A relocated dish typically becomes the basis for a similar but distinct dish, or some raw materials are incorporated. The same holds for ingredients. Tomatoes are indigenous to the Americas, but they've made their way into the cooking of Italy, India, and Southeast Asia. By now, the mere presence of tomatoes in a dish signifies nothing. By the same token, beyond the presence of the sitar there is nothing particularly "Indian" about the Beatles' "Norwegian Wood" or Tom Petty's "Don't Come Around Here No More" (1985).

Lisa Heldke argues that appropriation of food succumbs to the exploitive ideology of colonization when diners actively seek out what is exotic for the sake of its exoticism, reducing the richness and significance of another culture to whatever is unfamiliar in the cuisine.[20] The problem is not appropriation itself. It is the attitude of exoticism that resists seeing the food as significant in social and religious rites or as demanding knowledge of how the foods are authentically prepared. It is the willful aestheticism that reduces a cultural product to its surfaces and to the pleasures of novelty, and thus the attendant refusal to hear what other subject positions impart to the product being consumed.

This problem rests with diners, not cooks. By analogy, with music we should worry more about the audience and less about the musicians. Stephen Davies stresses this point in exploring the same comparison between music and food: "A person who listens to Balinese [music], neither knowing nor caring why the sounds follow each other in the order they do, is someone who interests herself not in the music, but in the noise it makes. Her pleasure is like that of the person who likes eating chocolate."[21] Her pleasure can only be an immediate pleasure in the pure sensuous flow of sound and, perhaps, in her private associations with that flow. But even with chocolate there can be an expressive dimension, as when it is given by one person to another in a red, heart-shaped box on Valentine's Day. Just as it would be callous and rotten to savor a box of chocolates delivered by a suitor whom one detests, it seems grossly disrespectful of others to reduce their cultural products to mere surfaces. With music, the problem arises when a person approaches all music as an item for pleasurable consumption, as if music were, say, of no more cultural significance than a candy bar that one buys for oneself at the market.[22] Modern capitalism makes it all too easy to treat both music and food as mere items for consumption, but that does not make the commodification of music the essential wrong.

So it turns out that the problem is not the ordinary ignorance and misunderstanding of cultural collisions. Instead, it lies in the wanton ignorance of audiences who pretend to care about music and so ought to know better. But if the problem is the thrill of exoticism and resistance to learning anything much about another culture, it suggests its own solution. Provided, of course, that we don't regard isolationism as the only way to resist colonialism.

Appeals to incommensurability and relativism are best answered by emphasizing that *several* norms are at play here. Because objections to appropriation cannot be grounded in a conflict between incommensurable standards, we should suspect that the more interesting problem is a conflict between competing intuitions enmeshed in the basic idea of artistic communication. One ideal regards artists as free agents who are not subject to our normal social constraints. It often goes under the heading of artistic autonomy. Narrowly construed, artistic autonomy licenses most appropriation. If *Graceland* is a Paul Simon album displaying sufficient artistry, then it simply doesn't matter how it was created or how he treated others in the process. But of course this attitude about artistry is precisely what we hope to counteract in identifying the wrong of wrongful appropriation.

The deeper problem with appropriation only emerges when we acknowledge that another ideal can counterbalance the excesses encouraged by artistic autonomy. Unfortunately, it is an ideal that gets too little attention. It is the ideal of audience responsibility. It might be called the ideal of audience deference. This ideal calls for understanding the cultural products of others on their own terms, as significant precisely because they are the creations of real persons who use art and music as a vehicle for engaging all others who join that artistic or musical community. If we participate by listening, seeking the music in the sound, then we also commit ourselves to understanding what we hear: we commit ourselves to hearing what the musicians are communicating in those sounds. For music with an expressive dimension, as is the case with most music that circulates as mass art, we commit ourselves to hearing the emotions and even the political ideas that are communicated in that music.[23]

Strictly speaking, the ideal of artistic autonomy does not conflict with the ideal of audience deference. The problem arises when we emphasize the former and forget about the latter. Hearing *Graceland* as the work of Paul Simon does not erase its attitude of exoticism (assuming, for the sake of argument, that it expresses such an attitude). If that attitude is part of the expressiveness of that music, then the audience can *and should* listen for it, and the audience is irresponsible if it ignores what is there to be found. However, I've also argued that any such attitude must be present as a higher-order property of the music. Because higher-order properties arise from the interplay of lower-order properties, their presence can only be demonstrated by *hearing them* in the music. Just as one cannot move from the fact that the Byrds recorded "Oh! Susannah" to the conclusion that the *Turn! Turn! Turn!* album ends on a racist note, one cannot assign an ugly colonialism to the music of Peter Gabriel or Paul Simon from facts about the creative process. The intellectual suspicion must be confirmed by finding something objectionable in the music.

At the same time, artistic autonomy does not imply that audiences should ignore the circumstances in which music is created. We only understand and appreciate a musical work by hearing the organized sounds as reflecting various historical and stylistic influences. So responsible listening places the music "against the background of the cultural heritage to which it gives expression."[24] Responsible listening is going to be easiest for those who simply listen to the most disposable and derivative pop music of their own place and time. It will be progressively more demanding as one listens to the music of remote cultures or music written many centuries ago. Hybrid music is going to be somewhere between these extremes.

Largely forgotten in the wake of recent theorizing about the "resistive," postmodern practices of the popular audience, the idea of audience deference still holds sway in mass art: it is the stance of the dedicated fan. The mass audience may be fickle, but there are still many fans of specific artists who regard new releases as additional chapters of a work in progress. Despite the collective creative process behind virtually all rock music, listening to a Patti Smith album as *hers* involves hearing it as grounded in a time and cultural moment. *Horses* is a debut, launched in the days when the music of Fleetwood Mac and Peter Frampton ruled the airwaves. *Gone Again* represents a mature artist, recorded just after the punk promise of the 1970s has proven hollow with the success and collapse of grunge. To listen in ignorance of these facts is to fail to appreciate much of what each says. The same point applies with cover versions. What the Rolling Stones mean by singing Chuck Berry in 1963 is rather different from what they mean by it two or three decades later. What the Sex Pistols "said" in performing Who and Small Faces songs in 1976 does not simply replicate whatever English mods found in them in the 1960s.[25]

The audience can choose to ignore such facts. Unfortunately, a large portion of the audience routinely does so. Worse yet, the recent tendency to congratulate audiences for appropriating mass art as a blank text for resistive pleasure minimizes audience responsibility to regard music as a directed utterance. It accepts, without restraint, the idea of an unlimited intertextuality in which texts circulate freely—which is really to say that audiences should feel free to appropriate anything that suits their purposes, origins and original meanings be damned. But music without history is music without meaning, and music without meaning cannot involve wrongful appropriation in any interesting way.

In conclusion, the appeal to cultural autonomy, as an essentially liberal ideal, leaves us completely indifferent about the specific cultural patterns people choose. We remain in a position to condemn fascism and apartheid as unacceptable curtailments of cultural autonomy, but unless we can make a similar case about rock's appropriations of African American and other musics, we have no reason to issue a sweeping condemnation of rock's love affair with the practice of appropriation. We can also condemn economic exploitation in which some musicians live in poverty while the music they made delivers fat royalty checks to someone else. While this evil of music's commodification is well known, it is more or less independent of the corrupting influence of *appropriation*, which has been my focus.

Yet we've also seen that the activity of seeking pleasure from music presupposes understanding the conventions governing that music. Understanding it as the music that it is assumes an engagement with the intentions and perspective of those whose music it is. The activity of listening, no less than the activity of music performance, presupposes audience responsibility. Audiences have a responsibility to attend to whoever has created it. Not that this means attending to the activities of artists apart from their musical activity (the way that some fans seem to think that every detail of the performer's life is equally important and equally their business), but at the very least it demands attending to them in the listening process. Seeking pleasure through music without making this effort demonstrates a profound contempt for other persons. This contempt for others, masquerading as a love of music, is probably the most serious wrong that typically arises as a consequence of musical appropriation.

While the risk of abuse is always present with appropriation, we have not arrived at any general wrong in media imperialism, the commodification of "folk" music, or the appropriation of musical styles. Indeed, the cultural differences and incommensurabilities that generate accusations of exploitive appropriation are ultimately factors that work against identifying any common pattern across all cases of appropriation. If we are going to point fingers, any criticism must be assigned on a case-by-case basis, sensitive to the dynamic patterns of living cultures.

PART

Gender

Can the Ethiopian change his skin, or the leopard his spots?

—Jeremiah 13:23

We created it! Let's take it over!

—Patti Smith concluding a performance of "My Generation," January 26, 1976

9

Act Naturally

Exile in Guyville

**I consider it self-evident that rock is "a white boy's club."
Why is another question.**

—Clinton Heylin

**As a fan, identifying across my gender was easy and fun.
For men, it appears not so. . . . It's interesting to note, for
instance, that the male fans Joni Mitchell and Madonna
boast seem to be disproportionately gay.**

—Barbara O'Dair

"When it comes to 'women in rock' nothing is very clear," warn
Simon Reynolds and Joy Press in *The Sex Revolts*. "Confusion
breeds confusion."[1] Slow to emerge in the spotlight, the topics of gender and "women in rock" confound anyone who
takes them on. I don't pretend to be the exception. In fact,
I must admit that I was personally rather slow to see that rock
has a serious gender problem. Having recognized it, I want
to suggest that several dimensions of the problem demand
more scrutiny than they commonly receive.

When I went off to college in 1975, a long day's drive
away from home, I was assigned to a dormitory and, with it,
to my first college roommate. We were not well suited. I was
a longhaired suburban kid whose stereo and record collection dominated half of the room. He was Jewish, from a family

with far more money than mine, was studying to become a dentist, and his principal entertainment was the small black and white television he'd brought from home. He called his mother the very first night to report that he'd been given a "hippie." Nonsense, I told him: my older brother was the family Deadhead. But since I liked to study while listening to music and he tended to spend his evenings watching television (a genuine conflict in the days before portable cassette and CD players), I looked for another place to study.

Luckily, I discovered a music listening room in the student union. Their sound system was a lot better than mine, and students could request specific titles from their stock of reel-to-reel tapes. I'd have chosen the Rolling Stones' *Exile on Main St.* (1972) and Joni Mitchell's *Court and Spark* (1974), the two albums that had dominated my listening during the summer I got out of high school, but the student union didn't have them. For most of the fall term my reading of Russian Literature and Plato's *Republic* was accompanied by two substitute albums that were available: the Stones' *Sticky Fingers* (1971) and Joni Mitchell's *Miles of Aisles* (1974). A newcomer to a strange city that I never learned to like, I felt at home whenever I listened to those two albums.

Sticky Fingers is bracketed by two of the Stones' finest moments; it opens with the unrelenting raunch of "Brown Sugar," a furious blast of guitar and saxophone and a classic bad-boy lyric, and it closes with "Moonlight Mile," a flowing yet languid track that is as feminine in tone as "Brown Sugar" is masculine. *Miles of Aisles* is basically a sampler of all the musical qualities that we thought of as appropriately feminine in the mid-1970s. The musical arrangements are far more restrained than in the infectious jazz-pop of *Court and Spark*, so that Mitchell's music remains solidly rooted in the earth tones and flow of folk music. In the words of one of the song titles, it's a portrait of a "woman of heart and mind." I was particularly enamored with "Real Good for Free," both for its swooning melody and its portrait of a brief moment of musical discovery in a strange city. I was on my own for the first time, and *Sticky Fingers* and *Miles of Aisles*, so utterly dissimilar in mood and sensibility, were my most frequent musical companions.

As the school year got going, I found plenty of outlets for my love of rock music. I subjected a very young Joan Jett to my not-much-older male gaze when she and the Runaways played at a fraternity party that fall. In the university library I tracked down the previous decade's published criticism on rock. I was able to expand my record collection by shopping in used record stores; I bought my first blues albums, and I found *The Stooges* (1969) and a mono copy of the Byrds' second album, *Turn! Turn! Turn!* (1966). Most afternoons after classes, I dropped by a room just down the hall that had the luxury of a refrigerator. Downing cold beer, we slipped into a ritual of listening to Pink Floyd or Queen before heading to the cafeteria for dinner. In the spring I saw a stadium show by the Who where Keith Moon was sober enough to deliver. (It was, I later learned, the very show at which Pete Townshend first experienced hearing loss.) Hanging out at the apartment of a girl I was getting involved with, I was impressed by the record collection of one of her black roommates, but I was also puzzled by the presence of Aerosmith and the Flying Burrito Brothers in a collection dominated by funk and disco.

As I got more heavily into music, I found less common ground with my roommate. Our differences created a rift that neither one of us made much effort to cross. I tended to hang out with others who shared my interests in music and beer, which meant that I was expected to accept the musical tastes of whoever happened to have beer to share. By the time I brought Patti Smith's first album back from the record store for a first listen, my roommate was spending his weekends at home, an hour away, rather than endure our coexistence and my horrible taste in music.

The situation made me more aware of the many cultural and social differences that estrange one sort of person from others—as did the fact that my school, USC ("University of Spoiled Children," the scholarship recipients joked), was a white bastion in an area of Los Angeles that was anything but Anglo. As I became dimly aware of racial issues, I also became more aware of the racial heritage of much of the music I was listening to. It took longer for issues of class and gender to make an impression on me. I loved *Court and Spark* as much as—perhaps more than—*Exile on Main St.* Others laughed at the Runaways in the autumn of 1975. I found them exhilarating. I was the first kid in the dorm to own a Patti Smith record; I had just gone through a phase of listening incessantly to Them and her cover of "Gloria" made perfect sense to me. At the same time I could not understand why one of my dorm friends wanted to get his ear pierced. Compared to the gender segregation of the dormitories and the way that the freshman cafeteria was neatly self-segregated into male and female zones, the world of rock seemed relatively integrated to me. The presence of a reggae rhythm in Patti Smith's "Redondo Beach" was far more notable than the fact that a woman was writing her own songs and leading her own band.

My first clue that I was missing something important was Ellen Willis's piece on Janis Joplin for the *Rolling Stone Illustrated History of Rock and Roll*, excerpted in *Rolling Stone* magazine in 1976. It was a lengthy rumination on Joplin's status as a woman singer in a male world, and I could not for the life of me see why Willis needed to go on about how "seeing Joplin" had liberated her by giving her the resolve not to get her hair straightened. I had the *Cheap Thrills* album and I loved Joplin's version of "Piece of My Heart." But Willis was writing about the *politics* of rock instead of about the music. It read like sociology, not criticism. Still clinging to the naive belief that a singer's performance is an act of pure, personal self-disclosure, I couldn't yet hear Joplin's performance as a self-effacement; the girl from Port Arthur, Texas, vanished into the willful counterculture construction of the hippie chick from Haight-Ashbury. It didn't help that I knew Haight-Ashbury firsthand, while Texas was more alien than the dark side of the moon. Stuck in the rhetoric of the day, I viewed the hippie as in touch with the natural self.

Later, when I understood that all music is coded discourse and that no music *directly* expresses anything, I saw that Willis was right: "Janis's femaleness complicated the issues, raised the stakes. She had less room to maneuver than a man in her position, fewer alternatives to fall back on if she blew it."[2] Her performances were less expressions of personal emotion than symbolic demands for the same level of individual liberation that young men were carving out for themselves in that time and place. She "was holding nothing back" when she sang.[3] Willis argues that, facing limited alternatives, Joplin's incessant display of struggle and drive conveys the idea that a woman might want *everything*, just like her male peers. (But, Joplin also implied, her male peers made sure that she had to try just a little bit harder than they did to get what she wanted.) My own failure to read gender where gender was so obviously part of the message is not, I think, unusual. It has been a persistent failing in most rock criticism and theorizing. Reflecting on the intersection of politics and music in the 1960s, Simon Frith likewise ignores gender when considering Janis Joplin. He sees her performances as remarkable for "her ability to use her emotions (which touched on self-loathing) to bind her listeners together."[4] Unlike Willis, Frith assigns no importance to the fact that it took the self-loathing of a woman to bind a predominantly male audience together.

If popular music and mass art simply reflect and reinforce our prevailing patterns of thought, what was reinforced all those evenings when my own listening alternated between the Stones and Joni Mitchell? That would depend, to a great extent, on the preconceptions that informed my listening. What is less clear is what those assumptions would be. If gender is organized as a strict dichotomy, what messages did I internalize? Equally important, what messages did I miss? Did I have any interpretive freedom in any of this?

Two Cultures? Some Central Issues

The universal social pressure upon women to be all alike, and do all the same things, and to be content with identical restrictions, has resulted not only in terrible suffering in the lives of exceptional women, but also in the loss of unmeasured feminine values in special gifts.
—Anna Garlin Spencer, 1912[5]

Chants and ripples, chimes and murmurs were the musical language this afternoon, definitely not shouts or scary electric guitars.
—Description of Lilith Fair, 1998[6]

I want to review some rather obvious points.[7] Sigmund Freud was wrong: anatomy isn't destiny. Psychological, social, and cultural differences between women and men are not the inevitable result of sex difference. Gender roles are not innate. Gender roles are not natural. Like an individual's ethnic or cultural identity, each individual's gender identity is a contextual matter of historical, social, and political positioning.

Yet in every known culture, biological differences serve as an excuse for imposing sharply distinct gender-role identities. From the moment of birth and first human interaction, baby boys and baby girls are treated differently, exposed to different environments, and evaluated according to different norms. Stereotypical masculine and feminine identities serve as blueprints for shaping and then policing the formation of genders that feel "natural" and inevitable. Judith Butler offers an acute example:

> When Aretha Franklin sings "You make me feel like a natural woman," she seems at first to suggest that some natural potential of her biological sex is actualized by her participation in the cultural position of "woman" as object of heterosexual recognition. . . . Although Aretha appears to be all too glad to have her naturalness confirmed, she also seems fully and paradoxically mindful that the confirmation is never guaranteed.[8]

Jonathan Culler amplifies Butler's point:

> [Aretha] seems happy to be confirmed in a "natural" sexual identity, prior to culture, by a man's treatment of her. But her formulation, "you make me feel *like* a natural woman," suggests that the supposedly natural or given identity is a cultural role, an effect that has been produced within culture: she *isn't* a "natural" woman but has to be made to feel *like* one. The natural woman is a cultural product.[9]

Granted, Aretha Franklin's performance is a powerful reminder that the seeming "naturalness" of gender requires a constant confirmation of our gender by those around us. But is it really a critique of gender? Is it a statement that the "natural" identity of "woman" is a cultural imposition that might be framed differently?

The "natural" linking of opposed gender-role stereotypes with two categories of biological sex serves two hegemonic functions. First, the pairs are typically opposed to one another as pairs of inverted opposites. The result is a downplaying of differences among members of the same sex, cloaking the fact that the range of difference is usually greater within each sex (between males as a group, and between females as a group) than between women and men. Relatively few men live up to the normative standards of masculinity; relatively few women live up to the normative standards of femininity.

The second function is to rank these stereotypes in a hierarchy of value, with the higher value assigned to the roles and traits defined as male. Against this male norm, female roles and traits are seen as marginal and even deviant. (Other roles become more marginal yet. As Butler remarks about Aretha's performance of "A Natural Woman," what if Aretha were singing to Butler, that is, to a lesbian?) By the age of two or three, boys and girls who adopt the normative gender-role stereotypes become oriented toward the world, particularly the social world, in some fundamentally distinct ways—perceptually, emotionally, and in all other areas of response.

So it is no surprise to find that empirical studies confirm that most women respond to cultural products, such as music and music videos, differently than most men. What women seek in music is different, what they enjoy is different, and what they derive from the experience of music is different. Women are more interested in *using* music as a means to an explicit end, such as for dancing or to set the mood for some other activity. Men are more likely to listen to the music for the sake of listening to the music (which may explain why musicologists—overwhelmingly male—have assumed that such listening is the best way to "use" music).[10] Female fans of specific artists act out their fandom quite differently than male fans, with female fans consistently engaged in "style imitation" as a major mode of fan response.[11]

Although significant numbers of males and females do not conform to these patterns, gender seems to be "a more important and clear-cut variable in terms of which to grasp the musical articulation of social and cultural realities . . . than class."[12] That is, gender is the best predictor of whether an individual will respond favorably to a new song by Metallica or Billy Joel. Take any brother and sister who are close in age, with comparable levels of education and similar jobs. The brother is far more likely to prefer the song by Metallica. The sister is far more likely to prefer the song by Billy Joel. Looking at the strong correlation between gender and preferences for various styles of music, researchers find that, "whatever mainstream (or *pop*) means, males tend to avoid it and females tend to gravitate to it." When it comes to musical taste, "there are really two cultures, a male and a female."[13]

So it seems that my teen enjoyment of the Rolling Stones, while not quite as predictable as snow in Minnesota in January, comes as no surprise. But notice that the link between gender and taste relates to *style*.

Studies have not revealed any significant connection between the gender of the listener and that of the musician. I was already a fan of the Stones, so there was no *musical* reason why I shouldn't respond to the hard rock of the Runaways and Patti Smith. What could not be predicted is that I should love Joni Mitchell's *Court and Spark*, the most radio-friendly album she ever made.

Reflecting on rock as a mass art rather than as a performing art, we realize another obstacle for women is that male and female fans seldom have the same access to the rock canon. Simon Frith remarks on how shopping for records has influenced his own tastes:

> Most of my life I've had to go to the record shop at least once a week. . . . *Record-shopping is a surprisingly sociable activity.* Propping up the counter (and I'm talking about small shops . . . not the audio hypermarkets) are disc jockeys, cultists, collectors, knowalls, obsessives, the unemployed. . . . The record shop is where gigs and clubs and musics are publicly discussed and placed, where changing tastes are first mocked and marked.[14]

Despite his frequent attention to sex and gender, Frith's paean to record shops never notes that this "active consumption" is almost exclusively masculine. Are the tastes being mocked female?[15]

Others have taken pains to note what Frith omits. Narrated by a man who owns an independent record shop, Nick Hornby's novel *High Fidelity* captures the masculinism of record collecting in one sharp paragraph:

> I get by because of the people who make a special effort to shop here Saturdays—young men, always young men, with John Lennon specs . . . and because of the mail order: I advertise in the back of the glossy rock magazines, and get letters from young men, always young men, in Manchester and Glasgow and Ottawa, young men who seem to spend a disproportionate amount of their time looking for deleted Smith singles and "ORIGINAL NOT RERELEASED" underlined Frank Zappa albums.[16]

To the extent that the world of record collecting is a male preserve, women are discouraged from participating in rock culture; they are left on the fringes, with "pop" music as their proper preserve.

Shifting our focus from consumption of music to its creation, we see that women face far more barriers to participation than do men. Hurdles range from active harassment to latent prejudice. David Lee Roth,

Van Halen's original vocalist, pinpoints the problem: "We don't have so many lead guitar women, not because women don't have the ability to play the instrument, but because they're kept locked up, taught to be something else."[17] As originally documented by Steve Chapple and Reebee Garofalo, the layers of gatekeepers involved in the production and circulation of mass music tend to keep women out of the game.[18] A quarter-century later, the situation is marginally improved. As documented in *Sexing the Groove,* many obstacles still block young women from the active participation that would allow them to pursue a career in rock.[19] The most obvious problems are institutional in nature, as when Melissa Etheridge notes that "Rock radio would say, 'We can't play that because we already have a woman on the radio,' and 'We couldn't play two women in the same hour. We might lose our male following.'"[20] Some obstacles are more subtle and indirect, as when gender norms dictating long fingernails for women interfere with learning to play most rock instruments.

There are signs of positive change: in the late 1990s, music purchases by women reached and then surpassed those of men. Many writers celebrate the liberatory potential of specific movements, particularly Riot Grrrl.[21] Punk is often celebrated as having made some difference by providing an outlet for musical novices with political agendas influenced by Marxism and feminism. However, it is a distortion of rock history to celebrate punk, as some do, as "the first form of rock not to rest on love songs."[22] (That would be folk-rock.) Although the Riot Grrrl movement generated a certain amount of media and scholarly attention, I do not believe that the mere increase in women's participation is significant as breaking down rock's male hegemony. Since the 1960s, each decade has seen the emergence of a new crop of female rock stars.[23]

By themselves, greater participation and a heightened profile do not automatically disrupt traditional gender norms. In recent years, the success of Lilith Fair illustrates that adult women are still most successful when they conform to the same "singer/songwriter/folkie lady" mode that represented the first significant wave of women's voices in rock.[24] The main alternative is the "diva" model of Whitney Houston, Cher, and Mariah Carey. In a tradition where an acoustic guitar and voice are not perceived as signs of *musicianship*, few women are known for their songwriting, their instrumental abilities, or as integral members of a group. If we consider the best-selling album and best-selling song from 1971 to 1997, thirteen of the top singles and eight of the top albums are the work of women or bands fronted by women. Yet nineteen of those twenty-one are women known almost exclusively for being vocalists. (Joan Jett and Carole King are the two exceptions.) No musical instrument is associated with Madonna, the Spice Girls, or Mariah Carey. There have been a few highly visible exceptions among women in rock: Maureen Tucker, Bonnie Raitt, Tina Weymouth, and Heart's Nancy Wilson. But until the 1990s, as players women were usually confined to that most domesticated of instruments, the piano: Aretha Franklin, Laura Nyro, Carole King. One wonders if it's really progress when Tori Amos takes the next step, overtly eroticising her piano bench.

These barriers are the active faces of a set of knee-jerk assumptions about sex and gender. Music is no less caught up in gender ideology than is any other sphere of symbolic interaction: "the goal of producing a commercially successful media product has colored the ways audiences are perceived and addressed . . . and revealed a design intent on perpetuating the social condition of gender inequality."[25] Because early rock and roll explored long-taboo subjects of sex and race, rock initially promised cultural disruption. But as the 1960s wound down, rock settled into a comfortable middle age and grew complacent about gender. In "Rock and Sexuality," originally published in 1978, Simon Frith and Angela McRobbie provided the first useful road map to rock's assumptions about gender.[26] Expanding on a theme that Ellen Willis had articulated in her Janis Joplin essay, Frith and McRobbie argued that rock's myth of sexual liberation was grounded in its audience's simplistic belief that rock expresses a "natural" sexuality. This belief made it easy to overlook the extent that "cock rock" bands like Led Zeppelin peddled traditional gender stereotypes. Yet the aggressive displays of male sexual prowess were never the sole option for male rock musicians. Frith and McRobbie itemized several modes through which rock constructs masculinity. However, this appearance of variety did not hide an underlying unity: as a form of sexual expression and sexual control, rock had become synonymous with a male-defined sexuality that sees women in light of a demeaning ideology of subordinate Other.

Women seeking avenues of expression in the traditional arts had already voiced parallel concerns. Many of them had concluded that nothing is gained by expressing progressive ideas about gender from within the established system:

> It is impossible for women within this structure to make statements which transcend gender. . . . When women set out in search of a new feminine self they are confronted with difficulties which are literally indescribable, for the medium "through" which we want to expose the fact that men have stamped the neutral concept of humanity with their own mark is itself a product of this process. This reduces our avenues of expression and confuses our thought.[27]

If rock music is lousy with patriarchal values, women musicians must turn to something else.

At least this was Lydia Lunch's conclusion. Lunch emerged in the second wave of New York punk with Teenage Jesus and the Jerks but did not find the punk scene to be genuinely progressive when it came to sexuality. She soon distanced herself from rock and pursued a career as a poet and performance artist: "Get rid of the fucking raunchy bad rock 'n' roll! That's where girls should wake up instead of trying to cop second, third and fourth generation rock 'n' roll licks that were terrible in the first place. Whey don't they just trade in their guitars for fuckin' Uzis?"[28] In her crude way, Lunch questions the possibility that any manifestation of rock can be nonsexist. So women should wash their hands of the whole mess: "to make nonsexist music it is necessary to use sounds, structures and styles that cannot be heard as rock."[29]

What will a genuinely nonsexist music sound like? In the 1970s, Olivia Records promoted the idea that it sounded like the folkish music of Holly Near and Cris Williamson. Others contend that it sounds like disco. Now that it has become something of an article of faith that nonsexist popular music cannot sound like the Rolling Stones, I want to retrace some steps and analyze the arguments supporting that conclusion. I think that they have limited merit. I will then review ways that rock music, as mass art, already contributes progressively to the formation of identity.

10

Così Fan Tutte Meets Tutti Frutti: Rock Performs Gender

Mannish Boys: How Is Rock Gendered?

You like to think of yourselves as blues musicians but you just prance around like little nance boys.

—Ian Stewart, the "sixth" Rolling Stone, expresses disapproval to Keith Richards

Women have seized rock 'n' roll and usurped it for their own expressive purposes, but we've yet to see a radical feminization of rock form in itself.

—Simon Reynolds and Joy Press, *The Sex Revolts*

For many women, rock's gender problem has been only too obvious in the music of the self-appointed "greatest rock 'n' roll band in the world," the Rolling Stones. Given their centrality to the rock formation, the Stones' frequent put-downs of women serve as a litmus test on the question of rock's general stance toward women. In the racist misogyny of "Brown Sugar" and "Some Girls," the Stones seem to have gone out of their way to live up to Clinton Heylin's description of rock as a "white boy's club." Their notorious early press headline of "Would You Let Your Daughter Go With a Stone?" gave way to "Can a Feminist Love the World's Greatest Rock and Roll Band?"[1] "Under My Thumb" and "Stupid Girl" were too ugly to ignore:

> To catalogue the anti-women songs [in rock] would make up almost a complete history of rock. This all hit home to me with knock-out force at a recent "Stones" concert when Mick, prancing about enticingly with whip in hand, suddenly switched gears and went into "Under My Thumb" with an incredible vengeance that upped the energy level and brought the entire audience to its feet dancing on the chairs. Mass wipe-out for women.[2]

Yet to love rock is to love the Stones (or Aerosmith, or Led Zeppelin, or Guns N' Roses, or some equally offensive group). It seems that loving rock means celebrating some of the most unpalatable abuse that men dish out for women. Some feminists who love the music of the Rolling Stones—their songs and sound, if not their message—report that submission to the phallic power of their sound can induce "spasms of feminist guilt."[3]

The most interesting critique of such music holds that the *music* is encoded as signifying masculinity. Since masculinity is the gendered face of patriarchy, then similar-sounding music will be no better simply because it is made by women. Susan McClary warns that when women employ the same musical styles and strategies as men, "masculine" elements of the women's music are likely to be put down as too aggressive and its "feminine" elements will be dismissed as trivial.[4] While I grant that lyrics and visual imagery attach gender stereotypes to various styles of rock, I am not convinced by McClary's further arguments: she advances the stronger claim that patriarchal *ideas* about sexual politics are deeply embedded in the *musical structures* of some popular music. All similar music within a specific musical tradition will inherit a set of inherited conventions whose meanings will be beyond any musician's personal control. I agree that meanings of "Under My Thumb" can't be collapsed into the intentions of Mick Jagger and Keith Richards. It doesn't follow that the music of "Under My Thumb" will "mean" the same thing as the Beatles' "All My Loving" or "Got to Get You Into My Life."

McClary claims that we hear most music as a narrative structure in which a harmonic progression is destabilized by ambiguous or dissonant elements. "The principal innovation of tonality," she claims, "is its ability to instill in the listener an intense desire for a given event: the final tonic cadence . . . called 'the climax,' which is quite clearly to be experienced as metaphorical ejaculation."[5] In rock music, she might have noted, we have no better example than the Rolling Stones' "Going Home," the long jam that occupies half of one side of *Aftermath:* "the manner in which the harp and drums continuously build while Keith Richards's guitar strokes to a furious conclusion is telling."[6]

There are two distinct claims advanced here. One concerns listening and audience reception, while the other is about music's capacity to convey a metaphor of male sexual response. According to McClary, intrusions that impede progress toward the climax are read "as Other and as an obstacle to the configuration defined as Self or identity." The effect is that "time becomes organized around the expectation of intensified conflict, climax, and eventual resolution." (In the absence of such elements, we are free to interpret "Going Home" as narcissistic self-love.) Assuming that stable elements are read as masculine and the less stable are read as feminine, tonality suggests a narrative which revolves around the violent purging of the tempting but dangerous Other.

But popular music seldom offers extended, teasing delays of anticipated musical events. So McClary qualifies her interpretation by noting that most popular music is harmonically simple and thus "avoids this schema." This indictment of rock music, however, is little more than guilt by association. True, the offending schema makes its way into a number of hard rock/heavy metal songs that McClary analyzes—made even more explicit in several Whitesnake videos. But her primary evidence is the predominance of similar narrative schemata in Western classical music, literature, film, philosophy, theology, and science.[7] Because rock partakes of European harmonies, rock seems determined to force upon its audience the cynical conclusion that lends its name to Mozart's great opera about men and women: *Così Fan Tutte* ("thus do all women" or "women are like that").

McClary is vague about the precise lesson to be drawn, but her analysis of several Madonna songs and videos makes it clear that she regards most segments of popular songs as having either "masculine" or "feminine" identities. By keeping such pairs of elements in constant play and resisting musical closure, Madonna escapes the "desire-dread-purge" narrative that implies masculine triumph over feminine Other. But several points work against drawing broad conclusions from these selected examples.

First, McClary's case rests on associating a specific message with the type of musical structure that occurs throughout European-based music of the modern period. In short, she grounds ideology in musical architectonic. But how well does this work for popular music, where musical interest is more likely to be directed at discrete, isolated musical "hooks" than harmonic resolution? If the popular audience has an "intense desire" for any aspect of the music, it is a desire to hear a song's hooks, its most memorable *moments*. It is not a desire to reach the final tonic cadence. Using traditional musicology to analyze the musical hooks of thirteen distinct melodies, Peter Mercer-Taylor demonstrates that they betray a common pitch configuration: "each features a step-wise ascent to a high tonic pitch followed by a drop of a fifth or more."[8] His examples include a song featured in the Disney animated film *The Hunchback of Notre Dame* (1996), the chorus of Elvis Costello's "No Action" (1978), Joan Osborne's "One of Us" (1996), an advertising jingle for Texaco gasoline, Cole Porter's "Bluebird," and a key moment in Brahms's Violin Concerto. While these hooks are structurally similar and provide points of intense musical interest, there is simply no common idea conveyed across the range of cases. Joan Osborne's metaphysical question ("what if God was one of us?") has nothing to do with the frustration and suggestion of violence that dominates Billy Joel's "Pressure" (1982), another of Mercer-Taylor's examples. While McClary pays too little attention to the hook element of popular music, such examples undermine her proposal that common musical strategies imply common meanings.

So it is not clear that the interplay of "masculine" and "feminine" carries the same weight and meaning in rock that it carried in the classical forms of the eighteenth and nineteenth centuries. Led Zeppelin's "Stairway to Heaven" is a classic example of an extended rock song that works slowly toward its triumphant climax. Yet its lyrics tend to work *against* a sexual interpretation of that climax.

Like "Stairway," many of rock's most triumphant musical climaxes belong to progressive rock, the rock genre that consciously imitates classical prototypes. As rock musicians in bands like Genesis and Yes experimented with longer instrumental forms, they established variety by borrowing from symphonic forms: "drawing on the legacy of nineteenth-century program music, progressive rock ... [introduced] systematic juxtapositions of what can best be termed masculine and feminine sections; while this approach is not unusual in symphonic music, it is rare in most other rock styles."[9] But a variety of strategies are employed in creating these contrasts between sections. Their "masculine" and "feminine" characters are not always a question of their relation to the tonic cadence. Contrasts of timbre, melody, meter and tempo are equally important devices: "acoustic sections tend to be slower and to feature longer, more lyrical melodies, simpler harmonic progressions, and more open textures, while electric sections tend to be faster and to emphasize less tuneful melodic material, denser textures, and more complex harmonies."[10]

Conflicts between these segments are not simply a matter of delaying the climax. Multiple climaxes are common. Finally, the lyrics frequently invite interpretations in terms of opposites, but not of male Self and female Other. Drawing on the themes and devices of religious texts, mythology, and fantasy literature, progressive rock has typically conveyed a struggle between dehumanizing modern life and some form of a humanistic, utopian alternative. Edward Macan is quite right to read progressive rock as rock's main alternative to heavy metal's crude glorification of the masculine. Yet prog-rock albums like Yes's *Tales From Topographic Oceans* (1973) and *Relayer* (1974) make more use of the struggle between the "masculine" and the "feminine" than can be found in the entire career of Whitesnake.

Second, there are questions of allusion and intertextuality as they play a part in generating meaning. McClary cites Bessie Smith and Aretha Franklin as evidence that African American music invites female participation "without the punitive, misogynist frame of European culture." Claiming that Madonna's "musical affiliations are with African American music," McClary concludes that Madonna's music escapes the codes of mainstream Western music.[11] But general affiliations (the level on which McClary makes the connection) hardly settle the matter if there are other, conflicting strains within African American music.

Tina Turner might have a different opinion about the status of women musicians in African American culture, a culture that is not so obviously free of misogyny. The back cover of Ike and Tina Turner's

River Deep, Mountain High album (1969), produced by Phil Spector and involving only token appearances by Ike, describes Tina as "a happily married mother of four!" Above this unknowingly ironic comment, a photograph of the pair places Ike at the piano. Tina is behind his chair, leaning over a tub of washing, singing along. The greater irony is that it took a white producer, Phil Spector, to unlock Tina Turner's potential as something more than a rhythm and blues screamer. Working with Spector, she later related, was both her first taste of personal freedom and her first experience of being treated as a professional musician.[12] Songs like "River Deep" also revealed the liberating possibilities of a broader range of musical expression. "To me, a lot of rhythm and blues is depressing," she explains. "The culture from which it descends is depressing." She also shatters McClary's idea that only European culture views women who take the stage as sexual commodities; whenever a woman "strut[s] about in some tiny skirt" on stage, Turner notes, "some men presume you are up for grabs."[13]

Furthermore, Madonna's appropriations hardly locate her *within* the African American tradition. To bell hooks, Madonna's appropriations of that tradition make her little more than a "plantation mistress" whose use of black culture is more "racist aggression" than true affirmation.[14] A related problem is that McClary's reading positions Janis Joplin and Polly Jean Harvey as at least as well situated as Madonna when it comes to African American music. But unlike Madonna, they appropriate the blues tradition. It is tempting to conclude that the blues appropriations of the Rolling Stones, Led Zeppelin, and Eric Clapton would also be free of "the demand within the discourse" that women, as Other, "be destroyed."[15] After all, the *musical structure* remains intact. It does not change with the musician's race and gender. The same blues progression is found in Etta James's version of "Tell Mama" and in Janis Joplin's cover version. The same blues progression is found in Memphis Minnie's "When the Levee Breaks" (1929) and in Led Zeppelin's cover version. The same basic schema runs through thousands of blues played by both blacks and whites. Yet white appropriations of blues structures are often reserved for overt misogyny and stereotypically masculine renderings of sexuality. Think of the Stones with "Stray Cat Blues" and Led Zeppelin's infamous come-on of "shake me 'til the juice runs down my leg" in "The Lemon Song"—basically Howlin' Wolf's "Killing Floor" with lyrics from Robert Johnson's "Traveling Riverside Blues." Several women's organizations called for a boycott of Eric Clapton's *Pilgrim* (1998) because of some standard blues tropes about shooting his woman. Clearly, one does not become subversive or buy into the ideology of a non-Western tradition simply by appropriating its songs or musical structures.

It remains doubtful whether a musical schema carries any strong implications about gender relationships. Discounting the extent to which songs and recordings remain open-ended, McClary underestimates the listener's "interpretive freedom."[16] This freedom is encouraged when performers engage in cultural appropriation, mixing together elements of different musical traditions. But appropriation (including Madonna's appropriations from African American dance music) can also generate interpretive confusion. Knowledgeable listeners often find themselves at a loss when faced with vague "affiliations" substituting for clear-cut musical competence.

We find an interesting test case in Janis Joplin's display of her own African American "affiliations" before a mixed-race audience in Memphis. The occasion was the Second Annual Stax/Volt Yuletide Show. Stanley Booth reports that Joplin was in fine voice that night, yet she bored the Memphis audience. They barely applauded her three songs and did not bring her back for an encore of her current hits. "At least they didn't throw things," Joplin said afterwards.[17] The audience, it seemed, had its own discursive tradition and its own assumptions about the meaning of the music. Joplin came across as sloppy rather than powerful, and the pastiche of styles incorporated into her musical arrangements came across as poor musicianship: "black audiences found little they recognized and nothing they wanted in Joplin's music."[18] The obvious lesson is that Madonna's equally selective use of African American musical sources neither increases nor decreases *her* capacity to convey an alternative story about desire and sexuality. It all depends on who's listening and their capacity to recognize specific intertextualities in what they hear.

One more factor weighs against locating rock's glorification of patriarchy in a general pattern derived from European classical music. There is the presence of the human voice, the centerpiece of popular music. "Even when treating the human voice as an instrument, in short, we come up against the fact that it stands for the person more directly than any other musical device. . . . The voice is a sound produced physically, by the movement of the muscles and breadth in the chest and throat and mouth; to listen to a voice is to listen to a physical event, to the sound of a body."[19] But not just a body. A *gendered* body. The music's "authorship" attaches to this gendered body regardless of our knowledge of its actual authorship. Because Tina Turner's husky voice conveys the torment of an adult woman, we hear "River Deep, Mountain High" as a woman's tale even if we regard Phil Spector as its *auteur.* Whatever persona the singer adopts, only the most extreme technological transformations of the voice can mask the sexed identity of the body producing it. Laurie Anderson, hardly mainstream, sometimes uses "audio masks" that make her sound male. But she is primarily a performance artist, and even here the audience is aware that a woman's body is the source of the voice they hear. Perhaps this is why she recruits Peter Gabriel and William S. Burroughs to provide vocals on *Mister Heartbreak* (1984).

I wager that virtually every member of the popular audience assigns gender to a piece of popular music according to the body whose voice provides the lead vocal. Apart from such identification, there is no presumption that the music speaks with the voice of a male Self. Janet Jackson's cover version of Rod Stewart's "Tonight's the Night (Gonna Be Alright)" is heard as a woman's seduction of another woman. The final cadence is not heard as a male climax and subordination of the Other. By the same token, there is nothing about the *music* that can tell us otherwise. When Annie Lennox sings "The Downtown Lights," inviting her lover for a stroll through the empty streets "in the cool evening," she soothes and reassures him, putting to rest any doubts about their love. In the Blue Nile's original version of the same song, Paul Buchanan leaves us unsure of their future. The same words, set to the same music and sung in much the same way, come across very differently when directed from different genders. This is not to deny that instrumental passages are important moments—even emotional highpoints—of many rock arrangements. Yet thanks to Joplin's titanic performance, the Self who narrates Big Brother's "Piece of My Heart" is consistently a woman; when Sam Andrew's crude guitar solo disrupts the vocal, it does not come across as a masculine element fighting with the feminine. Its rough howls come across as a pre-linguistic utterance by the same woman.

We thus arrive at a fresh puzzle. We have found nothing in the combination of some very general patterns of musical organization and the frame of European culture to show that rock music expresses the ideology of male dominance. As a consequence, that ideology is present only if it is constantly reaffirmed in the face of threats from marginalized voices. (The resulting insecurity probably contributes to the exclusionary practices found throughout so much of rock culture.) However, if this ideology of male dominance is so fragile, why is rock so slow to abandon it? Why is a mass art so unwilling to permit the expression of multiple voices? Where women's voices are heard as diverse expressions of "the feminine," men's voices are heard chanting endlessly on the same note. Why, as the audience for popular music fragments into a series of isolated audiences, is there such uniformity of mind when it comes to gender?[20]

Boys Keep Swinging: Masculinity Writ Large

You listen to something like what we do to enjoy it and have fun. If you're listening to something to diss it and to ridicule it, why are you listening to begin with? It's supposed to be a fun thing to begin with and that's what sexual lyrics are all about. . . . That's what rock 'n' roll's all about.

—Joey Kramer defends Aerosmith's lyrics against charges of misogyny[21]

The most durable reason offered to explain the continuing appeal of aggressive music and crude lyrics about masculine domination is that they express an essential truth about masculinity, particularly male adolescence. On this model, rock's most aggressive displays of misogyny are not just one mode of masculinity, nor simply fringe cases that push the envelope of acceptable representations of women. The worst excesses of "cock rock" are regarded as a frank display of the very core of patriarchal culture, whose central value is an exaggerated disavowal of all things female. When Mick Jagger "pretends" to be the rapist of "Midnight Rambler," his representation of the extreme is to be understood as normative, not marginal. At the same time, Jagger's performance of gender is itself an assault on women. There is no pleasure in his performance except by complicity in the assault.

I think that almost everything I've just summarized is false. Seeing where it goes wrong will be useful, I believe, in rehabilitating this music. But that requires digging a bit deeper into the story that has been told in order to damn this music.

Three ideas contribute to the position I've summarized. First, whatever the cultural influences on gender difference, it is assumed that aggression and a desire to dominate are essentially male. Second, it is thought that rock music is irrevocably linked to a specific ideology of sex. Third, it is taken for granted that a single general context informs interpretation of all cultural expression.

The first premise, linking aggression with masculinity, is particularized in the view that men are essentially rapists. Or, in the words of Susan Brownmiller, rape "is nothing more or less than a conscious process of intimidation by which *all* men keep *all* women in a state of fear."[22] All men, in being men, participate in the violent project of keeping women in their place through humiliation, degradation, and defilement. While violent pornography is "an extreme example," popular culture is saturated with entertainment through which men gain their "sense of power from viewing females as anonymous, panting playthings, adult toys, dehumanized objects to be used, abused, broken and discarded."[23] Surveying examples of mass art that glorify violence against women, Brownmiller describes Jagger's performance of "Midnight Rambler" in great detail. Mick Jagger's rapist is offered as the *truth* about masculinity, not a mere play-acting.

One could, I suppose, advance this line of analysis without holding that men are biologically driven to be aggressors.[24] One might say that it only describes our prevailing ideal of masculine identity, treating it as essential to *that* historically contingent meaning of "man." But if "all men" threaten "all women" with rape under a contingent ideology, we're merely engaged in semantics: which sense of "man" does Jagger exemplify when he performs songs like "As Tears Go By," "Wild Horses," and "Angie," in which he's not threatening or humiliating women? The fact that the Rolling Stones create such songs undercuts the assumption of a universal pattern to men's (or women's) lives. Or do we fall back on the old dogma that "Midnight Rambler" is more authentic, more sincere, than the sentimental ballads? Yet it remains the case that one of Jagger's poses, the sensitive side, is that of a man refusing to be a man. That suggests that neither sense of "man" has any claim to priority.

Harder to pin down is the second contributing idea that locates songs like "Midnight Rambler" as central rather than peripheral to rock. It is most clearly articulated in Catharine MacKinnon's argument that principles of free speech do not protect messages that degrade women. As weapons for dehumanizing women, speech acts are as powerful as physical acts. MacKinnon draws on the obvious fact that words are not opposed to deeds: words alone can constitute harm, as in verbal sexual harassment. As actions, the *wrongness* of a demeaning speech act is identical with the wrongness of a physical rape. Both express the demeaning attitude toward women that permeates patriarchy. To treat women as inferior to men simply because they're women is to act unjustly. To *portray* women as inferior is likewise to *act* unjustly (and one way to portray all women in this way is to portray an individual woman in this way).

The crux of the problem with "Midnight Rambler" is not its subject matter so much as the *use* that's made of that subject matter: there is a long tradition in which rock "means" sex. Rock is also heir to a tradition that endorses a specific ideology of sex. MacKinnon argues that the liberal ideal of free speech wrongly assumes that subordinated groups *have* a capacity to speak in the public arena. Yet as long as Mick Jagger is free to "pretend" to be a rapist, endorsing the dehumanization of women, society forces all women to accept defamation and the suspension of their own civil rights.[25] The deeper problem with "Midnight Rambler" is the context in which it's launched into the world.

The third assumption now emerges. It is that a common intention is manifested by all similar speech acts within this very general context. When sex is part of the message, we currently have only one context: an ideology of male domination and female subordination.[26] Within this context, to depict a woman as sexually exploited is already to have sexually exploited women.

This analysis derives from feminist critiques of pornography in which the most excessive pornography is regarded as continuous with the mildest versions. MacKinnon has been a major player in shaping American law on sexual harassment, and her views gained a good deal of publicity in the 1980s when she advocated a definition of pornography under which porn would be legally banned as a civil rights violation.[27] (The proposal became the model for ordinances in two American cities, Minneapolis and Indianapolis, but the ordinances were declared unconstitutional. Canada's Supreme Court was swayed by MacKinnon's ideas and banned hardcore pornography.) In this approach, pornography is a civil rights violation because it is a discriminatory practice. It treats women, as a class, as less than persons. As a speech act, pornography's force is to *subordinate* women.

Several points complicate this argument, primarily the misleading suggestion that only sexually explicit lyrics and images are being attacked. The Rolling Stones' infamous advertising campaign for *Black and Blue* (1976) might very well be censored under this ordinance; magazine advertisements and a Sunset Strip billboard showed a bound, beaten, smiling, and almost naked woman. "I'm 'Black and Blue' from the Rolling Stones—and I love it!" she says.[28] Or perhaps the ads were not sexually explicit enough to violate women's civil rights. Yet surely the wrongness of an image does not turn on the amount of nipple revealed. It turns out that MacKinnon originally pulled her punches because she hoped to build a coalition with conservatives who had more puritanical objections to pornography, so she misleadingly restricted its censorship to "graphic sexually explicit" material.

MacKinnon has since made it clear that the problem (and the proposed censorship) extends to any material that eroticizes forced sex or any other subordination of women, because eroticizing subordination "thereby legitimizes" it.[29] Subtract the words "graphic [and] sexually explicit" from MacKinnon's definition of porn, and most hard rock and rap lyrics and music videos must be condemned as equally offensive acts of misogyny—a position recently endorsed in Sheri Kathleen Cole's extended analysis of two Duran Duran videos that are neither sexually explicit nor violent.[30] A performance of "Midnight Rambler" is just as bad as the *Black and Blue* advertisement in the way that it eroticizes forced sex. It therefore subordinates women. As would many, many other songs and videos. MTV comes off as little more than a network specializing in hate crimes.

This argument is not hypothetical. A popular sociology textbook claims that "most [rock] videos combine sexual images with acts of violence," generating "callousness toward women" and, perhaps, creating "an environment in which males become indifferent to or mildly supportive of violence, especially sexual violence directed against women."[31] In short, MTV is a how-to manual for misogynists and rapists.

Dreamworlds, a documentary video, forcefully advances the same argument. Marketed to women's studies programs, the video is used in many universities for consciousness raising about the ideology of rock music and music videos. Using highly selective clips from a wide range of videos, it argues that rock portrays a dream world in which all women are masochistic nymphomaniacs, available to be used, abused, and degraded by men.[32] Drawing directly from feminist theory and recent discussions of the male gaze, *Dreamworlds* complains that rock reduces women to body parts and thereby renders women into passive "things" to be consumed. Videos by Prince, the Cars, U2, Van Halen, Whitesnake, Aerosmith, and John Mellencamp are criticized as presenting a false and dangerous story about sexuality. Deprived of clothing, dignity, and self-control, the women in their videos are depicted as lacking personal subjectivity. Made within a male system, rock videos *must* endorse a masculinist ideology and the subordination of women, even to the point of sexual violence.

An obvious attraction of this mode of content analysis is that it simply ignores the actual consequences of viewing such material. It does not investigate how the audience interprets or responds to these associations of sound and image. Material is dismissed as noxious without demonstrating that specific physical or mental harms result from it. Worse yet, the argument also assumes that the mere inclusion of certain content matter *automatically constitutes* a message that discriminates against or harasses all women. Material is assumed to subordinate women whenever a woman is presented in postures of sexual submission ("Under My Thumb" would seem to be a good candidate), or as a dehumanized commodity (engaged in prostitution, for instance, as with Donna Summer's cover photo for *Bad Girls*).

However, the danger of this position is aptly demonstrated when *Dreamworlds* proclaims that the "provocative sexual imagery" of Madonna's "Express Yourself" video is evidence that rock subordinates women. Because Madonna's video for "Express Yourself" features her in a posture of sexual submission (crawling animal-like along the floor and wearing an iron collar, chained to a bed), its message is equated with the worst hard-core pornography. Due to two scenes among many, the video is criticized as endorsing male domination. But Madonna's video does no such thing. Confusing real life with its video representation, Madonna's own defense of it misfires when she emphasizes that she was in control during the making of the video: "I have chained myself, though, . . . I'm in charge, okay?"[33] Surely the explanation of why these songs and video images do not endorse subordination must hinge on something that the audience can *hear* and *see*, rather than on the unseen process of their production. The audience has to *experience* Madonna playing multiple roles, controlling and controlled, blocking any suggestion that one or another is more appropriate to her sex.

More urgently, we must resist the dogma that there is only one context for interpreting such images. For that dogma goes hand in hand with the dubious assumption of an essence of masculinity. We must resist the dogma that every portrayal of the degradation of a woman must itself degrade women, or that every depiction of a woman as sexually exploited must sexually exploit women. As I have argued all along, meaning arises from specific contexts more readily than from a general context, and the interplay of elements within a work of mass art is itself one of the contexts shaping the meaning of the parts.

I am not denying that many rock videos are appalling. But dogmatic assumptions can obscure the way that masculinity is deconstructed and subverted in some surprising ways. Unfolding in time, later elements of a song or video can shatter and undermine the expectations aroused by earlier moments. If we see subversion in Madonna's juxtaposition of contradictory messages about gender and sexuality, we might also recognize that similar subversions gradually emerge in Aerosmith's video for "Sweet Emotion" (1991). Its standard performance footage emphasizes horseplay among the five band members, establishing a "boys club" atmosphere. To provide a heterosexual dimension to this overtly male world, Steven Tyler's phallic microphone thrusts are intercut with glimpses of an adolescent male's telephone call to a "phone sex" worker. But the concluding scene of this narrative is a reversal, revealing that the boy's fantasies about the sex worker are utter fabrications. The video ultimately challenges male viewers to confront their own narrow, predictable standards of female sexuality. To the extent that Tyler's own phallic preoccupations parallel those of the young man in the narrative, the video implies that Tyler's own poses are those of a fantasy world.

The bias against recognizing such messages is most obvious when *Dreamworlds* focuses on Aerosmith's three videos with Alicia Silverstone, an important factor in the group's massive popularity in the 1990s. Consider their 1992 video for "Cryin'," voted the number-one "All Time Favorite Video" by MTV in 1994. It stars Silverstone as a girl who threatens suicide; as she perches on the railing of a freeway overpass, her former boyfriend is summoned to talk her down. Upon his arrival, she leaps backwards to her death. The boyfriend (played by Stephen Dorff) looks down over the railing, only to see that she is attached to a bungee cord. Reveling in her stunt, she flips him off. This summary skips many details, but what it captures is the crucial resolution of the video's narrative (like "Sweet Emotion," the song itself lacks a story). The girl emerges in control after the breakup, not the smug, rejected boyfriend. Ignoring this element of the video, *Dreamworlds* isolates two scenes as evidence that rock ideology regards women as nothing more than bodies that serve as "the ground on which [male] action takes place." But the two scenes—she receives a tattoo and then a body piercing—offer no such message. These men are not agents who use her body as the ground for their actions. She is the agent, taking possession of her own body (taking it back from her boyfriend). Rather than signaling that her body is for the use of male viewers, she proclaims that her body is her own, just as her bungee jump at the end proclaims that her life is her own! Similarly, *Dreamworlds* ignores the narrative of female bonding at the heart of the "Crazy" video, in which Silverstone and Liv Tyler manipulate men—men who regard them as mere sexual objects—in order to create a space for their own rebellion.

The obvious point is that isolated elements cannot be assigned an ideological import apart from their combination in a total speech act. Think of the song "Singin' in the Rain" and the two famous film sequences in which a character is portrayed as singing that song. As introduced by Gene Kelly in the MGM film of the same name, the song accompanies his dance through the puddles in a downpour. It expresses the character's high spirits. Is this the only use for the song, guaranteed by its presence in any subsequent film? Certainly not. In the Stanley Kubrick film *A Clockwork Orange*, the character Alex sings it as he kicks a drunken tramp to death. Here, the song emphasizes the character's utter indifference to human life and not the character's celebration of life.

Narrative is used to structure the subject matter of a great deal of popular art. Narratives feature characters and portray those characters as having various attitudes. But each film or song has a further content, namely its *own* attitude toward its represented subject matter (where the latter includes its characters, their behaviors, and their attitudes). Because a representation's attitude need not match its character's attitudes, the work does not automatically endorse a character's offensive attitudes. Taken as a whole, *A Clockwork Orange* seems to present a critical vision of the instability and moral corruption that tend to arise in a free society. Alex's indifference to human life is explained without being excused. *Context* makes all the difference in deciding whether the work *endorses* what it portrays (in deciding if what is represented is also endorsed).

Thus, Paul Siebel's "Louise" (best known in Bonnie Raitt's 1977 version) is the story of a young woman dehumanized by prostitution. Needless to say, the song does not endorse her degradation. It invites us to empathize with her plight. Richard Thompson's version of his own "Don't Tempt Me" portrays a jealous man threatening to attack another man flirting with his woman; instead of endorsing the use of violence to preserve the man's rights over "his" woman, Thompson's song and performance invite us to laugh at his display of masculinity. Similarly, the video for "Cryin'" does not subordinate women. It invites *all* viewers to adopt the subject position of the Alicia Silverstone character, defiant in the face of a culture that assumes she needs a man in her life to make her world right.

None of this is to deny that a great many songs and videos are objectionable. The video for Billy Idol's "Cradle of Love" (1990) includes brief sequences in which the female lead, having stripped to her underwear in a wild abandon caused by Idol's music, crawls across the floor. Isolated from their structuring narrative, these segments are virtually identical to scenes of Madonna crawling across the floor in the "Express Yourself" video. Given a different context, Madonna's use of the same image implies that women are forced into submissive positions by a larger power structure. However, the Billy Idol video contains nothing to subvert its presentation of the theme that the woman, as irresponsible temptress, corrupts the man. The video contains numerous views of the woman through a window and its open horizontal blinds, emphasizing viewer voyeurism that disrupts any identification with the writhing young woman.

In short, the *presence* of specific words and images involving or depicting the subordination of women does not automatically count as an endorsement of such subordination. This conclusion parallels the earlier point that neither musical structures nor the sound of women's and men's voices are *automatically* anything. Intentions and meanings emerge from the complex interplay of many different aspects of the piece, providing unpredictable opportunities to shade meaning and even to reverse ordinary associations with stock phrases, images, and musical gestures.

So far, I have argued that prominent accounts of rock masculinity risk essentialism, leaving us pessimistic about the possibilities for progressive voices in rock. Even when they avoid treating sex as destiny, they too often downplay the possibility of multiple "voices" within mass art. The worst case promotes the idea that representations of specific gender roles carry a fixed message, grounded in the male essence of predator and rapist. There is also a tendency to condemn material for including representations of a specific subject matter—because, say, its portrayal of women fits a certain profile. As an antidote, we must keep in mind that we often miss the message when we pin meaning on the

presence or absence of specific subject matter. Where there is a dominant message within a genre, we should acknowledge the cases that
exploit audience expectations to present a more interesting message.
To the extent that the "Cryin'" and "Crazy" videos are gendered, they
either allow a women to inhabit a "masculine" position ("Cryin'") or
present a double-voiced discourse that addresses both masculine and
feminine desire ("Crazy").

To what use, then, does Mick Jagger put his portrayal of the rapist in
"Midnight Rambler"? While the character has a horrific attitude toward
women, it does not automatically follow that Jagger's performance
thereby expresses approval. Jagger's portrayal of Lucifer in "Sympathy
for the Devil"—a prototype for "Midnight Rambler," released on the
Rolling Stones' previous album—does not express approval for Lucifer's
"glee" over political assassination and the slaughter of millions in European wars. In the larger context of other songs and performances by the
Rolling Stones, Jagger has crafted a more complex, ambiguous stance:
"his male/female persona serves to eroticise the songs by making him
both the titillating/submissive woman and the male perpetrator of violence. . . . It could be argued that Jagger's sense of ambivalent sexuality
opened up definitions of gender which . . . provide a framework within
which the male performer and fan alike can find a range of heterosexual and homosexual expression."[34] One of the first serious discussions
of the Rolling Stones (written when they'd only been together five years)
noted that the Stones repeatedly foreground the social taboo of mentioning sexual inequality. By constantly making public what is normally
relegated to "private" life, "inequality is *de facto* denounced."[35] In other
words, Jagger uses the Stones as a framework for *calling attention* to and
thus questioning various persona, none of which can be taken as an
expression of his own position on these matters.

Without the regular check of interpretation of individual examples,
we easily become prisoners of a questionable essentialism. Feminist
criticism has done a valuable service in revealing the unequal, asym-
metrical power relations implicit in many mass media texts. Yet we cannot assume that every Aerosmith song and video has the same misogynist message. ("Janie's Got a Gun" is hardly interchangeable with the
sexist leer of "Love in an Elevator.") Paraphrasing a famous line from

the Enlightenment, we might say that interpretation without theory is blind, but theory without cases to interpret is empty. We need an ongoing interplay between theory and interpretation. To put it crudely, theory is too often employed because it is "interesting" or novel, without checking its insights against the real world. Cultural critique without empirical verification invites us to ignore the differences among voices in the popular arts. To assume that a song or a video is sexist because it is part of the rock formation is to argue in a circle. One must be able to show that the rock formation is a sexist context before one can decide how to "read" an ambiguous case, yet one can only know that the rock formation is a sexist context by looking at a cross-section of examples. If more than a few token songs or videos advance complex attitudes toward women, then the move of appealing to the general culture is empty, for the rock formation has a complex relationship to the general culture. That complexity, in turn, is our primary reason to think that women in rock can be heard in a voice that does not simply reinforce traditional notions of the masculine and feminine.

‖

Rebel Rebel: Proliferating Identities

Turn the Beat Around

The master's tools will never dismantle the master's house.
—Audre Lorde

Alanis Morissette came in and her record blew open the doors of every single radio station and showed programmers that, yes, people are interested in hearing women sing and, yes, women have something fresh to say. Well, surprise, surprise!
—Shirley Manson, vocalist for Garbage

We get a lot of mail from women inspired to form their own bands, learning to be aggressive instead of oppressed. Like the empty dance-floor metaphor, it always takes one to go out and start the dancing.
—Lori Barbero, drummer in Babes in Toyland

Truth be told, popular music will always be more popular as a resource for circulating familiar ideas than as a source of new ideas. When mass art tries to express unfamiliar ideas, it becomes less cognitively accessible—fewer people grasp it—and fewer people will embrace it. What's at issue, then, is what can be done within the context of rock to resist its conservative impulses as a mass art while recapturing some of its earlier, disruptive power.

These problems currently inspire two schools of thought. One celebrates gender solidarity. The other calls for gender transgression. I will
contrast crude approximations of each before moving to a more sophisticated statement of each position. Both positions recognize that
the problem is not merely, nor even primarily, how the music sounds.[1]
No progress is possible as long as audiences, musicians, management,
and critics respond to music in terms of concepts and categories that
reflect and reinforce the preferences of men, reflecting narrow norms
of masculinity.[2]

The gender solidarity faction holds that we cannot see past sexual,
bodily differences. Even if there are no "natural" differences between
the cultural expressions of men and women, cultural practices shape
them as different. Since we cannot or will not erase cultural constructions of identity grounded in sexual difference, the goal must be to
change our cultural practices, forcing us to clarify and revalue those
norms. Women's ways of being in the world will remain fundamentally
different from men's, so the proper strategy is to highlight what is distinctive about women's "different voice" and to valorize it. The only
basis for directing this change lies with women's own experiences as
women. Here, the primary problem is finding a way to communicate
those experiences in a media world that panders to a male audience.
Popular artists must find ways to present discovery signs, the sign systems identified by Lisa Lewis as ones that "refer to and celebrate dis-
tinctly female modes of cultural expression and experience."[3] But Lewis
found them only in the visual signs accompanying the music and the
musicians. Are there discovery signs within the sound of the music?

The second camp, the school of gender trouble, worries that any celebration of women as women merely reinforces existing patterns of
oppression. "It's starting to worry me," observes Tracy Bonham, "when
people decide that they're going to compare women just because they're
women, not because of the music. I'm starting to get a lot of that."[4]
What's needed is a disruption of the view that there are distinctively
female modes of identity. Gender trouble acknowledges that gender is
a social construction, but worries that we are still too eager to suppose
that sex difference is not. In practice it remains all too easy to continue
to polarize the sexes and to align sex with characteristics derived from

gender roles, reinforcing the binary opposition of men and women. Even if Bonham's music resists some of the usual stereotypes of "women's music," emphasizing her biological status as woman has the effect of limiting her disruption of gender norms. If we cannot see past sexual, bodily differences, it is because we deem those differences to be central constitutive components of identity. I will defend a version of this second position, exploring it more fully in the next chapter.[5]

Gender solidarity is the more established of the two traditions. Over the course of several decades it has worked to articulate a female aesthetic or *écriture féminine* (a form of writing thought unique to women): "Women-identified music has developed a suitable musical idiom that serves to express the creative side of women's lives. Feeling, thoughts, interests, and experiences of women, interpreted by women, addressing the areas of women's lives that do not deal with men nor seek their approval are, and will continue to be, the essence of women-identified music."[6]

Whatever women-identified music may sound like—from Sleater-Kinney's standard drums and guitar to Tori Amos's occasional assaults on a harpsichord—a female aesthetic tries to describe, justify, and celebrate a distinctively feminine articulation of women's experiences. A core doctrine of this new aesthetic is the demand for self-definition of women by women, which can only occur in their relationships with other women. "Woman can only develop her new relationship to herself through her relationships with other women. Woman will become the living mirror of woman in which she loses herself in order to find herself again. The relationship of woman to herself . . . is so new that it cannot be defined yet."[7] A female aesthetic is thus important for the way it refuses to see "woman" as the negative inversion of "man." It is not satisfied with a mere inversion of masculine norms. It cannot settle for Kristen Hersh's notion of "feminine" popular music: "The rule of pop is to be masculine, solid and predictable. The feminine . . . sounds deviant."[8]

A robust female aesthetic poses problems for celebrations of Riot Grrrls and "angry women of rock" as a paradigm of women in rock. For instead of exploring new realms of emotion, their music expresses a limited range of emotion. Worse yet, they too often define significant female experience as a *response* to the male world. Although Riot Grrrls aimed to build a grassroots community of women, their musical and political activities were constantly framed as a reaction to male oppression—in the rock community and the larger society—rather than in relation to other women. Young women have every reason to feel anger and rage, but Lori Barbero's pride in inspiring women "to be aggressive" overlooks the need to build a community that solidifies itself through internal relationships. There may be all sorts of good reasons why some young women have been swept up by the music of Riot Grrrl, but explanations of why female fans identify with such music are not always good reasons for celebrating that identification.[9]

In supporting a forum of women's voices *as* women and *for* women, a female aesthetic is less committed to exploding canons than to finding its own paradigms for expressing and reconstructing female experience. Its early formulations often resorted to gender essentialism. Committed to essences that make each thing the sort of thing that it is, gender essentialists hold that men are born men and women are born women. Change is possible, but only within biologically predetermined limits. So when children grow up and become fully socialized, their true selves remain unchanged—merely hidden beneath the limited range of characteristics emphasized as valuable. Gender essentialists generally trace men's power over women to biological differences and inequalities. Although social conditioning influences particular expressions of masculinity and femininity, patriarchy (and thus women's oppression) is the natural order of male/female interaction. Women's oppression is thus the most universal and fundamental mode of human oppression: "A long history has put all women in the same sexual, social and cultural condition. Whatever inequalities may exist among women, they all undergo, even without clearly realizing it, the same oppression, the same exploitation of their body, the same denial of their desire. That is why it is very important for women to be able to join together, and to join together among themselves."[10] But then, of course, interaction through male-identified music can only undermine this joining together and the exploration of woman-to-woman relationships.

At a more mature stage, essentialism gives way to pluralism.[11] But a new problem emerges. As optimism about a distinctive voice translates into artistic exploration of a plurality of "women's lives," the unifying category is called into question. Many voices have emerged, none more authentically "woman" than any other. The relationship of woman to woman turns out to be endlessly complicated by the ways that age, ethnicity, class, and sexual orientation impart their own differences of cultural identity. So a robust pluralism within a project of solidarity faces its own obstacles, for where is the foundation for the construction of commonality and alliance?[12]

If there are neither biological essences nor universal social positions that fix the nature of "woman," there are no guarantees that any one woman could relate to every other. Possession of a uterus did not give Bonnie Raitt any special insight into the *African American* voice of blueswoman Sippie Wallace's "Women Be Wise" or "Mighty Tight Woman" (nor did Raitt's Quaker upbringing and subsequent college years at Radcliffe). Yet, with Wallace's blessings, Raitt recorded both songs. Raitt faced as many initial obstacles in taking on Wallace's voice as did, say, Mick Jagger or Eric Clapton in taking on Robert Johnson's. Each person operates from a range of social positions; in negotiating these differences, each person's response is informed by a complex network of social positions.

But if there is no universal "woman" that Raitt can tap into, then it is all too easy to suppose that sex and gender provide no foundation for bridging differences between distinct social positions. Raitt's appropriations of the music of black women might be challenged both as a falsification of her identity as a white women and as "theft" of an African American voice. However, I have already taken some pains to discredit this line of argument, for it strikes me as one of the most dangerous traps in recent debates about mass art. Treating cultures as coherent monoliths, it assumes that participation in one culture demands adherence to practices and values that *cannot be shared* with other cultures.[13] It also assumes that ugly consequences will not follow when exclusionary practices are used in the service of liberation, as though our current problems stem from our current ideology and not from exclusionary practices themselves. But only practices that make their way into everyday life can liberate or harm real people, and practices have consequences that defy the neat logic and coherence of a priori speculation.

Unfortunately, the very attempt to carve out a separate sphere of cultural practice—whether to unify women by distinguishing them from men or to unify black women by distinguishing them from white women—reinforces the very problem that it hopes to solve. As long as identity is constructed by seeking a "different voice," identity is defined by contrast with the practices and norms of others. Such tactics only signify opposition to those who understand what is thus absent; the liberating gesture of shunning electric guitars and guitar solos *requires* an opposed tradition in which electric guitar and guitar solos are phallic gestures. But practical success demands something more. It demands the audience's prior endorsement of liberation from masculine displays and prevailing gender norms. Providing a "different voice" to a hostile audience creates a situation in which the audience may understand and yet reject what is opposed to established norms. (We'd do well to remember that seemingly open-minded audiences can turn reactionary in the face of unfamiliar practices; when the Clash played New York City in 1981, the audience hurled garbage at their opening act, Grandmaster Flash and the Furious Five.) Instead of disrupting or redefining the meanings displayed by the dominant group, oppositional practices often *consolidate* and *reinforce* those meanings.

Suppose Bonnie Raitt decided to convey her solidarity with other women by abandoning her instrument of choice, the electric guitar. Suppose she also stopped singing songs like "Women Be Wise" so that African American women will again possess their own songs and voice. These symbolic exclusions would clarify her position as "woman" and as "white," but they do nothing to change the fact that as "white" she is culturally advantaged in relation to African Americans and that as "woman" she is subordinate to men. All existing categories and norms remain in place. *Self-definition through exclusion reinstates and sustains the very same relationship of dependency that it seeks to overcome.* Exclusionary strategies fortify existing "categories of true sex, discrete gender, and specific sexuality" that oppress persons assigned certain identities in the existing gender hierarchy.[14]

In celebrating an unthreatening model of tuneful sisterhood, Lilith Fair positioned itself against all the other traveling rock festivals—

against H.O.R.D.E. and Lollapalooza and their mosh pits, ear-splitting volume, and other signs of masculinity. For all its economic and media success, Lilith Fair quickly came to stand for rock's safe, nondisruptive analogue of the *écriture féminine*. Trying to avoid the niche of women who sing for other women, both Ani DiFranco and Tori Amos pointed to Lilith Fair as representing what they are not. "Lilith Fair—right away, by the name," remarks DiFranco, "you know they aren't pushing the envelope hard enough."[15] A major profile of Tori Amos described the Lilith crowd as "mild-mannered Pottery Barn poets," while Amos herself worried that such festivals cannot sustain the focus and psychological intensity necessary for her art: "my shows are theater. . . . This isn't just about eating chicken and hearing a few of your favorite female singers."[16]

My sympathies are with DiFranco and Amos: the most liberating move is a refusal to respect our current signifiers of "feminine" and "masculine" qualities. Although their music sounds nothing like traditional rock and roll, those two singers deliver at least a bit of rock and roll's original thrill of transgressive expression. Only now the transgression is more fundamental, for they are disrupting the standard practice of aligning sex with gender. From Little Richard to David Bowie to Marilyn Manson, many male rock musicians have attempted a similar disruption. How much difference have they made? Is there any reason to suppose that female musicians will have as much impact? A deeper impact?

The more fundamental question is how they might do so, for we seem to have arrived at a double bind. Female self-definition and affirmation through exclusion merely confirms the power of the dominant discourse, consolidating women's position as excluded and dominated "Other." But embrace of the dominant discourse leaves everything just as it was: "the codes of mainstream rock are maybe too conservative, too rigorously male-defined for a woman to find a comfortable place."[17]

Sexx Laws: Butler on Gender Identity

Those of us who understood [David Bowie] seemed to find each other. It was the first time (of many) that music I listened to defined me—the first time I was part of a community formed by music *outside* of the norm.

—Tara Key[18]

I'm not into the all-male, all-female thing. Where's Dionysus? Where's Hades? You can't cut out the testosterone. And we need some pansy-ass people, too, like little camp Hermes.

—Tori Amos[19]

We have arrived at the crucial question. Although rock is not intrinsically masculine in gender, how can rock be something more than just another conduit for traditional gender identities? Given rock's history, how can rock provide a voice to those who are currently defined as "Other" within the existing rock formation?

It's not enough that there are women in rock: their presence must *disrupt* rock's dominant masculinity. This task is twofold: "The first move toward such disruption is to open up the gendered meaning of rock by returning 'woman' to it. At the same time, the term 'woman' must be opened up, or at least made permeable. . . . the definition of women must, as [Judith] Butler reminds us, be constantly scrutinized."[20] In other words, inclusion is not sought for its own sake. If Madonna can succeed commercially and artistically, and (for those who believe that commercial success is equivalent to artistic ruin) if Riot Grrrls can succeed artistically, then what are we fighting about? If they can make it, the argument runs, we cannot complain that rock is masculine. "If women have in fact achieved the same status as men in art," Linda Nochlin warns art historians who work to elevate neglected women artists into the canon of Western art, "then the status quo is fine."[21] If rock accommodates women's voices and yet those voices express femininity *as ordinarily constructed*, what's gained?

To bring it down to specifics, what was Jewel communicating to the world when she made her first Grammy appearance (1997) in a sheer dress that pandered to the sexual desires of heterosexual men? Is Ani DiFranco a traitor to feminism if her visual image becomes less confrontational, she enters into a long-term heterosexual relationship, and her music becomes more conventional? (Many of her fans think so, an issue she grapples with in *Little Plastic Castle* [1997], whose cover pictures her as a lipsticked goldfish in a glass bowl.) As long as the feminine is constructed as the deficient Other, women's voices will simply confirm the male misogyny already rampant in rock: "To do so would further sediment the gendered meanings of both women and men in rock."[22] The process of opening rock up to women must be followed by ideas and practices that pry open our ideas of masculinity and femininity. What we need, then, is genuine gender trouble.

Judith Butler's work on gender provides insights that may partially vindicate rock. I have already employed Butler's argument that gender solidarity merely reinforces the existing sex-gender system. It is time to examine her theoretical reflection on the subversive power of gay and lesbian voices. While I certainly don't endorse all that Butler says, she highlights several useful themes. Insisting that no system of discourse can nail down the range of meanings it can generate, Butler's arguments imply that the rock formation is not doomed to serve as just another tool of patriarchal oppression. But mere potential is hardly what we seek. I want to use her arguments as a basis for looking for subversions of patriarchy that really do take place in rock.

Drawing on J. L. Austin's theory of speech acts, Butler argues that personal identity is always constructed through "a regulated process of repetition."[23] An action that is so unique that it lacks iterability is an event that cannot be interpreted. The fundamental idea is that individuals quite literally assume their identity through the repetition of actions. There is no stable "self" in advance of its public articulation. Gender is something that we do, not something that we *have* in advance of culture.[24] We construct our own identity in the same public process that announces that identity to others. If music is ordinarily understood to play a role in the articulation of identity, there is no good reason to deny such a role to popular music. Unless one is hostage to the myth of pure, authentic self-expression, it is obvious that musicians and other performers construct an identity through the repetition of certain choices, such as songs performed, mode of dress, and so on.

Members of the audience for popular culture also "perform" identity, articulating personal identity in each act of consumption: purchasing a CD, getting up to dance to a certain song at a club, singing along on the car radio. As they come together in the formation of popular taste, the two processes of discovery and revelation are really one and the same. Roger Scruton makes essentially the same point: only social conventions make our gestures comprehensible, and thus make sincere (or insincere) expression possible in the first place. There is literally nothing to reflect on about one's identity prior to positioning oneself in relation to such public "gestures" as forming an interest in certain musical forms and styles. In forming preferences, we address basic questions of identity: "what kind of a person must I be . . . in order to sympathize, or identify, with *this?*"[25]

Consequently, what our musical choices say about us is not simply a matter of what we intend to announce. There is an interesting scene in the film *Jerry Maguire* (1996) when sports agent Jerry Maguire is alone in his car. He has just lost his job with a major agency but through some desperate scrambling has managed to secure a crucial verbal agreement and will continue to represent a college football star who is ready to turn professional. Believing he might be able to salvage his career, Maguire heads home. He turns on the car radio and begins to sing along. Pounding out the rhythms on the steering wheel, he finds that he doesn't know the words to the Rolling Stones' "Bitch" and switches stations; he quickly flips again when he encounters Merilee Rush's "Angel of the Morning" (because it's so obviously a woman's song?) and then again at Gram Parsons's "She" (a slow country-rock ballad). But the fourth station has Tom Petty singing the line "I'm breaking her heart." The song is "Free Fallin'" (1989). Maguire throws back his head to join Petty on the chorus: "And I'm free, I'm free fallin'." Responding to the song, he declares his independence from his old life; less consciously, he identifies the perils of his situation. The line that initially got his attention turns out to be no less crucial to his character, foreshadowing the story's other central complication.

I want to pause long enough to differentiate Butler's constructionist proposal from the common idea that we respond to music that mirrors our identity. The latter idea assumes that we seek and value discourses that represent ourselves to us.[26] Butler's point is that identity is not discovered through a process of self-reflection and self-recognition. (Turning inward, observed David Hume more than two centuries ago, never reveals a stable self. It reveals a chaotic flux of changing emotions and thoughts.) The important distinction here is the difference between expression and performativeness. Behavior only counts as an expression of identity if there is a stable, "natural" self that is altogether independent of our intelligible discourses. But even if this were the case, there is no process by which an essentially "private" self could become intelligible to others, much less to oneself. In order to be understood, identity is conceptualized through concepts embedded in an acquired language. Or, as Butler puts it, "Language is not an *exterior medium or instrument* into which I pour a self and from which I glean a reflection of that self."[27]

In short, culture neither mirrors nor "mires" the subject. Culture does not simply restrict and oppress the individual. Most of what counts as individual identity depends upon participation in social acts within practices of *signification*. By repeating actions that are intelligible according to regulated norms, one establishes an identity: a good mother, a heterosexually desirable object, a fit worker.[28] These repetitions are evaluated against identities assigned according to such contingencies as family of origin, birth order, and sex. By conforming to or rejecting the socially expected codes of action, individuals perform and construct socially intelligible identities. Personal identity is fundamentally performative: the fact of identity cannot be distinguished from the communicative acts that announce it. An individual's identity is "neither fatally determined nor fully artificial and arbitrary."[29] Identity only arises against the backdrop of a public language, and thus identity is intrinsically connected to a history of actions with a public character. The "I" referred to in "I don't like Madonna" has no hidden metaphysical unity; that unity arises from our tacit collective agreement that certain acts contribute to a better or worse performance of a recognized ideal or regulatory fiction. Identity comes to seem natural only through repetition of various actions that approximate an established ideal, such as a gender norm. The body is therefore central to an individual's identity, for it is literally the site grounding that identity.

It is no surprise, then, that actions signifying sex and gender are among the most seriously policed. As Butler points out, "we regularly punish those who fail to do their gender right."[30] According to Butler, "The cultural matrix through which gender identity has become intelligible requires that certain kinds of identities cannot 'exist'—that is, those in which gender does not follow from sex and those in which the practices of desire do not 'follow' from either sex or gender."[31] Punishment and reprisal greet anyone who transgresses the established binary categories by refusing to "perform" an assigned pairing of sex and gender. Punishment can be relatively mild, as when parents ask "When are you going to get married?" and bestow favor on their "normal" children. Or it can be harsh, as with domestic violence and gay bashing. At the same time, identity can become multiple if the embodied self performs actions that signify discrete identities: Tina Turner is a singer *and* a vegetarian *and* a battered wife who left her abusive husband. At the same time, her identities of woman, wife, and mother are regarded as "following" one another in a way that those of singer and vegetarian are not.

Gender trouble arises when actions involve a "subversive repetition" within the continuities among sex, gender, and desire that define heterosexual practice. With its strong iterability, successful mass art provides the repetition. In some cases it also supplies the subversion. When Elton John's much-anticipated *Caribou* album entered the pop charts at number one in 1974, listeners were confronted with "The Bitch Is Back." The song opens with a guitar-driven rock sound that matches any number of Rolling Stones classics, and Elton's voice gleefully announces "I'm a bitch, I'm a bitch." The song's success confronted millions of listeners with a hard rock sound and a man identifying himself as a bitch. In 1974 it was subversive repetition.

Pop culture also exploits visual dissonance. When Patti Smith's raised arm reveals armpit hair on the cover of *Easter* (1978), it sharply deviates from the overtly "feminine" display of her torso. In an image that sharply contrasts with the androgyny featured on her two earlier album covers, Smith's posture and camisole top emphasize her breasts and nipples. The pose highlights her sexual identity while the unshaven armpit creates a dissonance within the visual display of that identity. Her gender is thus revealed to be a contingent element of her identity.

Through a "radical proliferation of gender," such dissonance reveals the fragility of the "natural" link between sex and gender: "In place of the law of heterosexual coherence, we see sex and gender denaturalized by means of a performance which avows their distinctness and dramatizes the cultural mechanism of their fabricated unity."[32] Repeated often enough, such dissonance has the power to *"displace* the very gender norms that enable the repetition itself."[33] In the 1950s and 1960s, women could sing rock music, but their music depended on the men who were the true creative forces (the Phil Spector or Berry Gordy behind the scenes). Beginning in the 1970s, Carole King, Joni Mitchell, Patti Smith, Joan Jett, and other prominent rock musicians demonstrated that the notion of male creativity in rock was a "fabricated unity" that lacked necessity.

But is it so clear that awareness of the contingency and instability of our standard concepts of gender will translate into revisions of the current system? Mass art is a powerful arena for presenting exaggerated, fragmented, and reconfigured performances of the prevailing gender system. But how does any of this translate into social change? The constructionist position must demonstrate that as new configurations of sex and gender proliferate, new gender norms displace the old ones and new identities become intelligible; new identities become possible. The challenge is to explain how this happens in popular culture and with mass art.

Middle of the Road

Are you customized or ready-made?

—Roxy Music, 1979

It might seem that we have wandered rather far from questions about "women in rock." In fact, we are now in a position to see how the dominant discourse might be turned against itself. Music is not itself a language. At best, it falls under the category of discourse, for it involves actions that are intelligible according to regulated norms. But where music is frequently treated as the expression of personality, a constructionist such as Butler would have us regard it as a performance of personal identity.[34] Therefore, questions about what counts as music are really questions about political control. Or, as Greil Marcus put it when explaining the power of the Clash in 1978, "apparently trivial questions of music and style profoundly threatened those who ran their society."[35] It is no wonder, then, that the performance of music is "policed" almost as thoroughly as the performance of gender. In many cases they are one and the same.

A case in point is the Rolling Stones' "Let's Spend the Night Together" (1967). A Columbia Broadcasting System censor would not permit the band to perform their new single on the *Ed Sullivan Show*, opening the way to one of the most subversive performances seen by a large national audience. Allowed to perform after changing the key line to "let's spend some time together," Jagger thrusts his face forward, dominating the television screen each time he reaches the sanitized chorus; rolling his eyes in an exaggerated act of helplessness, he clearly signals his amusement and disgust to anyone who knows the real lyrics. Lacking a similar substitute, many radio stations would not play the song and it faired poorly on the American pop charts. These acts of censorship are hardly surprising for 1967, for the song frankly conveys the singer's seduction of the woman he addresses. It conveys masculinity and heterosexual desire.[36] In 1967, the song also may have been shocking for the narrator's promise to "satisfy your every need," a candid admission that women have sexual needs.

That reading hinges on contingencies of two very specific performances, one broadcast on television by Ed Sullivan and one recorded in the studio for commercial release. The presence of heterosexual lust rests on a specific reading of who the narrator is (Jagger) and whom the narrator addresses (one or more women). But as David Bowie sings it on *Aladdin Sane* (1973), "Let's Spend the Night Together" displays or "performs" a more eccentric sexual desire. The music is taken too fast and the vocal is both hysterical and demanding. It feels as if there is no time for seduction; the singer has to proposition someone quickly, then consummate the illicit act without delay. Also, Bowie's lust seems directed at another man.

It is not simply that the track appeared at a time when Bowie was openly bisexual. It is largely a matter of how he sings the lyric, with an affected, arch tone that is quite at odds with the aggressive phrasing of *Aladdin Sane*'s "Watch That Man" and "The Jean Genie." Bowie's performance carries an element of camp (the sudden falsetto of "oh my my"), but it also carries a touch of menace. The musical arrangement is no less relevant to these effects, as coyness gives way to a hint of something darker in Mick Ronson's guitar—particularly in the bridge. In much the same manner, k. d. lang's 1997 cover version of Steve Miller's "The Joker" (1973) subverts Miller's macho boast; the irony will be clear to lang's lesbian fans while the general audience, unaware of her sexual orientation, will be confronted by a dissonance between the voice and the gender performance if they impose a heterosexual reading.

Such ironic reversals support Butler's proposal that phallocentric discourse provides the means to perform subversive acts. But are irony, pastiche, and parody the only weapons at our disposal? I do not think so. Let us assume that Bonnie Raitt "performs" her assigned gender when she performs a song like "Cry on My Shoulder" (1989). On first listen, it conforms both lyrically and musically to the norms of heterosexual femininity. Performing the gentle, piano-driven ballad, Raitt convincingly assures her man that she will always be there for him. Indeed, the presumption that she addresses a man is so strong that Barbara Bradby found some lesbians would not listen to *Nick of Time* because it was about "Bonnie's heterosexual relationships."[37] In contrast, Butler's notion of gender trouble is invoked to demonstrate the political force of Madonna's videos for "Express Yourself" and "Justify My Love."[38] Their deliberate confusions of sex and gender seem made to order as illustrations of the idea of gender trouble. Madonna routinely provides gender trouble. Raitt's "Cry on My Shoulder" offers gender conformity.

The uncomfortable question is whether Madonna's work is progressive only through a selective reading of Raitt and other "mainstream" rock women. Theorists and critics may be paying too much attention to self-consciously experimental work that is designed to shock mainstream audiences. Following the assumptions of a century of avant-garde artists who believed that disruptive artistic practices could disrupt social norms, it is assumed that only direct confrontations of audience expectations can dislodge hegemonic interests. These ideas have remained in circulation in the rock formation decades after

they have fallen from favor in the world of high art. Notable rock precedents of direct audience confrontation are the Doors and the Mothers
of Invention; Jim Morrison's inflammatory antics at a Miami concert in
1969, which led to his arrest for indecent exposure, appear to have
been inspired by his attendance at six avant-garde Living Theater performances in the week before the concert. Yet the continuing popularity of the Doors gives credence to Rick Ocasek's remark that "even
political songs become pop songs after they're old."[39] Morrison's identity as "erotic politician" has evaporated. He is now just another sexy
dead rock star, singing "Light My Fire" on the car radio for the thou-
sandth time.

If calculated outrage has little of the transformative power so often
claimed for it, it's possible that less overt disruptions have more power
than we commonly suppose. Examined more closely, the song "Cry on
My Shoulder" reveals a less obvious bit of gender trouble, present in
the song's title. Although the female protagonist conforms to gender
stereotypes, she also conveys the message that real men do cry (at least
when alone with the women who love them). Masculine norms are thus
subverted. When it comes to breaking down the prevailing norms of
heterosexual relationships, mixed messages about men and masculinity are as important as similar messages about women and femininity.
Raitt's performance of "Cry on My Shoulder" is thus of a piece with
the leering swagger of "Thing Called Love" or the wanderlust of "The
Road's My Middle Name"—appropriations of stereotypically masculine
roles that accompany "Cry on My Shoulder" on the *Nick of Time* album.
Readily perceived as a heterosexual white woman, Raitt's eclecticism
genuinely confuses gender norms.

In this light, consider *The Bonnie Raitt Collection* (1990), the "best of"
compilation released after the success of *Nick of Time*. Raunchy blues
that treat men as sex objects are followed by "white" folk cadences.
Yearning love songs are juxtaposed with convincing declarations that a
woman has no need for any man that mistreats her.

By embracing contradictory public faces, Raitt's performance of femininity can "denaturalize" gender for a segment of the audience that has
no use for Madonna. Taken individually, none of Raitt's performances
on *Nick of Time* exhibits any sense of parody or exaggeration (that is, the

sorts of repetitions that Butler identifies as subversive). Yet the very breadth of subject positions, *delivered by the same voice,* has the effect of challenging the stability of any identity that we might assign to her. This seems to be the meaning of singers as different as Shirley Manson and Linda Ronstadt when they declare that they reveal nothing about themselves (their identities away from the spotlights) in their performances.[40]

Some of the most striking gender transgressions involve gender slippage, as when masculine discourse is delivered in a woman's voice.[41] Destabilization of gender occurs whenever a female voice delivers a song that is already associated with a masculine identity. The content does not have to be overtly confrontational; the act of appropriation is sufficient. I've already mentioned "The Joker" as performed by k. d. lang. It's easy to forget that Aretha Franklin's titanic, defiant version of "Respect" (1967) is a cover version of one of Otis Redding's 1965 hits, and her action of appropriating "his" song was originally an important element of its affective power. But once we look for them, we discover similar examples by the score. These are not simply cases of women covering songs written by men, but cases of women performing songs already popularized by and strongly identified with male performers:

Rod Stewart's "Tonight's the Night" as performed by Janet Jackson
Simon and Garfunkel's "A Hazy Shade of Winter" and Big Star's "September Gurls" as performed by the Bangles
The Beatles' "I Don't Want to Spoil the Party" as performed by Rosanne Cash
Jimi Hendrix's "May This Be Love" and "Room Full of Mirrors" as performed by the Pretenders
Led Zeppelin's "Rock and Roll" and "The Battle of Evermore" as performed by Heart's Ann and Nancy Wilson
Bob Dylan's "Man in the Long Black Coat" as performed by Joan Osborne
Nick Drake's "Which Will" as performed by Lucinda Williams
Buddy Holly's "That'll Be the Day" and the Rolling Stones' "Tumbling Dice" as performed by Linda Ronstadt
The Rolling Stones' "Angie" and Nirvana's "Smells Like Teen Spirit" as performed by Tori Amos

Bowie's "Rebel Rebel" and Jimi Hendrix's "Up From the Skies"
    as performed by Rickie Lee Jones
The Lovin' Spoonful's "Darling Be Home Soon" (popularized by
    Joe Cocker) as performed by Anne Richmond Boston
T. Rex's "Bang a Gong" and Iggy Pop's "Funtime" as performed by
    Blondie
The Clash's "Train in Vain" and Al Green's "Take Me to the River"
    as performed by Annie Lennox
The Rolling Stones' "Sister Morphine" and John Lennon's "Working
    Class Hero" as performed by Marianne Faithfull
Marvin Gaye's "What's Going On" and Prince's "When You Were
    Mine" as performed by Cyndi Lauper
Tom Waits's "The Heart of Saturday Night" as performed by Shawn
    Colvin
The Flying Burrito Brothers' "Hot Burrito No. 1" as performed by
    the Cowboy Junkies
The Police's "King of Pain" as performed by Alanis Morissette
"Spanish Harlem" as performed by both Aretha Franklin and
    Laura Nyro
Cheap Trick's "I Want You to Want Me" as performed by Letters
    to Cleo

These and countless other gender reversals of familiar songs are an
important subclass of access signs. A visual mode of gender performance identified by Lisa Lewis, access signs "are those in which the
privileged experiences of boys and men are visually appropriated. . . .
Symbolically, they execute take-overs of male space, effect the erasure
of sex roles, and make demands for parity with male-adolescent privilege."[42] Lewis is writing about music videos. But symbolic take-overs
can be auditory as well as visual, and literal take-overs of male-identified
songs are an important tool for demanding parity. Despite all the theorizing about how Madonna's message stems from her control of her own
productions and career, in practical terms one of her boldest moves was
her 1999 cover version of Don McLean's "American Pie" (1971).
"American Pie" is, of course, a selective history of the first decades of
rock music. In selecting some verses while jettisoning others, Madonna's

performance is a classic access sign that communicates the power of women musicians to remake rock through selective appropriation.

People Got to Be Free: Cultivating an Atmosphere of Freedom

It is essential that different persons should be allowed to lead different lives.

—John Stuart Mill, 1859[43]

I could say I was anything. I learned that from Andy [Warhol]: Nobody knows. You could be anything.

—Lou Reed[44]

The value of relatively "mainstream" music is often overlooked in the rush to celebrate edgy and provocative musicians. Yet the proliferation of gender does not succeed if gender trouble only arises at the margins of cultural consciousness. (It certainly does not succeed if it only takes place in academic theorizing; cultural theory will not itself destabilize sex and gender in everyday life.) Marginalized perversity is too easily "naturalized," stereotyping recognizable segments of the population and confirming their marginal identity. Worse yet, any assault on one set of gender norms is merely symbolic as long as "artificial" norms are opposed to some "natural," precultural mode of sex and desire. But rock has typically represented this very disjunction, selling itself as a path back to a "natural" self and sexuality in the face of society's corrupt conventions and false constraints.

Although they were pioneers in pointing out the social construction of gender in relation to rock music, even Simon Frith and Angela McRobbie had imagined "that sexuality has some sort of autonomous form which is expressed or controlled by cultural practice."[45] They assumed that *some* expressions of sexuality and desire (the really liberating ones) were authentic, original, "natural." They spoke for a generation that hoped rock's prevailing mode of masculinity would be unmasked as working against genuine sexual liberation. But they also thought that musicians would then, in the words of Jim Morrison, "break through to a cleaner, freer realm ... with maybe an element of purity."[46] True children of Rousseau, most of rock's first generation of ideologists had a vague faith that a noble savage lurks in each of us: thinking that African American music was a way to "get back to the primitive," they assumed rock's audience would be free, "the natural man living in the state of society."[47] Two decades later, we've abandoned the idea that we only have to throw off cultural impositions in order to arrive at something better.

Today, the mass audience faces related dangers in fandom organized around the gender perversions of specific artists, such as Madonna or k. d. lang, or of any one movement, such as Riot Grrrls. When we celebrate a specific artist or style as the expressive embodiment of a perverse identity, we demarcate a certain identity and position it against the dominant ideology. When David Bowie, Lou Reed, and the New York Dolls exploited a camp sensibility and wore "female" makeup in the early 1970s, their glitter-rock involved gender perversion. But of course it wasn't simply a matter of their appearance. It was a matter of the way that visual inversions of gender clashed with the sound of the music. Muscular, guitar-drenched music dominated glitter/glam classics like Bowie's *Aladdin Sane* (1973), Lou Reed's over-the-top *Rock N Roll Animal* (1974), Mott the Hoople's double-whammy of *All the Young Dudes* (1972) and *Mott* (1973), early Queen, and everything by the New York Dolls.[48]

Unfortunately, such epiphanies do not last. Although their contemporaries perceived glam rockers as androgynous and disruptive, extensive repetitions of their tactics by some heavy metal artists recast such signs as indicators of "glam" metal. No longer cutting edge, glam metal repositioned these signifiers as the less masculine, less threatening wing of 1980s metal. Robert Walser suggests that these visual appropriations of feminine identity, conjoined with a relative lack of musical virtuosity, constitute a "tactic for dealing with the anxieties of masculinity. . . . In their bid for greater transgression and spectularity, the men onstage elevate important components of many women's sense of gendered identity." At the same time, Walser notes that fans of "harder" heavy metal bands "are often frantic in their denunciations of androgyny."[49] Far from *disrupting* "natural" codings of gender, a predictable genre arose from the close identification of "female" makeup with stylistic markers that placed bands like Poison at the "light" end of heavy metal. Walser never quite explains how the codified practices of glam metal bands remain subversive when they become so regularized that they serve as reliable markers for an established genre. Instead, he observes that the combination "signals the extent to which a linkage of 'feminine' semiotic instability with monolithic, phallic power is deemed impossible" within the world of heavy metal.[50]

These factors make glam metal rather different from its 1970s glam progenitors. Not that all glam rock combined guitar-heavy rock and roll with female clothing and makeup. Roxy Music's first two albums juxtapose a camp sensibility, Brian Eno's androgyny, and the hyperfemininity of the women on the album jackets. Yet the band never presented a *unified* image, switching visual styles with each subsequent release. Early press reports suggest that most of the band wore makeup during live performances to support the first album, and reviewers remarked on their "carnival" elements and "disjointed," uneasy mixture of visual and musical styles.[51] As a result, gender contradictions were highlighted within the group itself. Yet no recognizable visual or musical style stuck around long enough to solidify a specific stance toward gender. The only aural constant is Bryan Ferry's voice, itself rather ripe and camp with its excessive vibrato. With Roxy Music, issues of gender remained ambivalent and constantly contested.

If subversive gestures become less subversive when they become the familiar signs of established musical styles, it also remains all too easy for the mass audience to ignore artists working at the margins. Thus, close identification with one subgroup often leaves an artist preaching to the converted.[52] When Christian fundamentalists made a fuss and prevented the openly lesbian Indigo Girls from playing shows at several American high schools in 1998, it's likely that most people who learned of the controversy through the news media had no clue about their music. But that music was now positioned as lesbian music, so that any high school student who listens to it risks punishment from parents and peers. Like Marilyn Manson, whose gender transgressions met with similar resistance in the same region, the Indigo Girls were an obvious, easy target and served as a rally point for repressive forces. Unless it makes regular inroads into the mainstream, subversion can thus reinforce prevailing norms of masculinity and femininity as "normal."

I do not mean to suggest that either the issues or ideas are new. Nor are the solutions. Not surprisingly, they all emerged at precisely the point when mass art posed its initial rivalry to high art. There is significant agreement between Butler's postfeminist constructionism and prominent strains of liberal theory. As John Stuart Mill warned Victorian England, the growth of mass media tends to stifle personal freedom by reducing individuality. We are not little gods, creating ourselves out of nothing; we arrive at our identities by drawing on available models. After repeated exposure to a limited range of acceptable behavior, people "speedily become unable to conceive diversity, when they have been for some time unaccustomed to see it." Behavior that does not conform to the prejudices of "the sovereign Many" is easily condemned as vice, so that "few now dare to be eccentric." (Mill even warns that the mass media are only too happy to hold up examples of subversive identity as warning cases whose "wild" and "erratic" behavior must be forced into a more familiar mold.) Strip away Butler's jargon and her emphasis on queer theory, and Butler's call for a proliferation of perversion is remarkably similar to Mill's call for eccentricity. "Precisely because the tyranny of opinion is such as to make eccentricity a reproach," Mill reasons, "it is desirable, in order to break through that tyranny, that people should be eccentric."

The core idea is that public discourse should present and endorse an ongoing proliferation of alternative models of identity. Ever the empiricist, Mill also saw that a person's "own nature" arises through a process of experimentation. But people do not buck tradition and culture in order to experiment with their own identity unless they "breathe freely in an *atmosphere* of freedom." Although most people will end up embracing traditional identities (leaving former Eagles drummer and vocalist Don Henley to whine about "a Deadhead sticker on a Cadillac"), tradition is modified and renewed by the presence of those who challenge established practice. Unfashionable as it may be, Mill argues that the most important tool in generating this atmosphere of freedom is the celebration of individuality. If individual liberty is not celebrated as one of the intrinsic values of human life, as an essential component of human happiness, then strategies for subversion amount to nothing.

In short, an artist's performance of eccentric identity is only a means to an end. That end is an atmosphere of freedom in which the audience will feel free to explore eccentric identities. We must be deeply suspicious of attempts to locate the pleasure of mass art in the audience's close identification with the identities assumed by artists. We must also resist the temptation to valorize some mass art as an expression of a *specific* identity. Finally, we must question any treatment of mass art that trivializes the mainstream ("pop") in order to celebrate the margins ("rock"), for this move usually locates value with expressions of oversimplified, extreme identities. When Butler concludes *Gender Trouble* by wondering what other local strategies might displace "gender norms as such," she implies that parody is merely one strategy. We need a constant array of disruptive reconfigurations, combining and recombining signifiers associated with different identities.

Unfortunately, Butler's own examples of subversive repetitions are largely confined to the cultural practices of drag and cross-dressing, emphasizing their deployment as a parody of gender norms. I have turned to Mill, an important nineteenth-century voice in challenging traditional gender norms, in order to emphasize that gender and sexuality are merely one dimension of a larger project of liberation. The real contribution of popular music may be its power to expose listeners to a vast arsenal of possible identities.

Singer/guitarist Tara Key recalls how chance encounters with different strands of rock music changed her sense of her life's potential. This process included her exposure to Neil Young, David Bowie, and Patti Smith:

> At three A.M. when I was eighteen, I was in my room partaking, when the local FM station played *Horses* in its entirety. My head was blown off before "Gloria" was over. I'd never heard a voice so like mine before—that is, *if I let myself go a little farther.* . . . She taught me about the beauty of collision—of words, sounds, thought—and, by her example, I gave myself permission to live passionately, permission to be an alien, permission to be self-confident.[53]

In allowing a listener to "inhabit" new positions without bearing any of their real-life consequences, mass art can suggest life options that were previously unthinkable. As Key observes, its very presence in our lives grants permission, suggesting that the master's tools can be used to dismantle the master's house.

Rock's performances of gendered homosexuality and female rage open up new possibilities, but such openings mean little unless there is an accompanying expansion of other performances of identity, continuously encouraging the audience to participate in multiple, shifting identities. If artists and audiences *proliferate* the identities with which we experiment, then there is less and less that will seem compulsory and "normal." But such a project demands constant exposure to a broad range of music styles and, through them, exposure to representations of various subject positions. In order to convey the plasticity of identity, it is also important to celebrate artists whose musical performances are unlikely to be taken as authentic expressions of the singer: we need both the Bruce Springsteen model of utter sincerity and the David Bowie model of ironic play-acting. (The danger comes from the common assumption that one musical style or even one artist is to be followed as real or genuine—commonly linked to the assumption that one style is more authentic than any other.) An interpretive "singer" like Dusty Springfield or Linda Ronstadt may be as central to the rock canon as an "artist" like Joni Mitchell and Patti Smith, and today we need the Spice Girls, Britney Spears, and Jennifer Lopez as much as we need Ani DiFranco and Tori Amos.[54]

12

Hello Stranger: Reaching the Uninitiated

Eyesight to the Blind: Getting Rid of Blinkers

Patriarchal blinkers cannot be taken off at whim.

—Silvia Bovenschen

To create genre out of gender is just horrible to me. . . .
There's a uniqueness in being a woman, but not that much.

—L7's Jennifer Finch

Those who bother to listen and look will find that rock exhibits a staggering variety of identities that can serve as models in the performance of personal identity. The main obstacle is that many listeners will not or cannot hear them speaking when they are present: the lesbian separatist who won't listen to Bonnie Raitt's *Nick of Time* and the working-class heavy metal fan who'd rather die than be caught listening to Barry Manilow. How does a mass artist, particularly one exploring the margins, avoid merely preaching to the converted? This question gets at the heart of the political dimension of mass art. How is consciousness raised if those who need it most won't listen? This is one of the most pressing problems confronting women artists; recall Melissa Etheridge's complaint that rock radio would not play her music because the presence of too many female voices alienates

217

male rock fans. Elton John lost many fans when he admitted that he was bisexual. "I had a couple of older brothers who had big record collections," recalled a female fan who'd driven two hundred miles to see her first Elton John concert. "They gave me all their Elton John albums when Elton announced he was bisexual. I guess that kind of freaked them out."[1] So how do straights hear the voice of an openly gay singer and not reject it as the voice of the hated enemy?

Some cultural theorists simply deny that they can. An emphasis on the audience has encouraged the pessimistic view that audiences can neither appreciate nor understand work that challenges an audience's community-specific assumptions.[2] Here we encounter a situation where personal experience is our best evidence against a theoretical conclusion. We must never lose sight of the fact that it *is* possible to hear and appreciate music that does nothing to confirm an individual's personal interests or idealized sense of self. In real life I avoid the self-righteous preaching of evangelical Christians, but Bob Dylan's "born again" shows at San Francisco's Warfield Theater in November 1979 were among the most enthralling slices of rock theater I've witnessed.[3] In everyday life I tend to avoid the glue-sniffing cretins celebrated by the early Ramones as well as the snotty boys populating the Beastie Boys' *Licensed to Ill* (1986). In everyday life I try to avoid the sorts of conversations captured by Joni Mitchell's "Raised on Robbery," a highlight of *Court and Spark* (1974). So how did I listen long enough to enjoy these and, much of the time, to experience empathy? Where is the reward? As with the classic question of how literary audiences can enjoy unpleasant material, we are left wondering why anyone responds with pleasure to representations of personae and events that would be met with suspicion or even hostility in real life.[4]

Simon Frith rejects the prevailing pessimistic view. He emphasizes two points that are relevant here. First, he reminds us that "tastes do not just derive from our socially constructed identities; they also help to shape them"—popular music has a special value for being able to "put into play a sense of identity that may or may not fit the way we are placed by other social forces."[5] Second, he recognizes that identity is not just a matter of the here and now: "identity is an ideal, what we would like to be."[6] Unfortunately, Frith does not really explain why or how listeners develop a taste for music that challenges their existing sense of identity, permitting them to embrace such music long enough to let it disrupt messages about identity that have already been internalized from other social forces. But my own experiences with popular music convince me that this possibility exists. What follows is an explanation (partly derived from Frith) of why and how listeners will sometimes allow music to shape their identity.

I want to endorse the strategy of disinterested listening as an important mode of listening.[7] Unfortunately, the phrase "disinterested listening" suggests listeners who are bored or find nothing of interest in what they hear. But disinterested listening does not imply an uninterested listener. Disinterested listening is a discovery process that encourages listeners to embrace music that lies outside their current estimation of their own tastes. In expanding their musical tastes, many listeners embrace music associated with otherwise unfamiliar or threatening identities. As a result, many listeners have a positive experience, even a sense of deep intimacy, with material associated with an otherwise forbidden or alien or unattractive identity.

Unfortunately, this proposal revives an idea that is decidedly unfashionable. Long a staple of aesthetic theory, the notion of disinterest assumes that it is both possible and advisable to disengage one's personal interests when occupied with music and other cultural products. It has been criticized and dismissed as a relic of patriarchal art practices. So I must be very careful here. It's not that disinterested listening is the only sort that ought to take place. Nonetheless, disinterest may play an important role in putting listeners in a position to hear and to respond to the presence of otherwise unwelcome perversions, subcultural identities, and gender trouble. But if all listening involves *interested* attention, many listeners will find it impossible to respond approvingly to music that *confronts* their sense of identity. Without disinterested listening, marginalized voices must remain marginalized in a way that can only reinforce the status quo.

This endorsement of disinterested listening requires seeing beyond its close association with strict autonomism. In the standard model of art and serious music that emerged in the nineteenth century, disinterest was yoked to the ideas of artistic autonomy and art for art's sake. The standard model insisted that good music is autonomous when it has no practical function. Appreciation was construed as attention to the exclusively "musical" features of a musical work. Musical value was divorced from functional value, from music's capacity to facilitate dancing, generate a mood in a movie soundtrack, or convey a message as a socially situated speech act. The appreciative listener could safely ignore the identity, politics, and standpoint of the music's writers and performers. Such features were dismissed as extrinsic to the music. Music was thus relegated to an autonomous realm of value: artistic activity was regarded as "a special sphere of human activity," detached "from the nexus of the praxis of life."[8] One's personal interests and social identity were treated as irrelevant to one's capacity for appreciating any given piece of music.

One lingering effect of autonomy theory is the idea that structure or design is the only real merit in music, so that strictly musical features of a song will account for its appeal. Frank Zappa was introduced to the doctrine in high school, when he took his favorite R&B tune to his band instructor. The song was "Angel in My Life," by the Jewels. Zappa relates their exchange:

"Listen to this," I said, "and tell me why I like it so much."

"Parallel fourths," he concluded.[9]

No thought was given to the lyric's theme or to the performers' vocal skills. Such teachers appear to have had a tremendous influence on Zappa, who regarded most of his own songs as unfortunate concessions to a mass audience incapable of dealing with instrumental music. Zappa generally preferred what he called "musically uncompromising boy-is-this-hard-to-play" music.[10]

The doctrine continues to surface in the most unlikely places, informing Courtney Love's primary advice to women interested in working in rock: "Learn how to write really good songs. I think it's a meritocracy. It's based on talent."[11] Imposing the standards of high culture onto the practices of mass art, the proposal that songwriting is what matters most is at odds with our main reason for being interested in Love's own career. On a meritocracy of writing talent, she wouldn't be on my own list of the one hundred best popular songwriters of the last

fifty years. As with Iggy Pop's and Jim Morrison's performances, Courtney Love's are more interesting than the artist's material. Although
some music has aesthetic value that transcends its specific origins, it
hardly follows that social and historical factors contribute nothing to
musical meaning and value.[12]

So I face two obstacles. One is the close association that has developed between disinterest and strict autonomism. The other is the suspicion that any endorsement of disinterest implies a hierarchy in which
disinterested attention is intrinsically superior to interested attention.
But if I can avoid both associations, then I can defend the proposal that
disinterested listening is valuable for the way that it empowers listeners to circumvent the "blinkers" of interested listening. In the case of
mass art, disinterested listening is most successful when listeners tran-
scend their disinterest.

Critics of disinterested attention emphasize the first obstacle. They
argue that it is not what it claims to be. Its mask of nonpractical, non-
moral, and nonegoistic judgment is really false neutrality. Like fine art
itself, such attention is regarded as politically tainted by its historical
associations with the rise of the middle class in eighteenth-century
Europe.[13] A kindred charge is that a feminist aesthetic is incompatible
with the traditional idea that works of art inhabit an "autonomous realm
of value."[14] Disinterested attention is challenged as masculine in gender, for it has been deployed within patriarchal art institutions as a justification for the objectifying male gaze. The neutrality of disinterest is
merely a subset of characteristics drawn from our cultural norm of masculinity; in a culture that simultaneously expects women to conform to
certain norms of femininity, "real" women are excluded from participation in activities suitable for "enlightened" audiences. A final obstacle to bringing disinterest to bear on the problem at hand is the general assumption that progressive theory must reject *all* aspects of
traditional aesthetic theory.[15] In sum, because traditional, patriarchal
models of art have proposed that disinterested aesthetic judgment is the
proper handmaiden for the autonomy of art, challenges to traditional
aesthetics have assumed that the pair must be thrown out together.

Just as feminist critics find reason to quarrel with the ways that aesthetic practices have been theorized, I want to question the "all or

none" mentality that treats autonomy and interest as mutually exclusive. Similarly, I'm suspicious of the tendency to posit an irreconcilable conflict between interest and disinterest, as well as between intrinsic and instrumental value. Strict autonomy may be ill suited to the consumption of popular culture and mass art, but there are other options. Instrumental autonomy and strict instrumentalism must also be considered.

For the sake of argument, suppose that musical value is strictly autonomous, resting exclusively in musical properties.[16] There are different views of what it means to value music in this way, but Gordon Graham does as good a job of it as we could hope to find. Graham offers this description of appreciating music's special character: "music is the 'foregrounding' of sound, the bringing to primary attention sound itself ... and aural experience becomes the focus of interest in its own right."[17] It appears that music's value has nothing to do with its being identified with contingently situated human authors or with the audience's predispositions about the music's subject matter. Appreciating a piece of music would be like appreciating a sunset or a waterfall, as sheer spectacle. We could point to reasons why we prefer one more than another, focusing almost exclusively on the music's structure. (Thus, a single Yes or King Crimson album would be more valuable than the collective works of Bob Dylan, Chuck Berry, and the Ramones.) However, our reasons would never refer to the music's capacity to express specific emotions, articulate identity, or comment on real life.

In contrast, the instrumental autonomist allows that one can value a musical work as an occasion for aural experience that is valued in its own right, but rejects this as inadequate—one *should* value music for its other dimensions, as well. It seems absurd to ignore these dimensions of meaning—surely we want to consider whether a particular song or performance is worth the effort we expend on getting at its meaning. *Musical* elements offer pleasure in and of themselves, but they generally serve as the means to a further, nonaesthetic end. Instrumental autonomism asks us to evaluate music for its nonaesthetic ends, for its aesthetic ends, and for the fit between sonic means and nonmusical ends.

The instrumental autonomist insists that music is valuable both intrinsically and instrumentally. In the words of Jerrold Levinson, we will approach a work of music "with a concern not only for its resultant, high-order qualities, meanings, and effects but also for the way these intertwine with and rest on the work's lower-level perceptual face . . . apprehending a work's content and character in relation to its concrete construction."[18] Musical pleasure should be a multilevel affair. This is only a little more complex than saying that meals can be evaluated on aesthetic grounds, according to presentation and taste, and on health grounds, according to their contribution to our diet. A concern for music should involve a concern for the way that the strictly musical level embodies the music's emotive and affective dimensions, such as the way Mick Ronson's guitar contributes to the camp tone of Bowie's version of "Let's Spend the Night Together."

But we must also consider the challenge presented by strict instrumentalism. Responding to the limitations of strict autonomy, some theorists go to the opposite extreme of endorsing entirely interested listening. Because appeals to parallel fourths and harmonic resolutions do not exhaust the appeal of popular music, some instrumentalists suppose that the practice of foregrounding aural experience—particularly musical form—contributes nothing of importance to the ordinary listening experiences of the audience for mass art. This model is influenced by the reader-response school of literary criticism, in which it is assumed that all consumers "hunt for histories that . . . trace a desire felt not by author but by reader, who is most acute when searching for signs of himself."[19] A text that cannot confirm the audience's sense of self is a text that cannot yield pleasure. The obvious consequence is articulated by David Sanjek: "we desperately need an ethnography of fanhood in order to discover what meanings specific individuals discovered in popular music and, even more importantly, what uses they made of those meanings in their lives."[20]

Unfortunately, the majority of fans are in the position of Frank Zappa confronted by "Angel in My Life," with no vocabulary for identifying how the construction of the music contributes to its appeal. Because most fans are not articulate about how their favorite music works to generate meaning, those features of the listening experience simply drop out of the ethnographic explanation. Recent examples include Lauraine Leblanc's *Pretty in Punk*, a sociological study of why some young women are so attracted to the male-dominated subculture of punk, and Daniel Cavicchi's *Tramps Like Us,* an ethnographic account of why ordinary Americans are drawn to the music of Bruce Springsteen.[21] Interesting as they are in illuminating the practices of actual listeners, such studies abandon the normative assumption that listening should be a multilevel affair.

In practice, therefore, strict instrumentalism pays little or no attention to the ways that musical features generate meanings. Yet some instrumentalists go another step and draw a normative conclusion that popular music should not be enjoyed for its own sake.[22] They do not deny the possibility of applying the norms of high culture to mass art. Rather, they contend that in doing so we filter the popular through a screen of assumptions and interests quite at odds with those of the mass audience.[23] What this flight from musical purism cannot explain, however, is why listeners ever tolerate music that challenges their current identities and social interests.

To some extent, strict instrumentalism reduces music listening to a juvenile or naive attitude. When my daughter was seven or eight, she seems to have lacked the ability to engage in disinterested attention. Like most children at that age, she also displayed little or no interest in instrumental music. But she was very fond of dogs and horses; she would ask to hear the songs "Old Blue" and "Old Paint" when nothing else by the Byrds or Linda Ronstadt interested her. She wanted to hear those particular songs because they are about a dog and a horse. Lacking a capacity for disinterested attention, she never betrayed the slightest interest in the Byrds' "Eight Miles High" or anything else by Ronstadt.

Suppose that strict instrumentalism captures everything of importance in audience appreciation of popular music. *Why would the popular audience ever listen to music that challenges their sense of identity?* We are back to men whose ideal of masculinity prohibits their enjoyment of the music of Melissa Etheridge and Elton John, and women who won't even listen to the Rolling Stones. If each genre of popular music yields pleasure according to one's identification with the effects it pursues, then we cannot expect anyone but the avant-garde listener to enjoy, *hear,* and profit from the proliferation of identity in popular music.[24] That is, unless there is pleasure to be had from popular music that is not simply the pleasure that comes when listeners feel confirmed in their identity.

I recommend that we endorse traditional aesthetics to the extent of granting that some aspects of music are of autonomous aesthetic value (some of the time, anyway), and that we are often in a position to appreciate such aspects apart from their contribution to the music's meaning. As instrumental autonomists, however, we will insist that a full and responsible evaluation will balance such value against the music's role as a speech act. The final stage of my argument aims to show that disinterested listening can play an important role in generating empathy for songs and thus subject-positions that do not confirm a listener's current ideal of self-identity. Disinterestedness is an important resource for furthering instrumental autonomy, and it is an important mechanism for reconfiguring patterns of sex and gender.

The Hunter Gets Captured by the Game

You know, the dangerous thing about listening [to music] is that you don't really know the effect it's going to have.

—Tori Amos[25]

You don't really criticize any author to whom you have never surrendered yourself. . . . You have to give yourself up, and then recover yourself, and the third moment is having something to say. . . . Of course, the self recovered is never the same as the self before it was given.

—T. S. Eliot on the practice of literary criticism[26]

Disinterested attention does not imply a lack of interest. It involves a specific focusing of attention, in which the audience adopts the aesthetic strategy of responding to a perceptible object while suppressing ordinary or "everyday" practical, moral, and social concerns.[27] Put crudely, it involves disciplining one's ordinary interests as they relate to a work's referential, representational and ideological aspects. "There is no purpose governing the experience," proposes Jerome Stolnitz, "other than the purpose of just having the experience. Our interest comes to rest upon the object alone."[28] Disinterested attention underlies the ability to evaluate an advertisement for hamburgers apart from the question of whether one actually likes hamburgers, or to see what's funny about a joke that pokes fun at something one holds dear.

In contrast, interested attention is firmly rooted in the audience member's personal, individual interests. In the absence of disinterest, the interested audience treats a representational work as a transparency *through which* attention passes. As when we look through the sheet of glass that protects a painting in order to see the painting, the focus is firmly on the content. Without disinterest, the audience's identification and involvement cannot go beyond the preferences exercised in ordinary life.

But interested attention involves more than just identification and involvement with subject matter as that has been treated in traditional content analysis. Interest is directed at all of the other "meanings" that accrue to a song or artist or style of music. When I was in high school, the Allman Brothers Band was the particular favorite of several unambitious guys whose lives revolved around racing their motorcycles on the weekend. Assuming that the Allmans spoke for bikers (an easy association after Duane Allman and then Berry Oakley died in motorcycle accidents) and not seeing myself in those terms, I simply would not listen to their music. I was then surprised to find that I liked "Blue Sky" and "Ramblin' Man" when I heard them on the radio. Similarly, prevailing prejudices about the music of the Carpenters and then disco meant that I would never be caught with either in my record collection, but I found that I really liked "Rainy Days and Mondays" and most of what I heard from Donna Summer. When I gave the music an opportunity to work on me, I found that I liked what it had to offer. But this did not happen until I stopped positioning myself in relation to the music according to preconceptions of who I thought I was and to whom I thought the music spoke. Some of what it had to offer was aesthetic in character, a point to which I'll soon turn.[29]

The main flaw with standard accounts of disinterested attention is that they attach it to one and only one goal. Why should we grant that the only legitimate model for musical listening is one in which listeners sustain a disinterested "aesthetic attitude" during the whole duration of every piece of music? Granted, this model is useful if one plans a steady diet of baroque fugues or if one subscribes to the aestheticism of experience for its own sake. But disinterested listening does not have to be yoked to strict autonomism. Disinterest can be a means to another end. The initial goal of becoming positioned to respond to the music as such ("just having the experience," as Stolnitz puts it) may open the way to responding more fully to its emotive and affective dimensions. Even fans of progressive rock, the genre that most closely approximates the autonomist ideals of high art, respond to the music as an expression of a counter-cultural ideology.[30]

Disinterested attention does not have to come about through a listener's conscious focus and concentration. The greatest irony of the Clash's career is that their only number-one chart position came about in 1991 when "Should I Stay or Should I Go" was used as the music for a United Kingdom television commercial for Levi's blue jeans. Once the music was detached from the Clash's original punk context, a new generation of fans responded without preconceptions. The single's success brought about a renewed interest in *all* of their music, and re-releases of several of their albums climbed the U.K. charts.[31] Although several members were embarrassed to find success through a television commercial, the Clash finally broke through to the masses who thought of them as an overtly anti-establishment punk rock band. The use of "Should I Stay or Should I Go" in the television commercial recontextualized it in a way that allowed less politically minded rock fans to really *listen* to it. It also didn't hurt that the song was chopped down to little more than its hook for purposes of the commercial, highlighting its most appealing qualities.

I have already emphasized that music is a multilevel affair. Disinterested listening usually involves concentration on the music's structural or syntactic features: harmony, dynamics, melody, and rhythm combine to produce a unique piece of music. But the listener ignores the music's full significance or meaning. However, a clear sense of what is syntactically unique about a piece of music will position the listener to notice "the way these intertwine with and rest on the work's lower-level perceptual face."[32] (How, for instance, the attitude of "Should I Stay or Should I Go" rests on its musical swagger, which rests on the interplay of guitar, bass, drums, and short moments of silence.) In short, disinterested attention—initially to a mere riff or snatch of melody—positions the listener to respond to the music for its own sake. But such listening can be the prelude to attending more fully (and with interested attention) to the complex interplay of music and lyric in the complete speech act. Since one must grasp that speech act to fully appreciate the music as the product of a socially situated voice, disinterested attention is not a mode of listening that blinds the audience to the music's political and intellectual dimensions. For listeners who move from a disinterested to an interested stance, the resulting interpretation will be richer than it will be with an experience that cannot include a stage of disinterested attention. The listener who balances interest with disinterest is "open to all the impressions that the work might provide."[33] In a very real way, disinterested attention *buys time* during which the listener becomes interested.

Because a song is a unity of music and words, the unwary listener who yields to the pleasure of a musical hook can easily engage in disinterested and selective listening. Words alone do not generate a song's meaning. At the beginning of the Who's "My Generation," Roger Daltrey stutters and thus extends such phrases as "f-f-f-f-fade away," "we all s-s-s-say" and "s-s-s-situation." Each time, the supporting instruments drop out and the stutter is supported by nothing but handclaps. The effect is an intense focus on the stutter, generating a momentary suspension of the time flow created by the music's amazing propulsion, teasing the listener with suspense. Then the song lunges forward again with its call-and-response pattern. The next time through the same lyric, Daltrey prolongs the stutter, so that the final word of the line now overlaps the response "talkin' bout my generation." This overlap foreshadows the purely musical conflict that soon emerges; at the end of the piece, Keith Moon's furious drumming and Pete Townshend's crashing guitar chords shatter the call-and-response that has been established as the song's dominant organization. But two upward key changes are introduced before that concluding instrumental chaos, heightening the arrangement's sense of expansive emotion. The effect is one of mounting urgency that culminates in confusion.

The immediate and seemingly "intuitive" appeal of a prominent musical hook invites repeated listening. While the increasing chaos of

"My Generation" was confrontational in 1965, listeners were hooked by the catchy chant of "talkin' about my generation" and the novelty of the stutter. For listeners interested in sonic adventure, there is the additional appeal of John Entwistle's virtuoso bass runs. (As originally written and presented to the band, "My Generation" was an unremarkable blues tune, very much in the style of Jimmy Reed. It had little chance of competing on AM radio.) The song's clever arrangement draws attention, positioning the listener to wonder why Daltrey is stuttering and why the piece breaks down at the end. The music generates interpretive questions that are never raised by the mere words on paper. To whatever degree the subject matter and perspective on that subject matter are conveyed through musical means, "expressed obliquely, in style,"[34] listeners who find musical rewards when employing disinterested attention will already have invested themselves in its message. For if one becomes interested in the music as music, one has already made an emotional investment in whatever else the music communicates. I'll wager that quite a few unwary listeners found themselves singing along to the "doot-da-doot" hook of "Walk on the Wild Side" (1972) on AM radio before catching on to its debaucheries. By then, however, it was clear that *the music* is relaxed about the lowlifes paraded through the verses. Mick Ronson's warm string arrangement cushions the harsh images, and the saxophone coda soothes any lingering doubts.

But what facilitates this transition from investing in the music to investing in the identity it articulates? Immanuel Kant, whose general theory of disinterest in aesthetic judgment has shaped all subsequent debates on these questions, offers a plausible path from disinterested attention to social identification.[35] Aesthetic rewards are not enough to do the job. His intriguing suggestion is that a lucky accident underlies any transition from disinterested, "pure aesthetic judgment" to interested engagement.[36] Kant proposes that disinterested attention can *create an additional interest* when two conditions are satisfied. First, our disinterested attention must reward us with pleasure. Second, we must grasp that the object of our attention communicates the feelings of another human being.[37] The first condition could be satisfied without the second: a severely autistic individual might exercise disinterested attention and never respond to music as anything but pure form, or an individual might adopt a stance of pure aestheticism. But continued detachment in the face of expressive art is an unnatural response, and it should not be the aim of disinterested attention. Kant contends that a "natural" response to a skillful communication of feeling leaves one "not satisfied . . . unless he can feel his liking for it in community with others."[38] Our common nature as social animals takes up where our disinterested, aesthetic response leaves off. The spirit of this proposal is just what we have been seeking to complement Butler and Mill.

Both Simon Frith and Greil Marcus independently endorse variations on this idea, repackaging it in more contemporary language. Trying to get a handle on the obvious fact that fans often abandon themselves to the pleasure of music whose meanings or message cannot account for its appeal, they turn to Roland Barthes's observation that "significance" does not account for the thrill or *jouissance* some music delivers.[39] Frith proposes that the significant aspect of the experience is its dimension of "self-abandonment, as the terms we usually use to construct and hold ourselves together suddenly seem to float free." He offers the example of the immediate appeal of Elvis Presley, whose music "was thrilling because it dissolved the signs that had previously put adolescence together."[40] We respond, in other words, to its sense of freedom and possibility more than to any "message." We are responding to what Barthes calls *signifiance:* "not to a sign but to 'the work of signification'—not to meaning, but to 'the making of meanings.' We do not respond to symbols . . . we respond to symbol creation."[41] We respond to a particular voluptuous combination of sounds, riffs, rhythms, and (in Barthes's famous phrase) "the grain of the voice." What exhilarates us about the combination is the very act of symbol creation. We respond to the intentionality of the act before we respond to the intentions we glean from it.

We might call this the "spoonful-of-sugar-helps-the-medicine-go-down" defense of disinterest. The promise of independent *musical* rewards can motivate a disinterested listener to invest enough *interpretive* energy to enter imaginatively into the world it represents. Musical structures are often autonomous in the sense of rewarding listeners who have little or no knowledge of their cultural origins. In the words of Keith Richards, "Why the keening sounds from Mississippi should strike notes of thrill and terror and wonder in hearts in the suburbs of London, I don't know. It can only be because it goes beyond color, blood—it goes to the bone."[42] The crucial point for popular song is that this pleasure is also bound up with the brute fact that the human voice, singing words, reflects purposeful human activity. This evidence confronts the listener quite apart from any recognition of what the words might actually signify (apart from understanding a lyric's representational or referential dimension). Thus, Patti Smith recalls the deep impression made by Little Richard: "I didn't know what I was hearing or why I reacted so strongly.... It was something new and though I didn't comprehend what drew me, drawn I was. Drawn into a child's excited dance. That was 'Tutti Frutti,' so alien, so familiar. That was Little Richard. That was for me the birth of rock and roll."[43]

To be "drawn in" by the music is to endorse the activity of its production. Insofar as Richards and Smith responded to the music without any clear comprehension of the identities expressed by that music, their pleasure came from disinterested listening. Smith articulates the further point that her disinterest compelled her to endorse the music's human agency before she discovered the identity performed in the complex interplay of its multiple levels.

So if disinterested attention buys listeners the time to become interested in the music as an intentional act of human signification, the listeners have already joined into a common community with the artist. Once the listener gets hooked into the bass line and sassy strut of Lou Reed's "Walk on the Wild Side" (1972) or Run-D.M.C.'s appropriation of Aerosmith's funky riff for "Walk This Way" (1986), the listener has already joined into community with a world of transvestites and Queens b-boys. In a very real way, disinterested listening can trick listeners into community with queers and weirdoes and ethnic groups and political radicals and all sorts of people they might ordinarily have nothing to do with.

All attention to music requires imaginative participation in the music. Imaginative engagement with the music and the intentionality behind it sets the stage for more active modes of participation, such as singing along or tapping a foot or dancing to the music. In many cases, direct engagement with the music is followed by the related activities of learning about the artist and seeking more of that artist's music, and perhaps branching out into the music of related artists and styles. (In my own case, an immediate attraction to the jangling guitar sound of the Byrds led me to acquire all of their albums; bearing traces of his roots in bluegrass music, Chris Hillman's songs on *Younger Than Yesterday* prepared me for the country immersion of *Sweetheart of the Rodeo*. *Sweetheart of the Rodeo* introduced me to Gram Parsons, influencing me to seek out his two albums with the Flying Burrito Brothers and then his solo albums; the solo albums, in turn, introduced me to Emmylou Harris—who sang, I soon realized, on Dylan's *Desire*—and her cover versions of "traditional" songs gradually led me into a body of music that I once sneered at: the Louvin Brothers, Bill Monroe, and Ralph Stanley.) Quite literally, if disinterested listening is a first step in broadening one's tastes, then it is also an invaluable means for broadening the community in which one sympathetically participates.[44]

Conversely, to *refuse* to listen to music because of its origins—whether "I don't listen to faggots like the Indigo Girls" or "I don't listen to Green Day and Everclear now that they've sold out to corporate rock"—is to *refuse community*. Experiencing peer pressure, many listeners are coerced into feeling ashamed for liking a certain piece of music, as when some heavy metal fans attack "glam" metal as the music of "fags." But pleasure is not entirely constrained by social pressure. The pleasure of music can encourage listeners to engage in a potentially disruptive project of integrating the different levels of music and performance of identity. To repudiate this community, listeners must deny some of what the music has already given them. In deciding whether to pursue further listening and other forms of engagement, "we are conducting an imaginative experiment: what kind of a person must I be, I ask myself, in order to sympathize, or identify, with *this?*"[45]

But if disinterested attention can lead to unexpected pleasures and thus unexpected alliances, its dangers should not be ignored. One price to pay is that each listener will, at times, take pleasure in material that imparts a noxious message. Instrumental autonomism thus explains the predicament of feminists who are troubled by the fact that they love misogynist rock music. They love the music as music but despise some of the ideas it so powerfully expresses. Recognizing the impulse to integrate a song's distinct ends and means, they thereby find themselves parties to an articulation of identity that affronts their current ideal identity. There is no need to appeal to any deep structures of the mind or any form of "false consciousness" to explain this conflict. It is only a little more mysterious than enjoying a wonderful meal despite one's guilt about its monetary and health costs, or admiring U.S. President Bill Clinton's communication skills while being disgusted by his frequent use of those skills to obscure the truth.

Offended by the idea that "driving" and "pounding" rock and roll cannot express women's sexuality, Terri Sutton encapsulates the dilemma that comes from instrumental autonomism:

> To question women's place in rock 'n' roll . . . we need to know why they love the music of Metallica despite (and it's not because of it; I reject that) the fact that Metallica call them sluts. There's a strong love there, and it's too big not to be tangled up in identifying with the crushing roller coaster of sound. I remember seeing the Clash when I was eighteen and coming out of the show buoyant and huge, . . . full of myself. A joy of loud driving chaotic music is part of me, part of my sexuality, and no one can theorize that away.[46]

Sutton does not simply ignore the offensive masculinity appended to the "roller coaster of sound." As her metaphor implies, the *music* transports women fans. The feeling is "too big" to deny, and the woman fan *identifies with* the mastery and power of the music. Women who respond to the drive and thrust of rock 'n' roll are thus invited to affirm that their bodies and sexuality need not be restricted to feminine stereotypes. Such music helps its women fans accept that they are capable of a sexuality normally reserved for the "masculine" end of the spectrum. Women can thus embrace identities without responding to the access signs and discovery signs that Lisa Lewis emphasizes as the main attraction of female musicians. Multiple feminine identities can emerge apart from explicit female-address from women to women about female experience.

Conflicts arise because Metallica yokes that expression of sexuality to a performance of masculinity that insists on the subordination of women. Unable to find a further, progressive end served by such performances of masculinity, we can be positioned to suffer the tensions of simultaneously loving and hating the music. As with most popular art that isn't disposable entertainment, aesthetic response must be weighed against moral and political standards.

I can recall when Guns N' Roses first began to break nationally and I found myself swept up in their undeniable power, only to be disgusted to have ever liked them when I heard "One in a Million" with its notorious rant about "immigrants and faggots." To the extent that the forceful affirmation of the music supports rather than erodes Axl Rose's ignorant rant, there is no room for pretending that elements of irony or parody subvert the overt message of hatred. Here is a case where one is forced to find some other means of repudiating community with its homophobic, xenophobic stance. One could maintain a high degree of disinterested attention, listening selectively, or one might look for *unintended* ideas in the content, reading against the grain. Or, more challenging still, one could reflect on the possibility of entering into community with someone whose sense of self is built on such hatred.

Under the instrumental autonomism that I have been describing, disinterested attention and any purely "aesthetic" reward are mere starting points in exploring music. When unfamiliar music provides *jouissance*, it promises further rewards that derive from a fuller, more complex understanding of its perspective on the world. Listeners who pursue this promise often confront and (perhaps) refashion their existing interests. Committed feminists will have to confront the misogyny of the Rolling Stones. But in confronting it, they will also grapple with the different messages in different songs, and might then puzzle even more about Aerosmith's stance toward sex and gender. Bringing very different interests to the same music, other members of the popular audience will confront identities that, from the perspective of their current interests, involve varying degrees of subversion. Disinterest thus positions one to reflect on self-identity and so, potentially, to alter one's performance of identity.

It is a mistake to dismiss disinterest as demanding a lack of interest or a detachment from real life, or as an endorsement of art for art's sake or formalism. Disinterested attention is a useful strategy for dealing with the limited blinders created by our interests. In much the way that some people refuse to taste certain foods because of their very literal origins (e.g., eel, squid, brains, and tongue), many listeners prevent themselves from hearing music about which they have certain preconceptions. The disinterested listener neither approves nor disapproves based on prior knowledge of the sources, intentions, or likely effects of listening. Disinterested listening is a tool for finding out what's what with a particular piece of music before deciding whether it is, all things considered, good or bad. Although engaged with the music, the disinterested listener refrains from making absolute value judgments or drawing definitive conclusions until a piece of music is really heard as the piece that it is. It by no means follows that the disinterested listener remains disinterested and ignores the fact that music reflects purposive activity by its very fallible human creators.

Conclusions and Consequences

This study of the complexities of identity performances in rock music has culminated in discussion of a paradox, an affective paradox. On the one hand, exposure to popular music cannot reshape a listener's identity unless that individual understands and identifies with an identity that the music "performs." On the other hand, many analyses of the mass audience insist that a listener will reject any music that does not reflect the listener's existing sense of personal identity. Taken together, these two assumptions tell us that popular music cannot form or shape a listener's identity. It can only communicate and reinforce identities shaped by other, nonmusical social forces, because listeners reject (and so cannot be influenced by) music that might contribute to a different identity.

Most of us can summon up personal experiences confirming the kernel of truth on each side of this dilemma. Music fans have no difficulty in identifying music that they like because it seems to speak on their behalf. At the same time, anyone who regards popular music as a politically significant element of daily life will also possess anecdotal evidence supporting the conviction that the music does shape the listener. The audience's position prior to reception will not foreclose on the transforming power of popular culture.

Unfortunately, a fair amount of theorizing about mass art's place in identity politics treats every question of identity as a question of group identity, as if the primary value of a Carlos Santana guitar solo is its statement of Hispanic identity. The positive influence of this approach has been to remind us that if race, ethnicity, and regional identity are communicated and contested in mass art, then so are sex and gender. Yet on this assumption, there's not a dime's bit of difference between the early recordings of Carl Perkins and Elvis Presley, or even between Presley and Ronnie Hawkins or some other lesser-known rockabilly cat.

Although many people lack the vocabulary to articulate the idea, most still believe that they have a stable, core identity and that it includes unchanging attributes of race, sex, and gender. As long as both audience and musicians approach popular music as the personal, sincere, "authentic" and artless expression of identity, most performance of identity in rock will only reward those who respond to it as a straightforward celebration of that identity. Unless the music is approached with some measure of disinterested attention, the audience's pleasure will always seem, to the audience, to be rooted in its messages about identity. As such, the bond between queer listener and queer performer or between female fan and female performer is no different in kind— and is neither better nor worse—than the bond between a brutal misogynist and the punk band X, whose antirape "Johny Hit and Run Paulene" has been misunderstood by the misogynist fan as an endorsement of rape. *Parody, irony, and other tools of subversion will be without force, and subversive speech acts will often boomerang, with hegemonic effects.*

I have attempted to uphold the formative, transforming power of popular song delivered through mass art by countering the affective paradox with a different paradox: without disinterested attention, most listeners cannot experience and become interested in a piece of music as the music that it is. But where there is no investment in the musical side of popular song, listeners have only the pleasure that accompanies the confirmation of established markers of identity. The subversive potential of popular music derives from the interplay of musical and nonmusical elements, where musical pleasure positions listeners to share community with persons performing otherwise threatening or previously unimagined identities. The musical payoff that allows a feminist to feel conflicted about liking the Rolling Stones is the same process that allows a homophobic teenage boy to feel conflicted about loving Queen's "Bohemian Rhapsody," allowing the latter to identify with queer identity and, perhaps, to become open to it. Any aesthetic of mass art that fails to endorse disinterested attention faces this problem: either provide some other mechanism that persuades us to embrace music that threatens our sense of identity, or assume that we do not willingly listen to music that disrupts our sense of identity as shaped by other social forces.

So we must look to the *musical* side of musical performance to make the difference in creating communities that do not simply replicate the divisions established by other social forces. However pure the musical impulse of a musician, the sphere of mass art requires popular artists to traffic in the performance of identity. But the reverse is equally true; popular artists who hope to address questions of identity had better offer some musical rewards. There is little reason to fear that encouraging disinterested attention will turn rock into mere entertainment, stripping away rock's capacity to challenge the audience by opening doors to new worlds. These incongruities—that disinterest produces interest and that ideas become more powerful in combination with powerful music—are illustrated everywhere in rock.

Musical meaning is a multilevel affair, so there is more than one way to sell the music short. I have been critical of responses to music that consist in nothing but approval or disapproval of the music's performance of identity. I've been equally critical of the opposite extreme, the aestheticism that seeks out music (especially nonmainstream music) as an exotic stimulus while ignoring its cultural complexity. One price to pay in encouraging a free proliferation of diverse identities in mass culture is the risk of constantly affirming the status quo. We buy the freedom to experiment with identity only by granting others a similar freedom, even at the cost of allowing that the resources of mass art will often make no difference. The good news is that it can, and sometimes does, make a difference.

Notes

Chapter One

Epigraph: Jones, as quoted in Stanley Booth, *The True Adventures of the Rolling Stones* (New York: Vintage, 1985), 146.

1. As quoted in Stanley Booth, *Dance with the Devil: The Rolling Stones and Their Times* (New York: Random House, 1984), 39.

2. As quoted in Robert Greenfield, "Keith Richard: 'Got to Keep It Growing,'" in Ben Fong-Torres, ed., *The Rolling Stone Interviews,* vol. 2 (New York: Warner Paperback, 1973), 222; original interview, 1971. In this interview, Richards says the meeting "was about 1960," but in 1960 Jagger was at Dartford Grammar and would have had no reason to be on the train to London. The most likely date for the encounter appears to have been 17 October 1961: see Christopher Sandford, *Mick Jagger: Primitive Cool* (New York: St. Martin's, 1993). Another biographer places the meeting sometime in December 1961; Christopher Andersen, *Jagger Unauthorized* (New York: Delacorte, 1993). Jagger and Richards have never agreed on which Chuck Berry album caught Richards's eye that day.

3. Keith Richards, "Muddy, Wolf, and Me," *Guitar Player,* September 1993, 88.

4. For instance, the index to Robert Palmer's history of rock shows that more space is devoted to explaining the influences on the Rolling Stones than to the Stones' own career, and more pages mention either Presley or the Sex Pistols than the Rolling Stones: Robert Palmer, *Rock and Roll: An Unruly History* (New York: Harmony Books, 1995).

5. Peter Van Der Merwe, *Origins of the Popular Style: The Antecedents of Twentieth-Century Popular Music* (Oxford: Clarendon, 1989), 213.

6. Donald Clarke, *The Rise and Fall of Popular Music* (New York: St. Martin's Press, 1995), 464.

7. As quoted in Chris Norris, "Aerosmith: Party of Five," *Spin,* May 1997, 126.

8. As quoted in Arlene Stein, "Androgyny Goes Pop," in Arlene Stein, ed., *Sisters, Sexperts, Queers: Beyond the Lesbian Nation* (New York: Plume, 1993), 103. 2 Nice Girls are a lesbian trio who playfully poke fun at straight relationships with songs like "I Spent My Last $10.00 (On Birth Control and Beer)" (1989).

9. As quoted in Dora Lowenstein and Philip Dodd, *The Rolling Stones: A Life on the Road* (New York: Penguin Studio, 1998), 28.

10. Popular music has never been synonymous with rock, which remains a minority taste even in the United States. How popular it is today depends largely on whether one distinguishes between rock and R&B (including hip-hop) and where one draws the line between rock and country. Examining available figures generated for a single week in May 1981, Charles Hamm notes that while radio is heavily slanted toward varieties of rock, television is not; that week, the *Barbara Mandrell Show* attracted more viewers than the combined audience for *Saturday Night Live* (featuring Devo) and Dick Clark's *American Bandstand* (featuring Rick Springfield and the Bus Boys). The top three shows of that week involving an appreciable amount of music featured easy listening and country music. See Charles Hamm, "The Measurement of Popularity in Music," *Putting Popular Music in Its Place* (Cambridge University Press, 1995), 127–28.

11. Charles Hamm, "Rock and the Facts of Life," *Putting Popular Music in Its Place*, 53. For Hamm, rock 'n' roll is the first wave of music to break sharply from earlier popular music in style and content; rock is the second distinctive wave of such music. See Charles Hamm, *Yesterdays: Popular Song in America* (New York: Norton, 1979), 441–42.

12. Steve Chapple and Reebee Garofalo, *Rock 'n' Roll Is Here to Pay: The History and Politics of the Music Industry* (Chicago: Nelson-Hall, 1977), 315. For studies of music in Nigeria and India, see Charles Keil, *Tiv Song: The Sociology of Art in a Classless Society* (University of Chicago Press, 1979), and Peter Manuel, *Cassette Culture: Popular Music and Technology in North India* (University of Chicago Press, 1993).

Garofalo's subsequent work often collapses differences among rock music, mass art, and popular music. For example, see Reebee Garofalo, *Rockin' Out: Popular Music in the USA* (Boston: Allyn and Bacon, 1997). Offered as a "social history of U.S. popular music since the invention of the phonograph in 1877," the book provides a discussion of the Flying Burrito Brothers but not bluegrass great Bill Monroe, of Frankie Valli and the Four Seasons but not Depression-Era crooner Rudy Valli, of M. C. Hammer but not Broadway writers Rodgers and Hammerstein. It is a social history of rock 'n' roll and related music, not of popular music.

13. Noël Carroll, *The Philosophy of Mass Art* (Oxford: Clarendon, 1998), 192. My formulations are often informed by Carroll's writings on film theory and mass art. There is one serious difference between Carroll and myself on the distinction between popular art and mass art; he believes that mass art has an identifiable essence, whereas I believe that his description is a well-informed generalization. Carroll rightly emphasizes that we should not overlook complications that arise from related classifications, such as folk art and middlebrow art, and that avant-garde artists have often employed mass technologies without thereby creating mass art.

14. Carroll, *Mass Art*, 188.

15. As quoted in Pete Welding, "Muddy Waters," in Pete Welding and Toby Byron, eds., *Bluesland: Portraits of Twelve Major American Blues Masters* (New York: Dutton, 1991), 143.

16. As quoted in James Rooney, *Bossmen: Bill Monroe and Muddy Waters* (New York: Da Capo, 1971; republication with author emendations, New York: Dial, 1971), 117.

17. Tony Kirshner, "Studying Rock: Toward a Materialist Ethnography," in Thomas Swiss, John Sloop, and Andrew Herman, eds., *Mapping the Beat: Popular Music and Contemporary Theory* (Oxford: Blackwell, 1998), 247–68. See also Ellen Willis, "Crowds and Freedom," in Karen Kelly and Evelyn McDonnell, eds., *Stars Don't Stand Still in the Sky: Music and Myth* (New York University Press, 1999), 153–59.

18. Greenfield, "Keith Richard," 233.

19. Nina Teicholz, "Name That Tune Dept.," *New Yorker,* 21 and 28 June 1999, 67–68. Teicholz notes that the Jefferson Airplane's "Somebody to Love" (1967) was chosen for karaoke performance by an Albanian cook.

20. Although it would be dangerous to generalize too broadly, there seems a tendency for mass art's audience to become more geographically dispersed over time. First a geographically concentrated fan base (perhaps only one city or region) supports a specific style, and then the base becomes dispersed. Universities have often served as a fan base for emerging styles, as have particular radio stations and club circuits. While the original fan base for progressive rock was a homogeneous subculture in southeastern England, its most active fans are now so geographically dispersed that "prog" bands formed after 1980 find it difficult to construct a feasible tour itinerary. See Edward Macan, *Rocking the Classics: English Progressive Rock and the Counterculture* (Oxford University Press, 1997), 151–52, 200–201.

21. See Theodore Gracyk, *Rhythm and Noise: An Aesthetics of Rock* (Duke University Press, 1996), chap. 1. On the type/token distinction as it relates to art, see Richard Wollheim, *Art and Its Objects* (Cambridge University Press, 1980).

22. Remixes and alternative editions of recorded music, like re-edited films, produce versions that introduce another layer of interpretation between the original first-stage object and the tokens delivered to consumers. However, these final tokens are not themselves interpretations. The interpretation arises at an intermediate stage of creating a type within a type, just as the dollar bills in my wallet are tokens of a type within a type (that is, the basic type of currency has been modified at various times, as has the flag of the United States when more states have been added).

23. I must qualify this argument by granting that singing a song can provide a genuine instance of the song, but the Sex Pistols' recording, as constructed with multiple overdubs in the studio with producer Chris Thomas, cannot be known through any recreation. See Gracyk, *Rhythm and Noise,* chap. 1.

24. Live recordings are, of course, further products of mass art, as are bootleg recordings of live performances.

25. As quoted in Clinton Heylin, *From the Velvets to the Voidoids: A Pre-Punk History for a Post-Punk World* (New York: Penguin, 1993), 98.

26. Joey and Johnny, as quoted in Timothy White, *Rock Lives: Profiles and Interviews* (New York: Henry Holt, 1990), 441 and 449, respectively; interviews were conducted in 1979 while the Ramones were promoting *Road to Ruin.*

27. Results of Soundscan study summarized in Roy Trakin, "The Money Tree: Who's Making What in the Music Biz," *Musician,* September 1997, 30.

28. As quoted in David Fricke, "Kurt Cobain: The Rolling Stone Interview," *Rolling Stone,* 27 January 1994; reprinted in Holly George-Warren, ed., *Cobain* (Boston: Little, Brown, 1994), 66.

29. Greil Marcus, *Lipstick Traces: A Secret History of the Twentieth Century* (Harvard University Press, 1989), 21.

30. As quoted in Jonathan Cott and Sue Clark, "Mick Jagger," in *The Rolling Stone Interviews* (New York: Warner Paperback, 1971), 160.

31. This story is slightly complicated by the fact that since 1995, when *Loaded* was reissued with all edits to the studio version of "Sweet Jane" restored, the shorter version used by Mott the Hoople has been commercially unavailable except on a Velvet Underground "best of" compilation.

32. See David Hatch and Stephen Millward, *From Blues to Rock* (Manchester University Press, 1987), 8–9.

33. Assuming that he must choose between notated or oral transmission, Charles Hamm treats rock as part of an oral tradition in which mass media are "an extension" of live performance. Hamm, "The Measurement of Popularity in Music," 119.

34. Walter J. Ong, *Orality and Literacy: The Technologizing of the Word* (New York: Methuen, 1982), 48.

35. Rooney, *Bossmen*, 103, 112. Son House and Memphis Minnie also left behind a few string-band recordings that feature mandolin. Ten years older than Muddy Waters, Sleepy John Estes remained a traditionalist and brought a mandolin player with him to perform blues at the 1964 Newport Folk Festival. Describing the Mississippi dance band that showed him the commercial value of country "blues," W. C. Handy recalls a trio of mandolin, guitar, and bass; *William Christopher Handy, Father of the Blues* (New York: Macmillan, 1941), 76. Handy does not offer a date for this crucial event, but it seems to have taken place around 1903.

36. Gary Giddins, "How Much Did Elvis Learn From Otis Blackwell?" in *Riding on a Blue Note* (Oxford University Press, 1981), 29. I do not mean to imply that rock musicians started this practice. For instance, when Alan Lomax first recorded Muddy Waters during a Library of Congress field recording trip in 1941, Waters performed a song "Country Blues" that was a thinly veiled reworking of Robert Johnson's recording of "Walkin' Blues." We know that Waters copied the recording, for he confirmed that he only saw Robert Johnson once, playing for change on a street, but had been too afraid of Johnson to go over and listen.

37. As quoted in Greil Marcus, Happy Traum, and John Grissim Jr., "Van Morrison: A Moondance Down Funky Broadway," in Ben Fong-Torres, ed., *The Rolling Stone Interviews,* vol. 2 (New York: Warner Paperback, 1973), 72; interview conducted by Happy Traum, 1970.

38. See Steve Turner, *Van Morrison: Too Late to Stop Now* (New York: Viking, 1993), 50–51, and Hatch and Millward, *From Blues to Rock,* 22–24. The 1927 version is by Papa Harvey Hull and Long Cleve Reed. But even Pink Anderson, the South Carolina bluesman who lent his first name to Pink Floyd, knew the Big Joe Williams version, singing it for Samuel Charters during a recording session in 1961.

Iggy Pop cites the Muddy Waters version of "Baby Please Don't Go" as the probable source of the Stooges' "I Wanna Be Your Dog" (1969).

Chapter Two

Epigraphs: Eduard Hanslick, *On the Musically Beautiful*, trans. Geoffrey Payzant (Indianapolis: Hackett, 1986), 70; Mills, as quoted in Paul Zollo, *Songwriters on Songwriting* (New York: Da Capo, 1997), 634.

1. Barry Shank illustrates this point with his detailed account of how bands that become popular in the club scene of Austin, Texas, must retool their sound in order to make their music comprehensible to "someone in Des Moines." See Barry Shank, *Dissonant Identities: The Rock 'n' Roll Scene in Austin, Texas* (Wesleyan University Press, 1994), chap. 7.

2. See Aaron Ridley, *Music, Value, and the Passions* (Cornell University Press, 1995), chap. 3, and Stephen Davies, *Musical Meaning and Expression* (Cornell University Press, 1994), chap. 7. These points will play an important role in my arguments in Chapters 7 and 8.

3. For a review of the relevant literature, see George H. Lewis, "Who Do You Love? The Dimensions of Musical Taste," in James Lull, ed., *Popular Music and Communication*, 2nd ed. (Newbury Park: Sage, 1992), 134–51. The notion of cultural capital stems from Bourdieu's *Distinction*; Bourdieu links it to formal education and subsequent social status, but it can be broadly understood to be education in and facility with the codes that permit individuals to gain social status. Empirical studies regularly demonstrate that age is one of the surest indicators of musical preference within popular music, suggesting that Bourdieu overestimates the importance of formal education and that he makes too few distinctions within popular culture. Because such codes must also be acquired informally, in order to operate within subcultures that have limited social status, we can also speak of subcultural capital; see Sarah Thornton, *Club Cultures: Music, Media, and Subcultural Capital* (Wesleyan University Press, 1996).

4. Patricia Herzog, "Music Criticism and Musical Meaning," *Journal of Aesthetics and Art Criticism* 53 (1995): 300. Compare: "Our interpretation of a work and our experience of its value are mutually dependent . . . simultaneously causing and validating themselves and causing and validating each other"; Barbara Herrnstein Smith, *Contingencies of Value: Alternative Perspective for Critical Theory* (Harvard University Press, 1991), 10–11.

5. Dave Laing, *One Chord Wonders: Power and Meaning in Punk Rock* (Open University Press, 1985).

6. As quoted in "Bob Dylan," in Kurt Loder, ed., *The Rolling Stone Interviews: The 1980s* (New York: St. Martin's/Rolling Stone Press, 1989), 96; interview conducted in 1984. Dylan is responding to Loder's attempts to construct a Zionist interpretation of "Neighborhood Bully."

7. As quoted in Mark Kemp, "Beck," *Rolling Stone*, 17 April, 1997, 94.

8. Deena Weinstein, *Heavy Metal: A Cultural Sociology* (New York: Lexington, 1991), 241.

9. Transcribed from "Punk," *The History of Rock 'n' Roll* television and video production (Time Warner, 1995), episode 9. Perhaps the only major critic to dislike the band, Dave Marsh dismisses them as tunelessly avant-garde and claims that their "failure to find an audience" is mainly due to "the band's utter failure to meet any

of the requirements of genuinely popular culture." Dave Marsh, "X," in Dave Marsh and John Swenson, eds., *The New Rolling Stone Record Guide* (New York: Random House/Rolling Stone Press, 1983), 560.

10. *History of Rock 'n' Roll*, episode 9. Kurt Cobain made a number of similar observations about punk/grunge fans of the 1990s.

11. Peter Manuel, "Gender Politics in Caribbean Popular Music: Consumer Perspectives and Academic Interpretation," *Popular Music and Society* 22 (Summer 1998): 17. The uncited quotations that follow are all from this page.

12. The relevance of these principles is explored by Ismay Barwell, "Who's Telling This Story, Anyway? Or, How to Tell the Gender of a Storyteller," in Stephen Davies, ed., *Art and Its Messages: Meaning, Morality, and Society* (Pennsylvania State University Press, 1997), 89–100. My summary of the principles also draws on Jerrold Levinson, "Messages in Art," also in Davies, 70–83.

13. For an interesting discussion of the issue, see Robert Kraut, "Perceiving the Music Correctly," in Michael Krausz, ed., *The Interpretation of Music: Philosophical Essays* (Oxford University Press, 1993), 103–16. Kraut argues that a degree of arbitrariness enters into every attempt to stipulate who counts as the relevant community and what counts as normalcy in that community.

14. E. D. Hirsch Jr., "Meaning and Significance Reinterpreted," *Critical Inquiry* 11 (1984): 205. Hirsch emphasizes that he now holds a different theory of meaning than the one defended in Hirsch, *Validity in Interpretation* (Yale University Press, 1967).

15. Hirsch, "Meaning and Significance," 206. It should now be clear that the issue I'm discussing has nothing at all to do with ambiguity or equivocation (intentional or otherwise).

16. George Lipsitz, *Dangerous Crossroads: Popular Music, Postmodernism, and the Poetics of Place* (New York: Verso, 1994), 109.

17. E. D. Hirsch Jr., "Coming With Terms to Meanings," *Critical Inquiry* 12 (1986): 627. Suzanne Langer's theory of art as unconsummated symbol has important similarities with Hirsch's proposal; Langer is cited to explain the power of pop songs by Ann Powers, "I'll Have to Say I Love You in a Song," in Karen Kelly and Evelyn McDonnell, eds., *Stars Don't Stand Still in the Sky: Music and Myth* (New York University Press, 1999), 187–90. However, Langer's theory is significantly flawed; see G. L. Hagberg, *Art as Language: Wittgenstein, Meaning, and Aesthetic Theory* (Cornell University Press, 1995), chap. 1.

18. Manuel does not describe it in this way, but this mode of interpretation seems to be operating in several of his explanations of how women can identify with sexist songs that degrade women. Where he goes wrong, I suggest, is in the claim that listeners find ways to respond to a song's "universal . . . sentiments"; Manuel, "Gender Politics in Caribbean Popular Music," 19. There is no reason to suppose that the sentiments will be universal, nor that the listener must identify with the song's subject position.

19. Hirsch, "Meaning and Significance," 209. Even direct speech acts can be open-ended in this way. As Noël Carroll observes, when somebody with an unlit cigarette asks "Do you have a match?" the question entitles one to produce a lighter. Taken as a request, the question has been understood perfectly well. See Carroll,

"The Intentional Fallacy: Defending Myself," *Journal of Aesthetics and Art Criticism* 55 (1997): 308.

20. As quoted in Greil Marcus, Happy Traum, and John Grissim Jr., "Van Morrison: A Moondance Down Funky Broadway," in Ben Fong-Torres, ed., *The Rolling Stone Interviews*, vol. 2 (New York: Warner Paperback, 1973), 71; interview conducted by Happy Traum, 1970.

21. Simon Frith emphasizes this point but then attempts to narrow the range of audience positions that shape the music's reception. Frith speculates that "these days" three overlapping "grids" of discourse influence the reception of all music; see Simon Frith, *Performing Rites: On the Value of Popular Music* (Harvard University Press, 1996), 26.

22. Lisa Lewis, *Gender Politics and MTV: Voicing the Difference* (Temple University Press, 1990), 220. Lewis challenges theoretical models that place undue emphasis on audience reception in order to show how female fans correctly perceive oppositional messages that female musicians place in their songs and videos.

23. As quoted in Paul Zollo, *Songwriters on Songwriting* (New York: Da Capo, 1997), 633.

24. In perverse reading, interpreters consciously impose their own perspective on a text, typically reversing the values they are expected to bring to it. See Bonnie Zimmerman, "Perverse Reading: The Lesbian Appropriation of Literature," in Susan J. Wolfe and Julia Penelope, eds., *Sexual Practice, Textual Theory: Lesbian Cultural Criticism* (Oxford: Blackwell, 1993), 135–49.

25. John Fiske distinguishes between a text's polysemic quality (polysemy as "structured into the text") and additional polysemic potential resulting from its intertextual relations. See John Fiske, *Television Culture* (New York: Methuen, 1987), 126–27. But no text is inherently polysemic, for all meaning of this sort is present or absent only through intertextual relations brought into play by the audience.

26. Tom Wolfe, "The First Tycoon of Teen," originally in *New York Herald Tribune* (1965) and frequently reprinted, including in Clinton Heylin, ed., *The Penguin Book of Rock and Roll Writing* (New York: Viking, 1992), 61, 63.

27. The empirical evidence suggests that most listeners ignore the lyrics most of the time. See John P. Robinson and Paul Hirsch, "It's the Sound That Does It," *Psychology Today*, vol. 3, no. 5 (October 1969), 42–45; Emily D. Edwards and Michael Singletary, "Mass Media Images in Popular Music," *Popular Music and Society* 9 (1984); Roger Jon Desmond, "Adolescents and Music Lyrics: Implications of a Cognitive Perspective," *Communications Quarterly* 35 (1987): 278; and Jill Rosenbaum and Lorraine Prinsky, "Sex, Violence and Rock 'n' Roll: Youths' Perceptions of Popular Music," *Popular Music and Society* 2 (1987): 85.

For an example of the effort to treat rock lyrics as poetry, see David Pichaske, *The Poetry of Rock: The Golden Years* (Peoria: Ellis, 1981).

28. The audience's ability to grasp the affective message of a recording's purely musical dimension (everything but the meanings of the lyrics) goes a long way toward accounting for the broad appeal of American and British music in countries where English is not the native tongue. See Simon Frith, *Music for Pleasure* (New York: Routledge, 1988), 154.

29. Writing about the song and album when they were new, Greil Marcus noted its disturbing lack of moral sensibility; see Marcus, "Love and Death in the American Novel," *Ranters and Crowd Pleasers: Punk in Pop Music, 1977–92* (New York: Doubleday, 1993), 130–34; originally published in *New West*, 25 August 1980.

30. See Randall R. Dipert, "The Composer's Intentions: An Examination of their Relevance for Performance," *Musical Quarterly* 66 (1980): 207–8. "Higher" and "lower" are relative terms here. An intention is higher-level if its communication depends on the communication of another, lower-level intention. Since I am concerned with mass art in a way that Dipert is not, I am treating the musicians who make a record as having the "authorship" role that Dipert assigns to the composer who produces a musical score.

31. Robert Christgau, *Grown Up All Wrong: 75 Great Rock and Pop Artists From Vaudeville to Techno* (Harvard University Press, 1998), 144–49.

Chapter Three

1. As quoted in David Dalton, *The Rolling Stones: The First Twenty Years* (New York: Knopf, 1981), 109.

2. Roland Barthes is a crucial source here. An accessible yet solid introduction to Barthes on "the text" is Michael Moriarty, *Roland Barthes* (Stanford University Press, 1991), chap. 8.

There is a standard distinction between utterance meaning (what a combination of symbols in a language, such as a sentence, would mean to the average native speaker) and utterer's meaning (what the speaker or writer means on the particular occasion of its production). The utterance meaning of the phrase "it's raining" is not sardonic, but in certain contexts (you've told me not to bother to close the car windows because you don't believe it will rain) its utterance meaning will bear such significance.

3. As quoted in Stanley Booth, *Dance With the Devil: The Rolling Stones and Their Times* (New York: Random House, 1984), 68–69.

4. Thus I am uncomfortable with Sheila Whiteley's citation of Brian Jones's stage behavior in her account of the bands' image of sexual aggression. His behavior may have contributed to their initial image for a very limited audience, but it cannot play any role in accounting for the messages that are understood by a mass audience ignorant of these distant events. See Sheila Whiteley, "Little Red Rooster v. The Honky Tonk Woman," in Whiteley, ed., *Sexing the Groove* (London: Routledge, 1997), 70.

5. It should be clear by now that I do not endorse all of the conclusions that are routinely derived from this slogan. By way of correcting the erroneous leap from textuality to the infinite play of texts, see John M. Ellis, *Against Deconstruction* (Princeton University Press, 1989), particularly chap. 5, and Peter Lamarque, *Fictional Points of View* (Cornell University Press, 1996), chap. 10.

6. Six other unacknowledged dichotomies that guide a good deal of writing on popular music are outlined and documented by Charles Hamm, "Modernist Narratives and Popular Music," *Putting Music in Its Place*, 1–27.

7. Barry Shank, *Dissonant Identities: The Rock 'n' Roll Scene in Austin, Texas* (Wesleyan University Press, 1994), 246. This tendency to adopt traditional ethnography is criticized by Tony Kirschner, "Studying Rock: Toward a Materialist Ethnography," in Thomas Swiss, John Sloop, and Andrew Herman, eds., *Mapping the Beat: Popular Music and Contemporary Theory* (Oxford: Blackwell, 1998), 247–68.

8. Shank, *Dissonant Identities*, 251. Lacking field data about participants in the Austin club scene during the period when disco brought about a financial crisis for honky-tonk clubs centered on live performances, Shank theorizes that "the gap between the performance of the music and its reception" made the audience narcissistic. Because the honky-tonk scene had emphasized a different set of core values, Shank assumes that any deviation from that core necessitates a false community, one incapable "of integrating elements from the everyday life of its audience"; Shank, 82. Shank adopts without scrutiny the assumption that Michelle Moody-Adams attacks as the dogma that cultural influence on participant belief and action must be understood deterministically; see Michelle M. Moody-Adams, *Fieldwork in Familiar Places: Morality, Culture, and Philosophy* (Harvard University Press, 1997), 21.

9. Roland Barthes, *S/Z*, trans. Richard Miller (New York: Farrar Straus, 1984), 10–12, 20–22. Lacking a mechanism for preserving texts without transforming them, an oral tradition lacks genuine intertextuality.

10. It is difficult to find a clear exposition of the claims made about intertextuality; the best source may be Jonathan Culler, *The Pursuit of Signs* (Cornell University Press, 1981), chap. 5. For an extended application to mass art, see Fiske, *Television Culture*, chap. 7. It should be noted that intertextuality is a doctrine about meaning, not about value; some highly intertextual rock songs, such as "American Pie," are clever without being particularly meritorious.

11. Ludwig Wittgenstein, *Philosophical Investigations*, trans. G.E.M. Anscombe (Oxford University Press, 1953; 3rd ed. 1967), 198.

12. The phrase is from Culler, *Pursuit of Signs*, 107.

13. Lisa Lewis, *Gender Politics and MTV: Voicing the Difference* (Temple University Press, 1990), 149, emphasis added. General intertextuality does not capture the highly focused references that emerge in "tertiary texts."

14. Specific intertextualities facilitate a text's subversive potential. Early in the development of deconstruction, Culler argued that parody and irony emerge only through specific intertextualities; Jonathan Culler, *Structuralist Poetics* (Cornell University Press, 1975), 145. In contrast, general intertexuality is supposed to be a form of quotation that is not a quotation of any specific precedent; e.g., Roland Barthes, *S/Z*, chap. 1. This proposal stretches the notion of quotation beyond recognition. In its place we can substitute the pair of notions, namely significant utterances that are recognizable tokens of a familiar type (one hears "Good morning" from someone one has never met before) and ones that follow a cultural rule without directly repeating any specific case (as with Wittgenstein's examples of solving a math problem one has not been shown before).

15. While Barthes is notoriously difficult to pin down, even he seems to have regarded both intertextuality and the death of the author as interpretive strategies, not as a descriptive theory. See Moriarty, *Roland Barthes*, 107–8.

16. This problem was first recognized by Wittgenstein, *Philosophical Investigations*, sec. 138–242. The solution is to see that a rule applies only insofar as there is a standard practice in following it. This emphasis on human practices will play an important role in my arguments in subsequent chapters.

17. As quoted in Paul Zollo, *Songwriters on Songwriting* (New York: Da Capo, 1997), 146–47.

18. Censorship also leads to interesting substitutions; British broadcasting regulations prohibit names of commercial products, so on British radio one hears Ray Davies singing "cherry cola" instead of "Coca Cola" in "Lola."

Chapter Four

Epigraphs: Corgan, as quoted in David Fricke, "Smashing Pumpkins," *Rolling Stone*, 16 November 1995, 59; Watt, as quoted in Mark Rowland, "Sideman: Mike Watt," *Musician*, December 1997, 12.

1. Stanley Fish, *Is There a Text in This Class? The Authority of Interpretive Communities* (Harvard University Press, 1980), and *Doing What Comes Naturally: Change, Rhetoric, and the Practice of Theory in Literary and Legal Studies* (Duke University Press, 1989).

2. Susan McClary, "Paradigm Dissonances: Music Theory, Cultural Studies, Feminist Criticism," *Perspectives of New Music* 32 (1994): 68. The same use of "paradigm" is found in John Covach, "We Won't Get Fooled Again: Rock Music and Musical Analysis," in David Schwarz, Anahid Kassabian, and Lawrence Siegel, eds., *Keeping Score: Music, Disciplinarity, Culture* (University Press of Virginia, 1997).

3. See Hannah Arendt, *The Human Condition* (University of Chicago Press, 1958), 52–53, 57. Arendt proposes that public art served in a similar capacity in the Greek city-states of antiquity, providing durable focal points in the face of "innumerable perspectives."

4. Thomas S. Kuhn, *The Structure of Scientific Revolutions*, 2nd ed., enlarged (University of Chicago Press, 1970), 175.

5. Kuhn, 10, 23, 43–44, 109, 175, 187, and 199–200.

6. Thomas S. Kuhn, "Comment on James S. Ackerman, E. M. Hafner, and George Kubler," *Comparative Studies in Society and History* 11 (1969): 412. In this article Kuhn again emphasizes that paradigms are not to be equated with theories, and that scientists are analogous to artists; consequently, his views do not suggest that interpretive theories or frameworks are paradigms.

7. Reebee Garofalo, *Rockin' Out: Popular Music in the USA* (Boston: Allyn and Bacon, 1997), 346.

8. Garofalo, *Rockin' Out*, 347. See also Tom Smucker, "Disco," in Jim Miller, ed., *The Rolling Stone Illustrated History of Rock and Roll*, 2nd ed. (New York: Random House/Rolling Stone Press, 1980), 432, as well as Susan McClary, "Same As It Ever Was: Youth Culture and Music," and Walter Hughes, "In the Empire of the Beat: Discipline and Disco," both in Andrew Ross and Tricia Rose, eds., *Microphone Fiends: Youth Music and Youth Culture* (Routledge, 1994), 32 and 147, respectively. McClary and Hughes contend that the slogan "Disco sucks" was a coded reference to the link between disco and male homosexuality. In the same collection of essays,

Lawrence Grossberg claims that the backlash against disco was because it was "too black." See Grossberg, "Is Anybody Listening?" 43.

9. George Lipsitz applauds mass art when "repressed elements of the past surge to the surface as part of the present." But he also condemns musicians who depoliticize music by obscuring its origins. See George Lipsitz, *Dangerous Crossroads: Popular Music, Postmodernism, and the Poetics of Place* (London: Verso, 1994); quotation from p. 18.

10. These claims are made by Roger Scruton, *The Aesthetics of Music* (Oxford University Press, 1997), 506.

11. As quoted in Clinton Heylin, *Never Mind the Bollocks, Here's the Sex Pistols* (New York: Schirmer, 1998), 124.

12. Noël Carroll, *The Philosophy of Mass Art* (Oxford: Clarendon, 1998), chap. 3.

13. See Stephen King and Richard J. Jensen, "Bob Marley's 'Redemption Song': The Rhetoric of Reggae and Rastafari," *Journal of Popular Culture* 29 (1995): 17–36.

14. Because the sources of samples are increasingly obscured in order to avoid the cost of paying for sample clearances, sampling has not fulfilled its early promise for conveying history. For further commentary on the importance of cover versions in keeping the past "culturally alive," see George Plasketes, "Like a Version: Cover Songs and the Tribute Trend in Popular Music," *Studies in Popular Culture* 15 (1992): 1–18, and "Look What They've Done to My Song: Covers and Tributes, an Annotated Discography, 1980–1995," *Popular Music and Society* 19 (1995): 79–106. Plasketes has not always done his homework: some songs that he calls covers were the first recorded versions (e.g., the Byrds performing Dylan) and he seems to think that Wilson Pickett recorded for Motown.

15. Lou Reed, *Between Thought and Expression: Selected Lyrics of Lou Reed* (New York: Hyperion, 1991), 159–61.

16. Greil Marcus, *Lipstick Traces* (Harvard University Press, 1989), 64; Marcus notes that Westerberg said this in 1986 but cites no source.

17. Patti Smith, as quoted in Gerri Hirshey, "Women Who Rocked the World," *Rolling Stone*, 13 November 1997, 73.

18. Seeing these problems in the work of other writers, I avoid building my theoretical position around the music that has meant the most to me. I might throw in the name of a beloved band like the Replacements or Roxy Music when nothing in particular depends on it, but I hope that nothing in my conclusions would be peculiar to Mott the Hoople, the Byrds, Joni Mitchell, the Blue Nile, and the bass playing of Duck Dunn.

19. Lester Bangs pokes fun at his own tendency to valorize marginal rock musicians in his comic tale of seeking a record by the Count Five; Lester Bangs, "Psychotic Reactions and Carburetor Dung: A Tale of These Times," in Greil Marcus, ed., *Psychotic Reactions and Carburetor Dung* (New York: Knopf, 1981), 5–19; originally published in *Creem*, June 1971.

20. The "as if" is crucial here, both for Kuhn and for the argument that follows. The very possibility of coming to share a currently unfamiliar paradigm presupposes that those who reject it already "live" in the same world as those who endorse it.

21. A position defended in relation to fine art by Robert Stecker, *Artworks: Definition, Meaning, Value* (Pennsylvania State University Press, 1996), part 2.

Chapter Five

Epigraphs: Wilfrid Mellers, *Music in a New Found Land: Themes and Developments in the History of American Music* (Oxford University Press, 1987; originally published 1964), 266; Richards, as quoted in Jenny Boyd with Holly George Warren, *Musicians in Tune: Seventy-Five Contemporary Musicians Discuss the Creative Process* (New York: Fireside/Simon and Schuster, 1992), 114.

1. Anthony Bozza, "Eminem Blows Up," *Rolling Stone*, 29 April 1999, 44. For a perceptive overview of the issues as they emerged in the rock and hip-hop world of the late 1990s, see Charles Aaron, "What the White Boy Means When He Says Yo," *Spin*, November 1998, 114–29.

2. Charles Aaron, "Chocolate on the Inside," *Spin*, May 1999, 104; Aaron called Eminem's debut album "the best rap album of this year."

3. See Charles Wolfe and Kip Lornell, *The Life and Legend of Leadbelly* (New York: Harper Collins, 1992), 52–56. Also see Francis Davis, *The History of the Blues* (New York: Hyperion, 1995), 169–70.

4. Davis, *History of the Blues*, 38. See also Paul Oliver, *Songsters and Saints: Vocal Traditions on Race Records* (Cambridge University Press, 1984), and Tony Russell, *Blacks, Whites, and Blues* (New York: Stein and Day, 1970), 25–47. These points suggest fundamental problems with Eric Lott's thesis that minstrel shows were America's only mode of "exchange of energies between two otherwise rigidly bounded and policed cultures"; E. Lott, *Love and Theft: Blackface Minstrelsy and the American Working Class* (Oxford University Press, 1993), 6.

5. A detailed discussion of the whole song family is provided by George M. Eberhart, "Stack Lee: The Man, the Music, and the Myth," *Popular Music and Society* 20 (1996): 1–70.

6. Jefferson's significance cannot be overstated, either in jump-starting the craze for "country" blues or in standardizing the style. His recordings were "unlike anything that had appeared on record before ... men who, unlike the classic blues singers, wrote almost all their own material"; Robert Dixon and John Goodrich, *Recording the Blues* (New York: Stein and Day, 1970), 34.

7. As quoted in Peter Guralnick, *Searching for Robert Johnson* (New York: Plume, 1998; rpt. of Dutton, 1989), 22.

8. Peter Guralnick, *The Listener's Guide to the Blues* (New York: Quarto Books, 1982), 20. Bing Crosby, the Andrews Sisters, and Guy Lombardo were among the many musicians to record cover versions of "You Are My Sunshine."

9. This formulation owes a good deal to Michelle M. Moody-Adams, *Fieldwork in Familiar Places: Morality, Culture, and Philosophy* (Harvard University Press, 1997). African American identity, argues K. Anthony Appiah, "cannot be seen as constructed solely within African American communities." Nor can it be seen as a shared set of beliefs, values, and practices: "what exists are African-American cultures, and though these are created and sustained *in large measure* by African-Americans, they cannot be understood without reference to the bearers of other American racial identities." K. Anthony Appiah, in Appiah and Amy Gutmann, *Color Consciousness: The Political Morality of Race* (Princeton University Press, 1996), 95–96, emphasis added.

10. Charles Keil, "People's Music Comparatively: Style and Stereotype, Class and Hegemony," in Charles Keil and Steven Feld, *Music Grooves: Essays and Dialogues* (University of Chicago Press, 1994), 199–200. For a fuller account of the degree to which the blues had a truly mixed ancestry in the musics of both whites and African Americans, see Peter Van Der Merwe, *Origins of the Popular Style: The Antecedents of Twentieth-Century Popular Music* (Oxford: Clarendon, 1989); Brian Ward, *Just My Soul Responding: Rhythm and Blues, Black Consciousness, and Race Relations* (University of California Press, 1998); Philip Tagg, "Open Letter: 'Black Music,' 'Afro-American Music,' and 'European Music,'" *Popular Music* 8 (1989): 285–98; Wilfrid Mellers, *A Darker Shade of Pale* (Oxford University Press, 1985); and David Hatch and Stephen Millward, *From Blues to Rock: An Analytical History of Pop Music* (Manchester University Press, 1987).

11. Transcribed from *Paul Simon: Born at the Right Time* (WNET/American Masters Special; commercial release by Warner/Reprise, 1992). Other information on Simon taken from Patrick Humphries, *Paul Simon: Still Crazy After All These Years* (New York: Doubleday, 1988), and Jon Landau, "Paul Simon: 'Like a Pitcher of Water,'" in Ben Fong-Torres, ed., *The Rolling Stone Interviews*, vol. 2 (New York: Warner Paperback, 1973), 389–430, interview conducted 1972.

12. As he would for Ladysmith Black Mambazo in 1986 and 1988, Paul Simon produced a 1972 album by Los Incas.

13. Landau interview, 399.

14. Paul Simon in *Paul Simon: Born at the Right Time.* Returning to his musical roots, Simon had the Everly Brothers contribute backing vocals to the album.

15. E.g., Steven Feld, "Notes on 'World Beat,'" in Keil and Feld, *Music Grooves*, 238–46. Another critic is George Lipsitz, who dogmatically insists that Simon violated the United Nations boycott. He criticizes intercultural collaborations like Simon's for failing to examine the power relations at work in such postmodern music; "however well-motivated," such music is insufficiently reciprocal and hides the "privileges, evasions, and contradictions" of American "whiteness." Lipsitz, *Dangerous Crossroads: Popular Music, Postmodernism and the Poetics of Place* (New York: Verso, 1994), 57, 63. See also Robert Christgau, "South African Romance," *Village Voice*, 23 September 1986, 71–3, 84, and Charles Hamm, "Graceland Revisited," *Popular Music* 8:3 (October 1989): 299–304.

16. Tony Mitchell, *Popular Music and Local Identity: Rock, Pop, and Rap in Europe and Oceania* (Leicester University Press, 1996), 83. As I later observe, this claim is really an unsupported complaint about the problematic content of Simon's message.

17. The first such song was the Kinks' hypnotic ballad, "See My Friends" (July 1965), which simulated the sound of a sitar through the use of a drone created from the feedback on an electric guitar. Within three months the Byrds used the same technique for "If You're Gone." For a discussion of this trend in British rock, with special emphasis on "See My Friends," see Jonathan Bellman, "Indian Resonances in the British Invasion, 1965–1968," in J. Bellman, ed., *The Exotic in Western Music* (Northeastern University Press, 1998), 292–306.

18. Peter Brown and Steven Gaines, *The Love You Make: An Insider's Story of the Beatles* (New York: McGraw Hill, 1983), 211.

19. David Crosby and Carl Gottlieb, *Long Time Gone: The Autobiography of David Crosby* (New York: Doubleday, 1988), 99. According to some accounts, Crosby also served as George Harrison's original introduction to the sitar, but Crosby himself is unsure and Harrison's account makes no mention of Crosby.

20. For a fuller account, see Jim Miller, "The Sound of Philadelphia," in Jim Miller, ed., *The Rolling Stone Illustrated History of Rock and Roll*, 2nd ed. (New York: Random House/Rolling Stone Press, 1980), 369–73, and Nelson George, *The Death of Rhythm and Blues* (New York: Plume, 1988), 142–46.

21. As quoted in Roy Carr and Charles Shaar Murray, *Bowie: An Illustrated Record* (New York: Avon, 1981), 72; from an interview in *Playboy* magazine, 1976.

22. Bruno Nettl, *The Study of Ethnomusicology: Twenty-Nine Issues and Concepts* (University of Illinois Press, 1983), 116. Following Wilhem Tappert, Nettl calls songs "the most indefatigable tourists of the world."

23. As quoted in Joe Smith, *Off the Record: An Oral History of Popular Music* (New York: Warner, 1988), 115.

24. Moody-Adams, *Fieldwork in Familiar Places*, 21. See also Hans-Rudolf Wicker, "From Complex Culture to Cultural Complexity," in Pnina Werbner and Tariq Modood, eds., *Debating Cultural Hybridity: Multi-Cultural Identities and the Politics of Anti-Racism* (London: Zed, 1997), 29–45.

25. Keith Negus takes pains to observe that Americans and Europeans are not the only ones engaged in such practices; Keith Negus, *Popular Music in Theory: An Introduction* (Wesleyan University Press, 1997), 170.

26. Because even early rock and roll drew on a variety of musical traditions and because only a small portion of rock music has ever been blues music as that is normally understood, it makes little or no sense for critics like Martha Bayles to insist that recent rock music can only regain its "soul" by returning to its blues roots. See Martha Bayles, *Hole in Our Soul: The Loss of Beauty and Meaning in American Popular Music* (New York: Free Press, 1994), 109. My thanks to Donald C. Meyer for getting me to clarify this point.

27. Timothy D. Taylor, *Global Pop: World Music, World Markets* (New York: Routledge, 1997), 40. Taylor also emphasizes that appropriation "betoken[s] old forms of racism, and long-standing western views of nonwestern peoples and cultures" (p. 201). Accusations similar to Taylor's are made by Rick Glanvill, "World Music Mining: The International Trade in New Music," in F. Hanly and T. May, eds., *Rhythms of the World* (London: BBC, 1989).

28. A good introduction is John Tomlinson, *Cultural Imperialism: A Critical Introduction* (Johns Hopkins University Press, 1991). Two interesting accounts of the Americanization of different cultures are Jonathan Zilberg, "Yes, It's True: Zimbabweans Love Dolly Parton," *Journal of Popular Culture* 29:1 (1995): 111–25, and Beverly James, "The Reception of American Popular Culture by Hungarians," *Journal of Popular Culture* 29:2 (1995): 97–108.

29. As quoted in Robert L. Doerschuk, "Frontman: David Bowie," *Musician*, April 1997, 11.

30. As quoted in Pete Welding, "Johnny Otis: The History of Rhythm and Blues," in Ben Fong-Torres, ed., *The Rolling Stone Interviews*, vol. 2 (New York: Warner Paperback, 1973), 320; interview conducted in 1971.

31. Charles Keil, "Dialogue Three," in Keil and Feld, *Music Grooves*, 315.

32. Charles Keil, *Urban Blues* (University of Chicago Press, 1966), 82. Marshall Chess observed his father's interactions with Waters on numerous occasions and responds to the idea of "Leonard as the plantation owner" with the observation that "Muddy probably never could have talked that way to a plantation owner," that is, without always agreeing. As quoted in Sandra B. Tooze, *Muddy Waters: The Mojo Man* (Toronto: ECW Press, 1997), 155.

33. The position that I am reading into Keil is outlined by John Tomlinson, *Cultural Imperialism*, chap. 4. A more generic version of the same idea is common in writing about rock. For a clear example, see Fred Goodman, *The Mansion on the Hill: Dylan, Young, Geffen, Springsteen, and the Head-On Collision of Rock and Commerce* (New York: Times Books, 1997). In response to Goodman, see Deena Weinstein, "Art Versus Commerce: Deconstructing a (Useful) Romantic Illusion," in Karen Kelly and Evelyn McDonnell, eds., *Stars Don't Stand Still in the Sky: Music and Myth* (New York University Press, 1999), 56–69.

34. Keil, *Urban Blues*, chap. 3; Amiri Baraka, "The Great Music Robbery," in *The Music: Reflections on Jazz and Blues* (New York: Morrow, 1987), 328–32. An excellent response to Baraka is Joel Rudinow, "Race, Ethnicity, Expressive Authenticity: Can White People Sing the Blues?" *Journal of Aesthetics and Art Criticism* 52 (1994): 127–37; reprinted in Philip Alperson, ed., *Musical Worlds: New Directions in the Philosophy of Music* (Pennsylvania State University Press, 1998), 159–69.

35. Keil, "Dialogue Two," *Music Grooves*, 170. Sounding remarkably like Theodor Adorno, Keil thinks that if it does not remain local, it risks becoming fascist. John Hutnyk contends that Adorno's position is really an attack on bourgeois taste directed at commodified music. But like Keil, Hutnyk contends that popular music cannot contribute to "revolutionary" politics as long as "the market remains intact." John Hutnyk, "Adorno at WOMAD: South Asian Crossovers and the Limits of Hybridity-Talk," in Werbner and Modood, *Debating Cultural Hybridity*, 106–36.

36. Keil, "Dialogue Three," *Music Grooves*, 321. Keil ignores the fact that some cultures treat songs as the unique property of specific individuals, so that it is wrong for anyone to ever sing another's song without an explicit transfer of ownership (e.g., among some Pacific Northwest Indians).

37. Keil, "Dialogue Three," 314. While I do not dwell on it in my argument, I do not want to overlook the fact that many African American musicians have been cheated by the music industry. On the other hand, the widespread practice of "pirating" recordings (copying and selling them without paying appropriate royalties) can be more harmful to local musicians than to international stars; see R. Wallis and K. Malm, *Big Sounds From Small People* (London: Constable, 1984), 138.

38. Keil, "Dialogue Three," 325.

39. As quoted in Smith, *Off the Record*, 114.

40. Peter Burger, *Pyramids of Sacrifice* (Harmondsworth: Allen Lane, 1974).

41. Jean-Jacques Rousseau, *Emile or On Education*, trans. Allan Bloom (New York: Basic Books, 1979), 341. Rousseau's critique of unnatural taste occupies much of the latter segment of book 4.

42. As quoted in Humphries, *Paul Simon*, 127. No source cited, but the remarks may have been at a London press conference. Orchestra Jazira, composed of

musicians from Ghana and Britain, similarly believes that African music can convey important messages to people outside Africa; see Charles Shaar Murray, "Orchestre Manoeuvres," *New Musical Express*, 5 March 1983, 16.

43. Keil, *Music Grooves*, 315.

44. Steven Feld, "Dialogue Three," *Music Grooves*, 311–18.

45. Davis, *History of the Blues*, 128.

46. See Lawrence N. Redd, *Rock Is Rhythm and Blues: The Impact of Mass Media* (Michigan State University Press, 1974), 130. Interviewing Crudup, Redd is explicitly searching for evidence that white musicians have "robbed" African American culture. Contrast Crudup's generosity with Public Enemy's single, "Fight the Power" (1989), which dismisses Elvis as a racist. The revisionist politics of their stance is documented by Ward, *Just My Soul Responding*, 134–42.

47. Rudinow, "Race, Ethnicity, Expressive Authenticity," 129–32.

48. E.g., Amiri Baraka, "Jazz Criticism and Its Effect on the Art Form," in David Blake, ed., *New Perspectives on Jazz* (Washington: Smithsonian Institution Press, 1990), 62. The same problem faces Redd's argument that "white America ... is guilty of robbing black America of one of its most treasured possessions—rhythm and blues," in *Rock Is Rhythm and Blues*, xiii. For Baraka's related argument that whites wrongfully promote a false history of black music, see "The Great Music Robbery" in *The Music*.

49. Rudinow, 130–31. It is difficult to judge how seriously we should take verbs like "steal" and "rob" in arguments against appropriation. Intellectual property is a tricky thing, and there is a very different dynamic at work in borrowing from a culture's music or cuisine and literally appropriating its mineral rights.

50. See Francis Davis, *History of the Blues*, 179–80.

51. This argument is particularly clear in Baraka, "Jazz Criticism," 60–64.

52. Armond White, "Who Wants to See Ten Niggers Play Basketball?" in William Eric Perkins, ed., *Droppin' Science: Critical Essays on Rap Music and Hip-Hop Culture* (Temple University Press, 1996), 199.

53. Rudinow, 134. See Dr. John (Mac Rebennack) with Jack Rummel, *Dr. John: Under a Hoodoo Moon* (New York: St. Martin's, 1994), and Grace Lichtenstein and Laura Dankner, *Musical Gumbo: The Music of New Orleans* (New York: Norton, 1993), 143–53.

Chapter Six

Epigraphs: Albert Goldman, *Freakshow: The Rocksoulbluesjazzsickjewblackhumorsexpoppsych Gig and Other Scenes from the Counter-Culture* (New York: Atheneum, 1971), 113. Goldman's answer is that they may do so as a "tentative identity" that will lead them out of the confines of middle-class culture and to nonimitative, authentic freedom. Armond White, "Who Wants to See Ten Niggers Play Basketball?" in William Eric Perkins, ed., *Droppin' Science: Critical Essays on Rap Music and Hip-Hop Culture* (Temple University Press, 1996), 201.

1. Amiri Baraka, "The Great Music Robbery," in *The Music: Reflections on Jazz and Blues* (New York: Morrow, 1987), 259, emphasis added.

2. The same fear lies at the heart of many criticisms of "world beat" and "world music." A fine overview is Steven Feld, "From Schizophonia to Schismogenesis: On the Discourses and Commodification Practices of 'World Music' and 'World Beat,'" in Charles Keil and Steven Feld, *Music Grooves: Essays and Dialogues* (University of Chicago Press, 1994), 257–89. Feld devotes the second half of this piece to a justification of his own participation in "commodifying otherness." See also Timothy D. Taylor, *Global Pop: World Music, World Markets* (New York: Routledge, 1997).

3. Clifford Geertz, *The Interpretation of Cultures* (New York: Basic Books, 1973), 89. See also Clifford Geertz, *Available Light: Anthropological Reflections on Philosophical Topics* (Princeton University Press, 2000). Unfortunately, Geertz undervalues the significance of behaviors as a fundamental element of culture and he tends to neglect the ways that systems of signs connect with the practical activities of daily life. Geertz's influence has been considerable. A summary and critique of this influence are found in Richard Biernacki, "Language and the Shift from Signs to Practices in Cultural Inquiry," *History and Theory* 39 (2000): 289–310.

4. John Tomlinson, *Cultural Imperialism* (Johns Hopkins University Press, 1991), chap. 3.

5. Arnold Schering, "Musikalische Symbolkunde," in Edward Lippman, ed., *Musical Aesthetics: A Historical Reader,* vol. 3 (Stuyvesant, N.Y.: Pendragon, 1990), 194.

6. As quoted in Peter Guralnick, *Feel Like Going Home: Portraits in Blues and Rock 'n' Roll* (New York: Perennial Library, 1989), 85.

7. James Rooney, *Bossmen: Bill Monroe and Muddy Waters* (New York: Da Capo, 1971; republication with author emendations, New York: Dial, 1971), 107, 112. Ironically, Waters had difficulty persuading Leonard Chess to record the full band that Waters used in clubs. Having established a successful formula with only a slight updating of the Delta sound, Chess was afraid that anything else would alienate the audience. Chess recorded Waters for four years before allowing a session that featured the more raucous sound of the full Muddy Waters and His Blue Boys.

8. The implications of this point are explored more fully in Chapters 7 and 8. An important exception may be the basic narrative of a typical Hollywood film. Details may be misunderstood, but it is doubtful that movies and TV could constitute such powerful forms of cultural imperialism if they were not accessible and engaging as narratives across cultural and class boundaries. See Noël Carrol, *Mystifying Movies: Fads and Fallacies in Contemporary Film Theory* (Columbia University Press, 1988), 208–25.

9. Alan Lomax, "Appeal for Cultural Equity," *Journal of Communication* 27 (1977): 125–39. Bruno Nettl documents eight different ways that a culture can respond to the threat of cultural grayout; Bruno Nettl, *The Study of Ethnomusicology: Twenty-Nine Issues and Concepts* (University of Illinois Press, 1983), 349–52. More recent variants of this position are summarized by Keith Negus, *Popular Music in Theory: An Introduction* (Wesleyan University Press, 1997), chap. 6.

10. Amiri Baraka, "Jazz Criticism and Its Effect on the Art Form," in David Blake, ed., *New Perspectives on Jazz* (Washington: Smithsonian Institution Press, 1990), 69–70. See also Franklin Rosemont, "Preface," *Paul Garon, Blues and the*

Poetic Spirit (New York: Da Capo, 1978), 7–8, and Mary Ellison, *Lyrical Protest: Black Music's Struggle Against Discrimination* (New York: Praeger, 1989), particularly chap. 2.

11. Baraka, "Jazz Criticism," 56. This white appropriation includes critics and other intellectuals who shape taste and write about the history of the music.

12. Tomlinson, *Cultural Imperialism*, 95.

13. Ibid., 96.

14. For an overview of attempts to stifle rock, covering the years 1954 to 1986, see Linda Martin and Kerry Segrave, *Anti-Rock: The Opposition to Rock 'n' Roll* (Hamden, Conn.: Archon, 1988). See also Brian Ward, *Just My Soul Responding: Rhythm and Blues, Black Consciousness, and Race Relations* (University of California Press, 1998), chap. 3.

15. As quoted in James Miller, *Flowers in the Dustbin: The Rise of Rock and Roll, 1947–1977* (New York: Simon and Schuster, 1999), 59.

16. Tomlinson, *Cultural Imperialism*, 97–98. In contrast, George Lipsitz maintains that the key question is always "the consequences of cultural collusion and collision," and appropriation is to be condemned when it does not "advance emancipatory ends." George Lipsitz, *Dangerous Crossroads: Popular Music, Postmodernism and the Poetics of Place* (New York: Verso, 1994), 56. As is so often the case, we find a clash between consequentialist and nonconsequentialist critiques.

What are the actual outcomes? Some empirical studies conclude that although much of the world's popular music now sounds like Western commercial pop music, it retains a decidedly local flavor and often serves as a vehicle for affirming cultural uniqueness; see Deanna Campbell Robinson, Elizabeth B. Buck, Marlene Cuthbert, et al., *Music at the Margins: Popular Music and Global Cultural Diversity* (Newbury Park: Sage, 1991).

17. Greg Shaw, liner notes to *The Roots of British Rock* (Sire Records, 1975).

18. Charlie Gillett, *The Sound of the City: The Rise of Rock and Roll*, rev. 2nd ed. (New York: Da Capo, 1996), 23–35; the relevant section is reprinted in Clinton Heylin, ed., *The Penguin Book of Rock and Roll Writing* (New York: Viking, 1992), 6–22. See also Peter Guralnick, "Rockabilly," in Jim Miller, ed., *The Rolling Stone Illustrated History of Rock and Roll*, 2nd ed. (New York: Random House/Rolling Stone Press, 1980), 61–65.

19. "I just had to tag along," sings Fogerty on his song of that title; John Fogerty, *Centerfield* (Warner Bros. Records, 1985).

20. John Morthland, *The Best of Country Music* (Garden City, N.Y.: Doubleday/Dolphin, 1984), 264.

21. Morthland, 241–42.

22. Bryan Ferry, as quoted in Timothy White, *Rock Lives: Profiles and Interviews* (New York: Henry Holt, 1990), 549. John Cale says, "every Friday night at 7:00, bingo, there would be Alan Freed. . . . The teddy boys came from that program and I was the local teddy boy." Cale is hardly known for such music, but there is his devastating take on "Heartbreak Hotel" on *Slow Dazzle* (1975). As quoted in Scott Cohen, *Yakety Yak* (New York: Fireside, 1994), 147.

23. Dick Hebdige, *Subculture: The Meaning of Style* (London: Methuen, 1979), 51–52. See Paul Rock and Stanley Cohen, "The Teddy Boy," in Vernon Bogdanor

and Robert Skidelsky, eds., *The Age of Affluence 1951–1964* (London: Macmillan, 1970), 288–320. Singer Ian Dury recalls the importance of films like *Don't Knock the Rock* in the cultural formation of the Teds; see Ian Dury, "The Fifties: Razors Out at Rock Riot," in Tony Stewart, ed., *Cool Cats: 25 Years of Rock 'n' Roll Style* (New York: Delilah, 1982), 9–10.

24. Chuck Berry, *Chuck Berry: The Autobiography* (New York: Harmony Books, 1987), 226.

25. Hebdige, *Subculture*, 82.

26. Bruno Nettl observes that the fundamental values of the field of ethnomusicology prejudice its practitioners against hybrid, "polluted" genres; they routinely dismiss hybrid styles "as resulting from events that should not have taken place." Nettl, *Study of Ethnomusicology*, 319.

27. As quoted in Steven Solder, "Rock News," *Rolling Stone*, 8 August 1996, 22.

28. As quoted in Robert Palmer, "Muddy Waters: The Delta Sun Never Sets," *Rolling Stone*, 5 October 1978, 56.

29. Will Kymlicka, *Liberalism, Community, and Culture* (Oxford: Clarendon, 1989), 190. Kymlicka carefully distinguishes peoples who have been forced to assimilate against their own wishes from those who have been segregated involuntarily.

30. Ibid., emphasis added. One implication is that subcultures of voluntary immigrants are seldom entitled to collective rights, because in most cases it would force the dominant culture to bear the cost of maintaining a context for choice that the immigrants have chosen to disrupt.

31. Ibid., 165.

32. The purpose of such treatment is "to help ethnic groups and religious minorities express their cultural particularity and pride without hampering their success in the economic and political institutions of the dominant society," in Will Kymlicka, *Multicultural Citizenship: A Liberal Theory of Minority Rights* (Oxford University Press, 1995), 31.

33. This situation is quite different from the issue of styles like Motown, soul, and funk supplanting the blues tradition within the African American community as arising from within the community itself.

34. Ibid., 167–68. As Jeremy Waldron puts it, "Cultures live and grow. . . . To preserve or protect [a culture], or some favored version of it, artificially, in the face of change, is precisely to cripple the mechanisms of adaptation and compromise . . . with which all societies confront the outside world." Waldron, "Minority Cultures and the Cosmopolitan Alternative," in Will Kymlicka, ed., *The Rights of Minority Cultures* (Oxford University Press, 1995), 110.

35. See Leslie Green, "Internal Minorities and Their Rights," in Kymlicka, *Rights of Minority Cultures*, 256–72. Such a refusal presumes some notion of irrevocable racial community that is incompatible with the position on ethnicity endorsed to avoid assumptions about biological race.

36. Ray Charles interview, *Playboy*, March 1970, 69. Johnny Otis complained that not enough "black cats" got work through such channels to justify white appropriations; as quoted in Pete Welding, "Johnny Otis: The History of Rhythm and Blues," in Ben Fong-Torres, ed., *The Rolling Stone Interviews*, vol. 2 (New York: Warner Paperback, 1973), 319.

37. See Peter Guralnick, "Ray Charles," in Miller, ed., *The Rolling Stone Illustrated History of Rock and Roll*, 109–12. Guralnick reports that Big Bill Broonzy was particularly angered by "I've Got a Woman" (1955). Charles was not the only African American listening to the Opry; the Chambers Brothers, whose psychedelicized soul music was so popular in the late 1960s, were regular Opry listeners and were great fans of the Sons of the Pioneers. The degree to which "white" pop music influenced African American musicians is explored in Ward, *Just My Soul Responding*, chap. 1.

But many African Americans were hostile to the same music; in the 1940s, an anonymous interviewee in the Delta told one visiting folklorist, "I don't like white music at all.... Sometimes I have the radio on and hear whites and turn it off." As quoted in William R. Ferris, *Blues From the Delta* (New York: Da Capo, 1984; originally published 1978), 92.

38. In Joe Smith, *Off the Record: An Oral History of Popular Music* (New York: Warner, 1988), 75.

39. Davis, *History of the Blues*, 237.

40. Charles Keil, *Urban Blues* (University of Chicago Press, 1966), 2.

41. As quoted in Sandra B. Tooze, *Muddy Waters: The Mojo Man* (Toronto: ECW Press, 1997), 168.

42. As quoted in Rooney, *Bossmen*, 146. Waters goes on to express the hope that young African Americans will outgrow disposable pop ("that James Brown beat") and will come back to the blues when they get older.

43. Stanley Booth, *Rhythm Oil: A Journey Through the Music of the American South* (New York: Vintage, 1993), 103. Anecdotal information suggests that in many American cities, King's audience is evenly split between whites and blacks. However, while King continues to attract white blues fans, most of the blacks who attend his concerts are middle aged or older.

44. Nelson George, *The Death of Rhythm and Blues* (New York: Plume, 1988), 108. He suggests that whites often do a better job of drawing on these discarded styles than do younger black musicians.

45. Baraka, "Jazz Criticism," 56, and William H. Grier and Price M. Cobbs, *Black Rage* (New York: Bantam, 1968).

46. Keil, *Urban Blues*, 42–43. Johnny Otis also disparaged most of Motown's production as "diluted" music; see Pete Welding, "Johnny Otis," 316.

47. E.g., Baraka, "Jazz Criticism," 62. Even if corporate practices "water down" the music, that charge must be distinguished from Baraka's charge that racism is to blame.

48. See Tony Mitchell, *Popular Music and Local Identity: Rock, Pop, and Rap in Europe and Oceania* (Leicester University Press, 1996), chap. 3 (focusing on rock music in the Czech Republic).

Chapter Seven

Epigraph: As quoted in James Rooney, *Bossmen: Bill Monroe and Muddy Waters* (New York: Da Capo, 1971), 104.

1. Timothy Taylor explicitly points to Peter Gabriel's "subject position" to demonstrate that "Come Talk to Me" is a contemporary form of imperialism; Timothy D. Taylor, *Global Pop: World Music, World Markets* (Routledge, 1997), chap. 2. Taylor also provides an extended description of the music and lyrics of "Come Talk to Me," but he offers no evidence that Gabriel's music (as opposed to Gabriel's studio practice) expresses disrespect toward the African drummers featured on the track.

2. A variant of the problem I've been highlighting can be found in a recent textbook on rock music that claims to teach "social history" through rock music; one chapter proposes that the white blues boom of the 1960s should be read in the context of escalating student unrest in response to Vietnam. Yet aside from selected song lyrics (not all of them from blues), the only evidence connecting the two trends is their general coincidence. See David P. Szatmary, *Rockin' in Time: A Social History of Rock-and-Roll,* 3rd ed. (Upper Saddle River, N.J.: Prentice Hall, 1996), chap. 10.

3. Bruno Nettl, *The Study of Ethnomusicology: Twenty-Nine Issues and Concepts* (University of Illinois Press, 1983), 259. How far can we push this attitude? "I felt that after the novelty had worn off the Americans didn't really understand our music or our culture," complains Kinks cofounder Dave Davies, *Kink: An Autobiography* (New York: Hyperion, 1996), 83.

4. This point harmonizes with Attali's claim that music arises when a structural code "tames" noise, with the obvious difference that I deny that any such code can be imposed on listeners. There are several interesting essays related to these themes in Thomas Swiss, John Sloop, and Andrew Herman, eds., *Mapping the Beat: Popular Music and Contemporary Theory* (Oxford: Blackwell, 1998).

5. Stephen Davies, *Musical Meaning and Expression* (Cornell University Press, 1994), 325, emphasis added. The same point is an important theme of Jerrold Levinson, *Music in the Moment* (Cornell University Press, 1997).

6. Jonathan Cott, "Leonard Bernstein," *Rolling Stone,* 29 November 1990, 83, 86. Explaining why he prefers the sounds of traffic to most Western music, John Cage tells the story of visiting African royalty who listens to a concert of classical music and afterwards asks why they kept replaying the same thing.

7. Martyn Evans, *Listening to Music* (London: Macmillan, 1990), 11.

8. Clifford Geertz, "Art as a Cultural System," *Modern Language Notes* 91 (1974): 1475, 1497; Geertz cites Nelson Goodman as an important influence.

9. Lawrence Grossberg, "Is Anybody Listening? Does Anybody Care? On the State of 'Rock,'" in Andrew Ross and Tricia Rose, eds., *Microphone Fiends: Youth Music and Youth Culture* (Routledge, 1994), 48.

10. Davies, *Musical Meaning and Expression,* 326.

11. For a summary of recent work on this topic, see Davies, *Musical Meaning,* chap. 5. See also Peter Kivy, *Sound Sentiment* (Temple University Press, 1989).

12. As quoted in Eric Tamm, *Brian Eno: His Music and the Vertical Color of Sound* (Boston: Faber and Faber, 1989), 17.

13. Rian Malan, "In the Jungle," *Rolling Stone,* 25 May 2000, 54–66.

14. As quoted in "Dialogue Three: Commodified Grooves," in Charles Keil and Steven Feld, *Music Grooves: Essays and Dialogues* (University of Chicago Press, 1994), 309.

15. Think here of W.V.O. Quine's situation of radical translation, of trying to produce a translation manual for a totally unfamiliar language, but in this case there is no opportunity to interact with a native guide.

16. These admissions do not imply that musical meanings are either arbitrary or subjective associations; whether a particular piece of music bears specific expressive qualities is as objective and as publicly accessible as the fact that two people are married or divorced. We might describe them as culturally emergent properties; see Joseph Margolis, *Art and Philosophy: Conceptual Issues in Aesthetics* (Atlantic Heights, N.J.: Humanities Press, 1980), 27–49.

17. Farrell (real name, Simon Bernstein) was interviewed by David Wojcik, *Punk and Neo-Tribal Body Art* (University of Mississippi Press, 1995), 28–31. In the late 1990s, trendy tattoos in the United States included Polynesian iconography and Chinese characters. Aerosmith and Madonna faced strong protests from Hindus when their ignorance about the visual symbols they borrowed bore sacrilegious implications; Aerosmith revised the cover of *Nine Lives* to correct the problem, while Madonna simply went on to plunder a different culture.

18. These charges against "uncomprehending appropriation" are from George Lipsitz, *Dangerous Crossroads: Popular Music, Postmodernism and the Poetics of Place* (New York: Verso, 1994), 169.

19. Incommensurability is the incomparability of competing values or value systems. For an extended discussion, see Ruth Chang, ed., *Incommensurability, Incomparability, and Practical Reason* (Harvard University Press, 1997).

20. Charles Keil, *Urban Blues* (University of Chicago Press, 1966), vii.

21. As quoted in Charles Aaron, "What the White Boy Means When He Says Yo," *Spin*, November 1998, 128.

22. Amiri Baraka, "Jazz Criticism and Its Effect on the Art Form," in David Blake, ed., *New Perspectives on Jazz* (Washington: Smithsonian Institution Press, 1990), 58.

23. This reading is inconsistent with an African American perspective that regards disco as an insipid white appropriation of black beats; whites confused disco with black dance music, and when market saturation led to a general backlash against disco, popular music became more racially segregated. See Rickey Vincent, *Funk: The Music, the People, and the Rhythm of the One* (New York: St. Martin's Griffin, 1996), 214–15. Disco, opines Vincent, "in fact, sucked."

24. Baraka, "Jazz Criticism," 56. I am going to ignore the intertwined argument that racist white audiences and critics routinely judge the music as inferior, since it is not clear why whites are so keen to steal something they regard as so inferior.

25. Taj Mahal (Henry St. Claire Fredericks), interviewed and as quoted in the liner notes for Taj Mahal, *Taj's Blues*, Columbia/Legacy Compact Disc (Sony Music Entertainment, 1992).

26. Baraka as LeRoi Jones, *Blues People* (New York: William Morrow/Quill, 1963), 217–19. Hastily jumping to the relativist's conclusion, Baraka says that only "black institutions" can "objectively" respond to black music; Baraka, "Jazz Criticism," 70.

Chapter Eight

Epigraph: Ry Cooder, as quoted in Joe Smith, *Off the Record: An Oral History of Popular Music* (New York: Warner, 1988), 317.

1. This formulation is adapted from David Whewell, "Aestheticism," in David Cooper, *A Companion to Aesthetics* (Oxford: Blackwell, 1992), 6. The same doctrine will be addressed as "strict autonomism" in the closing chapter.

2. As quoted in Greil Marcus, *Ranters and Crowd Pleasers: Punk in Pop Music, 1977–92* (New York: Doubleday, 1993), 304. Strummer followed with a dig at the Police's "white reggae" by asking, "You hear that, Sting?"

3. T. S. Eliot, *Notes Towards the Definition of Culture* (New York: Harcourt Brace, 1942), 63–64.

4. Harrison's comment about Presley is from *VH1: 100 Greatest Artists of Rock and Roll* television broadcast, 15 September 1999.

5. As quoted in Jock Baird, "Peter Gabriel's Visitation," *Musician*, June 1989, 38.

6. See Pete Welding, "Johnny Otis: The History of Rhythm and Blues," in Ben Fong-Torres, ed., *The Rolling Stone Interviews*, vol. 2 (New York: Warner Paperback, 1973), 317. If Otis were more reflective about such matters, we might call him a race traitor.

7. Review of Captain Beefheart's *The Spotlight Kid*, in Robert Christgau, *Christgau's Record Guide: Rock Albums of the Seventies* (New Haven: Ticknor and Fields, 1981), 74.

8. Some musicians work over recordings of another culture's music, as Peter Gabriel did for "Come Talk to Me" or as Joni Mitchell did for "The Jungle Line" (1975), but the resulting multilayered recording is no less a hybrid as a consequence.

9. Jerrold Levinson, *Music in the Moment* (Cornell University Press, 1997), 32; Frank Sibley, "Making Music Our Own," in Michael Krausz, ed., *The Interpretation of Music: Philosophical Essays* (Oxford University Press, 1993), 173–74. The discussion of basic musical understanding that follows owes an obvious debt to Levinson. In an exchange in 1998, he remarked that once you have basic musical understanding, "you have 90 percent" of what there is to get out of a piece of music. I won't quibble about the precise amount, but it strikes me as a good ballpark estimate.

10. In an important respect, therefore, musical appropriation is free of Orientalism as defined by Edward Said, *Orientalism* (New York: Vintage, 1979), 1–5.

11. George Lipsitz, *Dangerous Crossroads: Popular Music, Postmodernism and the Poetics of Place* (New York: Verso, 1994), 61.

12. I do not reduce organization to form. Tone color, tempo, and volume are equally important elements of organization in popular music, facilitating expressiveness. See Theodore Gracyk, *Rhythm and Noise: An Aesthetics of Rock* (Duke University Press, 1996), chaps. 4 and 5.

13. A position that I defended earlier in Chapters 2 and 3.

14. But this does not imply that listeners must be able to articulate precise relationships holding between a piece and its historical precedents; not every Cream

fan can (or should) aspire to the level of detail in Dave Headlam, "Blues Transformations in the Music of Cream," in John Covach and Graeme M. Boone, eds., *Understanding Rock: Essays in Musical Analysis* (Oxford University Press, 1997), 59–92. I concur with Stephen Davies that knowing some relevant musical history is far more important than having a technical vocabulary. See Davies, *Musical Meaning and Expression* (Cornell University Press, 1994), 369.

15. Judith Butler, *Excitable Speech: A Politics of the Performative* (Routledge, 1997). See also Lawrence Grossberg, "Another Boring Day in Paradise: Rock and Roll and the Empowerment of Everyday Life," in Grossberg, *Dancing in Spite of Myself: Essays on Popular Culture* (Duke University Press, 1997), 35.

16. See Eric Lott, *Love and Theft: Blackface Minstrelsy and the American Working Class* (Oxford University Press, 1995), chap. 7.

17. As Michael Baxandall notes in his celebrated discussion of Piero della Francesca's *The Baptism of Christ*, no modern viewer will ever possess a "participant's" grasp of the culture and values expressed in that painting. Nonetheless, visitors to London's National Gallery have the opportunity to test their "observer's" knowledge of that world against the rich and subtle participant's knowledge expressed in the insider's behavior of painting that particular canvas. See Michael Baxandall, *Patterns of Intention: On the Historical Explanation of Pictures* (Yale University Press, 1985), chap. 4.

18. Both the contradictory position being described and the specific examples are from Timothy D. Taylor, *Global Pop: World Music, World Markets* (Routledge, 1997), chap. 3.

19. Davies, *Musical Meaning*, 272.

20. Lisa Heldke, "Let's Cook Thai: Recipes for Colonialism," unpublished manuscript. See also Dorothy Lee, "Cultural Factors in Dietary Choice," *Freedom and Culture* (Prospect Heights, Ill.: Waveland, 1987), 154–61.

21. Davies, 326.

22. Timothy Taylor comes very close to making this point in his discussion of world music promotion that emphasizes the music's "sheer freshness"; Taylor, *Global Pop*, 20.

23. I extend this argument in Chapter 12 when I consider the implications of identifying with the music one hears.

24. Davies, 380. While historical information will be needed (as in the earlier example of the war in Vietnam as a background for interpreting certain songs), stylistic precedents are no less essential to an understanding of musical expression, a point that I defended in Chapters 3 and 4.

25. If we follow Stephen Davies's additional suggestion that we understand the music only by working out the musical "question" to which it might be the "answer," then we can also ask about the "question" to which the choice of a particular cover version is the "answer." It is sometimes legitimate to wonder what "question" is implicit in Patti Smith's decision to cover Bob Dylan's "Wicked Messenger" in 1996, as opposed to the Faces' decision to cover the same song in 1970. Is there a different "question" in place simply because a woman chooses to perform it? See Davies, *Musical Meaning and Expression*, chap. 7.

Chapter Nine

Epigraphs: Clinton Heylin, "Introduction," *The Penguin Book of Rock and Roll Writing* (New York: Viking, 1992), xvi; Barbara O'Dair, "Across the Great Divide," in Karen Kelly and Evelyn McDonnell, eds., *Stars Don't Stand Still in the Sky: Music and Myth* (New York University Press, 1999), 250.

1. Simon Reynolds and Joy Press, *The Sex Revolts: Gender, Rebellion, and Rock 'n' Roll* (Harvard University Press, 1995), 234.

2. Ellen Willis, "Janis Joplin," in Jim Miller, ed., *The Rolling Stone Illustrated History of Rock and Roll*, 2nd ed. (New York: Random House/Rolling Stone Press, 1980), 278.

3. Simon Frith, "Rock and the Politics of Memory," in Sohnya Sayres et al., eds., *The 60s Without Apology* (University of Minnesota Press, 1984), 66.

4. Ibid.

5. Anna Garlin Spencer, "Woman's Share in Social Culture," in Miriam Schneir, ed., *Feminism: The Essential Historical Writings* (New York: Vintage, 1994), 285.

6. R. J. Smith, "Lilith Fair," *Spin*, September 1998, 90. Smith's summary will strike Lilith fans as simplistic, but it captures mainstream reaction. At the same time, the three compilations of live Lilith recordings have done little to refute Smith's description.

7. These points are explored more fully in any standard introduction to the subject. See, for instance, James A. Doyle and Michele A. Paludi, *Sex and Gender: The Human Experience*, 4th ed. (Boston: McGraw-Hill, 1998).

8. Judith Butler, "Imitation and Gender Insubordination," in Diana Fuss, ed., *Inside/Outside: Lesbian Theories, Gay Theories* (Routledge, 1991), 27. Butler's main point is that if the "natural woman" is a cultural product, so are sexual categories themselves; we have no neutral way of delineating what's biological (sex) from what's social (gender). The same point is argued by Alison M. Jaggar, *Feminist Politics and Human Nature* (Totowa, N.J.: Rowman and Littlefield, 1983), 106–13.

9. Jonathan Culler, *Literary Theory: A Very Short Introduction* (Oxford University Press, 1997), 14.

10. W. Gantz, H. Gartenberg, M. Pearson, and S. Schiller, "Gratifications and Expectations Associated With Pop Music Among Adolescents," *Popular Music and Society* 6 (1978): 81–89.

11. Lisa Lewis, *Gender Politics and MTV: Voicing the Difference* (Temple University Press, 1990), chaps. 7 and 8.

12. John Shepherd, "Music Consumption and Cultural Self-Identities: Some Theoretical and Methodological Reflections," *Media, Culture, and Society* 8 (1986): 328. A confirmation of this finding is found in Gregory T. Toney and James B. Weaver III, "Effects of Gender and Gender Role Self-Perception on Affective Reactions to Rock Music Videos," *Sex Roles* 30 (1994): 567–83.

13. Peter G. Christenson and Jon Brian Peterson, "Genre and Gender in the Structure of Music Preferences," *Communication Research* 15 (1988): 298, 285. Examining British dance clubs and raves in the 1980s and early 1990s, Sarah Thornton found that when subcultures fear "their" taste is becoming mainstream, they distance

themselves from it. The older trend is then "feminized" (dismissed as appealing to white, heterosexual, working-class girls). See Sarah Thornton, *Club Cultures: Music, Media, and Subcultural Capital* (Wesleyan University Press, 1996), chap. 3.

14. Simon Frith, *Music for Pleasure: Essays in the Sociology of Pop* (New York: Routledge, 1988), 183.

15. See Will Straw, "Sizing Up Record Collections: Gender and Connoisseurship in Rock Music Culture," in Sheila Whiteley, ed., *Sexing the Groove: Popular Music and Gender* (Routledge, 1997), 3–16.

16. Nick Hornby, *High Fidelity* (New York: Riverhead, 1995), 37.

17. As quoted in Dave Marsh, *The First Rock and Roll Confidential Report* (New York: Pantheon, 1985), 165. I was made aware of this quotation in Susan McClary, *Feminine Endings: Music, Gender, and Sexuality* (University of Minnesota Press, 1991), 151.

18. Steve Chapple and Reebee Garofalo, *Rock 'n' Roll Is Here to Pay: The History and Politics of the Music Industry* (Chicago: Nelson-Hall, 1977), chap. 8. Music is so fundamentally social and public that women's efforts are blocked more effectively than with many other modes of expression. With writing, for instance, women often have turned to journals, letters, and other "private" forums for recording their responses to the world and their place in it.

19. Whiteley, *Sexing the Groove,* especially Sara Cohen, "Men Making a Scene: Rock Music and the Production of Gender," 17–36; Mavis Bayton, "Women and the Electric Guitar," 37–49; Norma Coates, "(R)evolution Now? Rock and the Political Potential of Gender," 50–64.

20. As quoted in Christina Kelly, "Melissa Etheridge," *Rolling Stone,* 13 November 1997, 159. In the same issue, Tori Amos recalls hearing very similar explanations of why her music was not played on the radio; Susan Cheever, "Tori Amos," 104.

21. The original Riot Grrrl movement peaked in 1992, when bands like Bikini Kill, Huggy Bear, and Babes in Toyland attracted so much media attention that they began to disavow the label. Yet five years later it peaked again, as Sleater-Kinney's *Dig Me Out* (1997) was ranked in the top five of the *Village Voice*'s annual critics poll. For more background on Riot Grrrl bands, see Lucy O'Brien, *She Bop: The Definitive History of Women in Rock, Pop, and Soul* (New York: Penguin, 1995), chap. 5, and Evelyn McDonnell, "Rebel Girls," in Barbara O'Dair, ed., *Trouble Girls: The Rolling Stone Book of Women in Rock* (New York: Random House, 1997), 453–63. For a theoretical discussion, see Mary Celeste Kearney, "The Missing Links: Riot Grrrl–Feminism–Lesbian Culture," in Whiteley, *Sexing the Groove,* 207–29; Marion Leonard, "'Rebel Girl, You Are the Queen of My World': Feminism, 'Subculture' and Grrrl Power," also in Whiteley, 230–55; and Neil Nehring, *Popular Music, Gender, and Postmodernism: Anger Is an Energy* (Thousand Oaks: Sage, 1997).

22. Simon Frith and Angela McRobbie, "Rock and Sexuality," in Simon Frith and Andrew Goodwin, eds., *On Record: Rock, Pop, and the Written Word* (New York: Pantheon, 1990), 384; originally in *Screen Education* 29 (1978).

23. For instance, Jim Miller, "Rock's New Women," *Newsweek,* 4 March 1985, 48–57; Miller endorses the orthodox position of the time, celebrating Cyndi Lauper as progressive while putting down Madonna as "fluffy" pop.

24. Frith and McRobbie, 377.

25. Lewis, *Gender Politics and MTV,* 5, 55. Lewis is summarizing the early years of MTV, but her argument also makes the case that MTV reflected the ideology of rock as something different from pop music.

26. Frith and McRobbie, "Rock and Sexuality," 372. In Chapter 11, I discuss Frith's acknowledgment that their position contains its own implicit essentialism.

27. Gisela Breitling, "Speech, Silence, and the Discourse of Art: On Conventions of Speech and Feminine Consciousness," in Gisela Ecker, ed., *Feminist Aesthetics,* trans. Harriet Anderson (Boston: Beacon, 1986), 164.

28. As quoted in O'Brien, *She Bop,* 149 (from an article in the *New Musical Express,* 1993).

29. Frith and McRobbie, "Rock and Sexuality," 372.

Chapter Ten

Epigraphs: Stewart, as quoted in Michael Cooper and Terry Southern, *The Early Stones: Legendary Photographs of a Band in the Making: 1963–1973* (New York: Hyperion, 1992), 76; Simon Reynolds and Joy Press, *The Sex Revolts: Gender, Rebellion, and Rock 'n' Roll* (Harvard University Press, 1995), 387.

1. Karen Durbin, "Can a Feminist Love the World's Greatest Rock and Roll Band?" *Ms.,* October 1974, 23, 24.

2. Susan Hiwatt, "Cock Rock," in Jonathan Eisen, ed., *Twenty-Minute Fandangos and Forever Changes: A Rock Bazaar* (New York: Vintage, 1971), 144.

3. Norma Coates, "(R)evolution Now? Rock and the Political Potential of Gender," in Sheila Whiteley, ed., *Sexing the Groove: Popular Music and Gender* (Routledge, 1997), 50. See also Terri Sutton, "Women, Sex, and Rock 'n' Roll," in Evelyn McDonnell and Ann Powers, eds., *Rock She Wrote: Women Write About Rock, Pop, and Rap* (New York: Cooper Square Press, 1995), 376–81; Renee Cox, "A History of Music," *Journal of Aesthetics and Art Criticism* 48 (1990): 395–409; and Eisa Davis, "Sexism and the Art of Feminist Hip-Hop Maintenance," in Rebecca Walker, ed., *To Be Real: Telling the Truth and Changing the Face of Feminism* (New York: Anchor, 1995), 127–41. Cox explores her attraction to music of the Rolling Stones and Davis explores her immersion in hip-hop culture in the face of their awareness that each denigrates women.

4. Susan McClary, *Feminine Endings: Music, Gender, and Sexuality* (University of Minnesota Press, 1991), 17–19.

5. McClary, *Feminine Endings,* 77–78.

6. Dave Marsh, "Onan's Greatest Hits," in Greil Marcus, ed., *Stranded: Rock and Roll for a Desert Island* (New York: Knopf, 1979), 227.

7. McClary, 156–58. Besides her appeal to music videos, McClary's overall argument depends heavily on the history of opera (Monteverdi's *L'Orfeo* and Bizet's *Carmen* receive individual chapters), suggesting that the visual dimension plays a central role in any musical construction of the "feminine."

8. Peter Mercer-Taylor, "Two-and-a-Half Centuries in the Life of a Hook," *Popular Music and Society* (Fall 1999): 1–15.

9. Edward Macan, *Rocking the Classics: English Progressive Rock and the Counterculture* (Oxford University Press, 1997), 43.

10. Ibid.

11. McClary, *Feminine Endings*, 153.

12. Gillian G. Gaar, *She's a Rebel: The History of Women in Rock and Roll* (Seattle: Seal, 1992), 89. See also Tina Turner, *I, Tina: My Life Story* (New York: Avon, 1987). Etta James also reports that the African American tradition granted her neither respect nor autonomy, but when she first worked with white musicians, "they all knew who I was and respected me. They more or less helped me learn how to be independent." As quoted in Katherine Dieckmann, "Etta James," *Rolling Stone*, 13 November 1997, 152.

13. Tina Turner, as quoted in Lucy O'Brien, *She Bop: The Definitive History of Women in Rock, Pop, and Soul* (New York: Penguin, 1995), 124, 126; O'Brien's source is an interview conducted by David Toop in 1992.

14. bell hooks, *Black Looks: Race and Representation* (Toronto: Between the Lines, 1992), 157, 159. Also see bell hooks, "Is Paris Burning?" *Zeta Magazine*, 6 June 1991, 60–64, where hooks likewise complains that Madonna is just another in a long line of whites who profit from their abusive appropriations. It is worth noting that Madonna's breakthrough single, "Holiday" (1983), was released in a sleeve that did not picture the singer. Drawing on the "Dance Music" of the New York club scene, Sire Records assumed that the song would not do well if club audiences knew that she was white.

15. McClary, *Feminine Endings*, 153.

16. Simon Frith, *Performing Rites: On the Value of Popular Music* (Harvard University Press, 1996), 104.

17. Stanley Booth, *Rhythm Oil: A Journey Through the Music of the American South* (New York: Vintage, 1991), 107. Booth saw the show, covering it for *Rolling Stone*.

18. Brian Ward, *Just My Soul Responding* (University of California Press, 1998), 248.

19. Frith, *Performing Rites*, 191.

20. Some theorists seek answers to these questions by hypothesizing about the human unconscious, employing a modified form of psychoanalytic theory to explain why popular culture is infused with portrayals that objectify and demean women. The most important model of such thinking is Laura Mulvey, "Visual Pleasure and Narrative Cinema," *Screen* 16 (1975): 6–18; reprinted in Mulvey, *Visual and Other Pleasures* (Indiana University Press, 1989). I am among those who regard this use of psychoanalytic theory as a mistake, believing that its theoretical claims lack adequate empirical confirmation.

21. As quoted in John Lamb, "The Nine Lives of Aerosmith," *High Plains Reader*, 30 April 1998, 5.

22. Susan Brownmiller, *Against Our Will: Men, Women, and Rape* (New York: Simon and Schuster, 1975), 15, emphasis as in original.

23. Ibid., 394.

24. Camille Paglia has revived the position of biology as destiny; see Paglia, *Sexual Personae: Art and Decadence From Nefertiti to Emily Dickinson* (Yale University Press, 1990), 21.

25. Catharine A. MacKinnon, *Only Words* (Harvard University Press, 1993). To put her point in technical terms, she believes that the general context ensures that

such expressions share a common illocutionary intention, aiming to do harm even if the speaker does not consciously intend it.

26. Catharine A. MacKinnon, *Feminism Unmodified: Discourses on Life and the Law* (Harvard University Press, 1977), 198–205.

27. See MacKinnon, *Feminism Unmodified*, 176, and *Only Words*, 121, n. 32.

28. With her clothing ripped, her legs forced wide apart, and her arms tied over her head, the woman is certainly made into a sexual display. A photograph of the billboard version, defaced by Women Against Violence Against Women to say "This is a crime against women," can be found in Dave Marsh and Kevin Stein, *The Book of Rock Lists* (New York: Dell/Rolling Stone Press, 1981), 451. The print version of the advertisement can be found in *Rolling Stone*, 1 July 1976, 79.

29. MacKinnon, *Feminism Unmodified*, 137. Since representations can eroticize a situation without being sexually explicit, sexual explicitness is a mere accidental property of the alleged problem with pornography.

30. Sheri Kathleen Cole, "I Am the Eye, You Are the Victim: The Pornographic Ideology of Music Video," *Enculturation* 2:2 (Spring 1999).

31. Linda L. Lindsey, *Gender Roles: A Sociological Perspective*, 3rd ed. (Upper Saddle River, N.J.: Prentice Hall, 1997), 325. Country music (and country music video) is charged with the lesser crime of presenting and reinforcing gender stereotypes.

32. Sut Jhally (writer and director), *Dreamworlds 2: Desire/Sex/Power in Music Video* (Northampton, Mass.: Media Education Foundation, 1995). The thrust of this critique is far removed from the mainstream, puritanical objections that originally greeted MTV; see E. Gelman, "MTV's Message," *Newsweek*, 30 December 1985, 54–56. Empirical data relevant to Jhally's analysis can be found in Rita Sommers-Flanagan, John Sommers-Flanagan, and Britta Davis, "What's Happening on Music Television? A Gender Role Content Analysis," *Sex Roles* 28 (1993): 745–53.

33. *Nightline*, ABC Television, 3 December 1990. Madonna appeared on *Nightline* to discuss the MTV ban on her video for "Justify My Love." For a more comprehensive discussion of Madonna's videos, see Cathy Schwichtenberg, "Madonna's Postmodern Feminism: Bringing the Margins to the Center," and Melanie Morton, "Don't Go for Second Sex, Baby!" both in Cathy Schwichtenberg, ed. *The Madonna Connection: Representational Politics, Subcultural Identities, and Cultural Theory* (Boulder: Westview, 1993), 129–45 and 213–35 respectively.

34. Sheila Whiteley, "Little Red Rooster v. The Honky Tonk Woman," in Whiteley, *Sexing the Groove*, 95.

35. Richard Merton, "Comment on Stones," in Jonathan Eisen, ed., *The Age of Rock: Sounds of the American Cultural Revolution* (New York: Vintage, 1969), 116; originally published in *New Left Review* 47 (1968). Merton thus attributes the same strategy to the Stones that Angela Davis attributes to blues singers like "Ma" Rainey and Bessie Smith. See Angela Y. Davis, *Blues Legacies and Black Feminism* (New York: Pantheon, 1998), 25–33.

Chapter Eleven

Epigraphs: Audre Lorde, "The Master's Tools Will Never Dismantle the Master's House," in Cherrie Moraga and Gloria Anzaldua, eds., *This Bridge Called My*

Back: Writings by Radical Women of Color (Watertown, Mass.: Persephone, 1981), 99; Manson, as quoted in Jancee Dunn, *Rolling Stone*, 13 November 1997, 137; Barbero, as quoted in Lucy O'Brien, *She Bop: The Definitive History of Women in Rock, Pop, and Soul* (New York: Penguin, 1995), 165. The quote comes from an interview conducted by O'Brien in 1993.

1. The two positions are loosely aligned according to the differences between second-wave and third-wave feminism. If first-wave feminism was unified by the project of attaining equal rights and equal access for women, then its successes set the stage for a second wave centered on issues of gender formation. In practical terms this meant that attempts to forge a feminist aesthetic invited reflection on the social institutions that impact the art practices; female artists and musicians became increasingly interested in employing art as a vehicle for exploring collective politics in the struggle for feminine identity. A third wave has now emerged. Less concerned with the task of theorizing problems, the third wave concentrates on the fit between feminism and the practices of everyday life (e.g., Riot Grrrl bands). See Rita Alfonso and Jo Trigilio, "Surfing the Third Wave: A Dialogue Between Two Third-Wave Feminists," *Hypatia* 12 (1997): 7–16.

2. For examples of the ugly essentialism that still haunts the discourse of male intellectuals when confronted by any incursion of "feminine" values into the rock formation, see Norma Coates, "Can't We Just Talk About Music? Rock and Gender on the Internet," in Thomas Swiss, John Sloop, and Andrew Herman, eds., *Mapping the Beat: Popular Music and Contemporary Theory* (Oxford: Blackwell, 1998), 77–99.

3. Lisa Lewis, *Gender Politics and MTV: Voicing the Difference* (Temple University Press, 1990), 109.

4. As quoted in Michael Saunders, "Tracy Bonham Fights the 'Angry Woman Rocker' Stereotype," *Sacramento Bee*, 2 August 1996, Ticket section, p. 16.

5. This is not the silly idea that discursive practices create bodies, but rather the idea that our discursive practices always invite us to pay selective attention to our bodies, so that some aspects are regarded as essential to our identity in a way other aspects are not. My warning here is meant to block the sort of misreading that Neil Nehring gives to Robert Walser's remark that experiences of physical and emotional gestures are "dependent" on the concepts and metaphors through which we interpret them. Nehring accuses Walser of believing that bodies do not exist apart from discursive practices; see Neil Nehring, *Popular Music, Gender, and Postmodernism: Anger Is an Energy* (Thousand Oaks: Sage, 1997), 147–48.

6. Karen E. Petersen, "An Investigation Into Women-Identified Music in the United States," in Ellen Koskoff, ed., *Women and Music in Cross-Cultural Perspective* (University of Illinois Press, 1989), 211.

7. Elisabeth Lenk, "The Self-Reflecting Woman," in Gisela Ecker, ed., *Feminist Aesthetics*, trans. Harriet Anderson (Boston: Beacon, 1986), 57.

8. Kristen Hersh quoted in Laura Post, *Backstage Pass: Interviews With Women in Music* (Norwich, Vt.: New Victoria, 1997), 211.

9. A cause is not a justification: one can understand why male fans identify with the rapist of X's "Johny Hit and Run Paulene" without supporting that identification. The distinction is not always recognized by Nehring, *Popular Music, Gender, and Postmodernism*, particularly chap. 7.

10. Luce Irigaray, *This Sex Which Is Not One*, trans. Catherine Porter (Cornell University Press, 1985), 164. See also Rosemarie Tong, *Feminist Thought: A More Comprehensive Introduction* (Boulder: Westview, 1998), chs. 3 and 4, and Nancy Holstrom, "Human Nature," in Alison M. Jaggar and Iris M. Young, eds., *A Companion to Feminist Philosophy* (Oxford: Blackwell, 1998), 280–88. For an introduction to writers exploring a female aesthetic through gender essentialism rooted in psychoanalytic theory, see Rosemarie Buikema and Anneke Smelik, eds., *Women's Studies and Culture: A Feminist Introduction* (London: Zed, 1993), chap. 13.

11. A central text in challenging the essential commonality of "woman's" experience is bell hooks, *Ain't I a Woman: Black Women and Feminism* (Boston: South End, 1982). Several important essays are collected in Claudia Card, ed., *Feminist Ethics* (University Press of Kansas, 1991). See also E. V. Spelman, *Inessential Woman: Problems of Exclusion in Feminist Thought* (London: Women's Press, 1990).

12. For recent work on this issue, see Naomi Schor and Elizabeth Weed, *The Essential Difference* (Indiana University Press, 1994).

13. The retreat from gender essentialism has posed the converse problem of cultural essentialism, in which the project of recognizing differences too easily emphasizes some cultural practices and values as constitutive of a culture (and thus as embraced by every individual within that culture) in order to distinguish it from others. See Uma Narayan, "Essence of Culture and a Sense of History: A Feminist Critique of Cultural Essentialism," *Hypatia* 13 (1998): 86–106.

14. Judith Butler, *Gender Trouble: Feminism and the Subversion of Identity* (Routledge, 1990), 128. Joanne Waugh advances a parallel argument; see Joanne B. Waugh, "Analytic Aesthetics and Feminist Aesthetics: Neither/Nor?" *Journal of Aesthetics and Art Criticism* 48:4 (1990): 317–26; reprinted in Peg Brand and Carolyn Korsmeyer, eds., *Feminism and Tradition in Aesthetics* (Pennsylvania State University Press, 1995). While I draw on various strands of Butler's thought, I largely agree with Martha Nussbaum's complaints about Butler's published work; see Martha C. Nussbaum, "The Professor of Parody," *New Republic*, 22 February 1999, 37–45.

15. As quoted in Jonathan Van Meter, "Righteous Babe," *Spin*, August 1997, 60.

16. Both quotations from Steven Daly, "Tori Amos: Her Secret Garden," *Rolling Stone*, 25 June 1998, 40.

17. O'Brien, *She Bop*, 130.

18. Tara Key, "The Things That Made Me Who I Am," in Scott Schinder, ed., *Rolling Stone's Alt-Rock-A-Rama* (New York: Delta, 1996), 216.

19. Daly, "Tori Amos," 40.

20. Norma Coates, "(R)evolution Now? Rock and the Political Potential of Gender," in Sheila Whiteley, ed., *Sexing the Groove: Popular Music and Gender* (Routledge, 1997), 56.

21. Linda Nochlin, "Why Have There Been No Great Women Artists?" in Thomas B. Hess and Elizabeth C. Baker, eds., *Art and Sexual Politics: Why Have There Been No Great Women Artists?* (New York: Collier, 1973), 5.

22. Coates, "(R)evolution Now?" 55.

23. Judith Butler, *Gender Trouble: Feminism and the Subversion of Identity* (Routledge, 1990), 145. The clearest statement of her position may be Judith Butler, "For a Careful Reading," in Seyla Benhabib, Judith Butler, et al., *Feminist Contentions:*

A Philosophical Exchange (Routledge, 1995), 127–43. Although Butler invokes neither author, the views of Aristotle and David Hume are important antecedents. A similar idea informs Dick Hebdige, *Subculture: The Meaning of Style* (London: Methuen, 1979).

24. Dorothy E. Smith, "Femininity as Discourse," in L. G. Rowman, L. K. Christian-Smith, and E. Ellsworth, eds., *Becoming Feminine* (London: Falmer, 1988), 37–59.

25. Roger Scruton, *The Aesthetics of Music* (Oxford University Press, 1997), chap. 11; quotation, 379. Given his credentials as a conservative theorist, Scruton likely would fault the proposal that his thought runs parallel to Butler's, but I think his only ground for objection would arise when the argument just sketched is supplemented with a discussion of the values that ought to be promoted through music and the other arts.

26. As in Toni A. H. McNaron, "Mirrors and Likeness: A Lesbian Aesthetic in the Making," in Susan J. Wolfe and Julia Penelope, eds., *Sexual Practice, Textual Theory: Lesbian Cultural Criticism* (Oxford: Blackwell, 1993), 291–306. The "truism" that music can neither communicate new meanings nor convey ideas that are unfamiliar to listeners is noted and challenged by Robert Walser, *Running With the Devil: Power, Gender, and Madness in Heavy Metal Music* (Wesleyan University Press, 1993), 34.

27. Butler, *Gender Trouble*, 145. Unfortunately, Butler takes her attack on the "abiding gendered self" as proof that there is no transcendental subject. However, the fact that determinate, empirical identities are performatively constituted by discursive categories is no evidence against a prediscursive, noumenal subject. For further criticisms of Butler, see Allison Weir, *Sacrificial Logics: Feminist Theory and the Critique of Identity* (Routledge, 1996), chap. 5; Penelope Deutscher, *Yielding Gender: Feminism, Deconstruction, and the History of Philosophy* (Routledge, 1997), chap. 1; and Herta Nagl-Docekal, "The Feminist Critique of Reason Revisited," *Hypatia* 14 (1999): 49–76.

28. Butler, *Gender Trouble*, 145.

29. Ibid., 147.

30. Ibid., 140.

31. Ibid., 17.

32. Ibid., 148. Similar ideas are advanced by Linda Hutcheon, *The Politics of Postmodernism* (Routledge, 1992), chap. 2.

33. Butler, *Gender Trouble*, 148.

34. Butler thus shares common ground with Jacques Attali, who contends that "the code of music simulates the accepted rules of society." Jacques Attali, *Noise: The Political Economy of Music*, trans. Brian Massumi (University of Minnesota Press, 1985), 26.

35. Greil Marcus, "The Clash," *Ranters and Crowd Pleasers: Punk in Pop Music, 1977–92* (New York: Doubleday, 1993), 29.

36. The music does so by refusing to resolve its harmonic progression with any sense of stability. Ironically, it thus employs a "feminine" mode. Paradoxically, this lack of resolution can be regarded as reflecting "masculine desire and frustration."

See Renee Cox, "A History of Music," *Journal of Aesthetics and Art Criticism* 48 (1990): 405–6.

37. Barbara Bradby, "Lesbians and Popular Music: Does It Matter Who Is Singing?" in Gabriele Griffin, ed., *Outwrite: Lesbianism and Popular Culture* (London: Pluto, 1993), 163.

38. E. Ann Kaplan, "Madonna Politics: Perversion, Repression, or Subversion?" in Cathy Schwichtenberg, ed., *The Madonna Connection: Representational Politics, Subcultural Identities, and Cultural Theory* (Boulder: Westview, 1993), 149–65; Sheila Whiteley, "Seduced by the Sign: An Analysis of the Textual Links Between Sound and Image in Pop Videos," in Whiteley, ed., *Sexing the Groove*, 259–76; and Lisa Henderson, "Justify Our Love: Madonna and the Politics of Queer Sex," in L. Frank and P. Smith, eds., *Madonnarama: Essays on Sex and Popular Culture* (New York: Cleis, 1994).

39. Transcribed from "Up From the Underground," *The History of Rock 'n' Roll* television and video production (Time Warner, 1995), episode ten.

40. See Jason Cohen, "Garbage: A Fiery Bird and Three Studio Blokes Bond in a Very Savvy Pop Band," *Request*, June 1998, 29, and Karen Schoemer, "Linda Ronstadt," in Barbara O'Dair, ed., *Trouble Girls: The Rolling Stone Book of Women in Rock* (New York: Random House, 1997), 201–2.

41. See Paula Bennett, "Gender as Performance: Shakespearean Ambiguity and the Lesbian Reader," in Wolfe and Penelope, *Sexual Practice, Textual Theory*, 94–109. Simon Frith makes a similar point but seems to restrict it to gay and lesbian singers; Simon Frith, *Performing Rites: On the Value of Popular Music* (Harvard University Press, 1996), 195.

42. Lewis, *Gender Politics and MTV*, 109.

43. John Stuart Mill, *On Liberty*, chap. 3. All further quotations from Mill are from this source. For an edition that includes critical essays responding to Mill, see John Stuart Mill, *On Liberty: A Norton Critical Edition*, ed. David Spitz (New York: Norton, 1975).

44. Lou Reed, as quoted in Robert Palmer, *Rock and Roll: An Unruly History* (New York: Harmony, 1995), 187.

45. Simon Frith, "Afterthoughts," in Simon Frith and Andrew Goodwin, eds., *On Record: Rock, Pop, and the Written Word* (New York: Pantheon, 1990), 420.

46. As quoted in Andrew Doe and John Tobler, *The Doors in Their Own Words* (New York: Perigee, 1991), 48.

47. Jean-Jacques Rousseau, *Emile or On Education*, trans. Allan Bloom (New York: Basic Books, 1979), 205.

48. See Robert Palmer, *Rock and Roll: An Unruly History*, chap. 7.

49. Walser, *Running With the Devil*, 128, 131. Walser makes no attempt to explain how the "glam" element arose within heavy metal, so there is no perspective for considering whether bands like Poison were appropriating (and neutralizing) the strategies of 1970s glam rock practitioners.

50. Walser, *Running With the Devil*, 128.

51. See Barry Lazell and Dafydd Rees, *Bryan Ferry and Roxy Music* (London: Proteus, 1982).

52. The same point is made by Arlene Stein, "Crossover Dreams: Lesbianism and Popular Music Since the 1970s," in Corey K. Creekmur and Alexander Doty, eds., *Gay, Lesbian, and Queer Essays on Popular Culture* (Duke University Press, 1995), 421. Ironically, some writers criticized k. d. lang for the way she "teased" her lesbian fans ("lang thangs") prior to outing herself in 1992, and then found her later, noncountry work less representative of a lesbian sensibility; see Martha Mockus, "Queer Thoughts on Country Music and k. d. lang," in Philip Brett, Elizabeth Wood, and Gary C. Thomas, eds., *Queering the Pitch: The New Gay and Lesbian Musicology* (Routledge, 1994), 257–71, and Stella Bruzzi, "Mannish Girl: k. d. lang—From Cowpunk to Androgyny," in Whiteley, *Sexing the Groove*, 191–206.

53. Key, "The Things That Made Me," 216, emphasis added.

54. See Greil Marcus on the Go-Go's, "Kiss Kiss Bang Bang," *Ranters and Crowd Pleasers*, 195–98.

Chapter Twelve

Epigraphs: Silvia Bovenschen, "Is There a Feminine Aesthetic?" trans. Beth Weckmueller, in Gisela Ecker, ed., *Feminist Aesthetics* (Boston: Beacon, 1986), 45 (originally published in German in *New German Critique* 12 [1977]); Finch, as quoted in Daina Darzin, "L7," *Rolling Stone*, 11 August 1994, 26.

1. As quoted in Chuck Klosterman, "Elton John Rocks Fargo," *Fargo Forum*, 26 October 1997, A1. Elton John revealed his sexual orientation in 1976. On first glance, such knee-jerk responses might suggest that many consumers of mass art do respond as Pierre Bourdieu hypothesizes: they respond first and foremost to content. Further reflection suggests that heterosexual rejection of gay-identified music and male rejection of "feminine" music is more properly a reflection of the listener's presumption of its content.

2. Locating interpretation in "acts of recognition," Stanley Fish endorses this extreme position. Whether responding to a text or to an interpretation of it, "You will agree with me (that is, understand) only if you already agree with me." Stanley Fish, *Is There a Text in This Class? The Authority of Interpretive Communities* (Harvard University Press, 1980), 173.

3. Professional critics, appalled by Dylan's message, failed even to acknowledge the musical intensity of these shows; see Clinton Heylin, *Bob Dylan: Behind the Shades* (New York: Summit, 1991), 332–33.

4. The classic formulation of the problem is David Hume's essay, "Of Tragedy." A fresh wave of discussion has been generated by Colin Radford, "How Can We Be Moved by the Fate of Anna Karenina?" *Proceedings of the Aristotelian Society*, supp. vol. 49 (1975), 67–80.

5. Simon Frith, *Performing Rites: On the Value of Popular Music* (Harvard University Press, 1996), 276–77, from an essay originally published as "Music and Identity," in Stuart Hall and Paul Du Gay, eds., *Questions of Cultural Identity* (Thousand Oaks: Sage, 1996), 108–27.

6. Frith, *Performing Rites*, 274. Exploring the theme of identity as an ideal, Christine Korsgaard argues that the contingency of our specific identities ("as a mother or a citizen or a Quaker") does not challenge Enlightenment conceptions of the self

and agency. See Christine M. Korsgaard, *The Sources of Normativity* (Cambridge University Press, 1996), chap. 3.

7. "Although the adoption of a stance of traditional disinterestedness is a masculinist approach . . . it is still a possible and appropriate, useful mode of experiencing a work of art, including feminist art." Peggy Zeglin Brand, "Disinterestedness and Political Art," in Carolyn Korsmeyer, ed., *Aesthetics: The Big Questions* (Oxford: Blackwell, 1998), 163. An earlier version of Brand's essay appeared as "Can Feminist Art Be Experienced Disinterestedly?" in David Goldblatt and Lee B. Brown, eds., *Aesthetics: A Reader in Philosophy of the Arts* (Upper Saddle River, N.J.: Prentice Hall, 1997), 532–35.

My arguments owe a very real debt to Brand's "revisionist feminist stance," but I want to avoid any implication that a text's status as art plays any role in this strategy. Where Brand emphasizes the utility of disinterested attention in allowing audiences to "strongly identify" with a work of art based on their existing interests, I want to explore the possibility that it allows audiences to identify with works that challenge those interests.

8. Peter Burger, *Theory of the Avant-Garde*, trans. Michael Shaw (University of Minnesota Press, 1984), 36. For a discussion of "autonomy theory" as it relates to music, see Rose R. Subotnik, *Developing Variations: Style and Ideology in Western Music* (University of Minnesota Press, 1991), chap. 1.

9. Frank Zappa with Peter Occhiogrosso, *The Real Frank Zappa Book* (New York: Poseidon, 1989), 35.

10. Zappa, 182. Also: "If a guy expects to earn a living by providing musical entertainment for folks in the U.S.A., he'd better figure out how to do something with a human voice plopped on it" (p. 185).

11. As quoted in Katherine Dunn, "Courtney Love," *Rolling Stone*, 13 November 1997, 166. See also Poppy Z. Brite, *Courtney Love: The Real Story* (New York: Simon and Schuster, 1997), 159–60; Love is quoted putting down "shitty band[s] with girls" who can't write a bridge for a song.

12. Thus, the impossibility of grasping meaning apart from knowledge of a work's historical and social origins is offered as evidence against traditional aesthetics; see Mary Devereaux, "Oppressive Texts, Resisting Readers and the Gendered Spectator: The New Aesthetics," *Journal of Aesthetics and Art Criticism* 48:4 (1990): 345; reprinted in Peg Brand and Carolyn Korsmeyer, eds., *Feminism and Tradition in Aesthetics* (Pennsylvania State University Press, 1995).

13. This position is independently articulated by both Pierre Bourdieu, *Distinction: A Social Critique of the Judgment of Taste* (Harvard University Press, 1984), and Terry Eagleton, *The Ideology of the Aesthetic* (Oxford: Blackwell, 1991).

14. Devereaux, "Oppressive Texts," 344. Devereaux's summary makes it clear that autonomy and disinterest are two very different doctrines. The doctrine of the autonomy of art addresses the question of artistic value, while doctrines about "neutral" or disinterested reception address the meaning (but not value) of texts. So they do not stand or fall together.

15. This position is articulated by Hilda Hein, "The Role of Feminist Aesthetics in Feminist Theory," *Journal of Aesthetics and Art Criticism* 48:4 (1990): 286 (also reprinted in Brand and Korsmeyer, *Feminism and Tradition in Aesthetics*). Hein

endorses feminist strategies that "abandon" traditional aesthetic problems. See also Joanne B. Waugh, "Analytic Aesthetics and Feminist Aesthetics: Neither/Nor?" *Journal of Aesthetics and Art Criticism* 48:4 (1990): 317–26 (also reprinted in Brand and Korsmeyer).

16. This is the position of strict autonomists. The categories employed to classify versions of autonomy theory are adopted from Casey Haskins, "Kant and the Autonomy of Art," *Journal of Aesthetics and Art Criticism* 47:1 (1989): 43–54. As a doctrine about music, it is sometimes known as musical purism or strict formalism; see Peter Kivy, Music Alone (Cornell University Press, 1990), 202, and Philip Alperson, "What Should One Expect From a Philosophy of Music Education?" *Journal of Aesthetic Education* 25 (1991): 220, respectively. I am sympathetic to the claim that the position is really a straw man created to win support for music's expressive character; see Wayne D. Bowman, "The Values of Musical 'Formalism,'" *Journal of Aesthetic Education* 25 (1991): 41—59.

17. Gordon Graham, "The Value of Music," *Journal of Aesthetics and Art Criticism* 53 (1995): 151.

18. Jerrold Levinson, "What Is Aesthetic Pleasure?" in *The Pleasures of Aesthetics: Philosophical Essays* (Cornell University Press, 1996), 7. For a related discussion of higher and lower levels of artistic intention, see Randall R. Dipert, "The Composer's Intentions: An Examination of Their Relevance for Performance," *Musical Quarterly* 66 (1980): 207–8.

19. This description celebrates the gay male reader in Wayne Koestenbaum, "Wilde's Hard Labor and the Birth of Gay Reading," in Joseph A. Boone and Michael Cadden, eds., *Engendering Men: The Question of Male Feminist Criticism* (Routledge, 1990), 176–77.

20. David Sanjek, "The Wild, Wild Women of Rockabilly," in Whiteley, *Sexing the Groove*, 159.

21. Lauraine Leblanc, *Pretty in Punk: Girls' Gender Resistance in a Boys' Subculture* (Rutgers University Press, 1999), and Daniel Cavicchi, *Tramps Like Us: Music and Meaning Among Springsteen Fans* (Oxford University Press, 1998). A telling example of Cavicchi's inability to get fans to talk about the "sound" of the music is offered on p. 112.

22. A further temptation is to reason that if musical structure is the chief value of the high-art tradition of instrumental music, then it cannot play any role in rock music, for rock inverts all the values of classical music. Consequently, rock critics and major rock publications often vilify progressive rock. Assumptions about the importance of "authenticity" and progressive politics also figure into the undervaluation of progressive rock. For an excellent survey of these issues, see Edward Macan, *Rocking the Classics: English Progressive Rock and the Counterculture* (Oxford University Press, 1997), chap. 8.

23. See John Fiske, *Understanding Popular Culture* (Boston: Unwin Hyman, 1989; rpt. Routledge, 1991), chap. 3. As John Frow puts it, employing the terminology of Pierre Bourdieu, "there is no escape from the consequences of possession of cultural capital, just as there is no way of getting outside the game of cultural distinction"; John Frow, *Cultural Studies and Cultural Value* (Oxford University Press, 1995), 168–69.

24. Frith recognizes "an avant-garde within popular music, offering musicians and listeners the pleasures of rule breaking"; Frith, "Towards an Aesthetic of Popular Music," 147 (a passage omitted from *Performing Rites*). But of course it is everyone else who concerns us here; how does a rock musician get a disruptive message to anyone who does not already identify with rule breaking?

25. As quoted in Susan Cheever, "Tori Amos," *Rolling Stone*, 13 November 1997, 104.

26. From a letter to Stephen Spender, May 1935, as quoted in "Remembering Eliot," Allen Tate, ed., *T. S. Eliot: The Man and His Work* (1966), 55–6.

27. While disinterest is a feature of many theories of taste originating in the eighteenth century, including those of the Earl of Shaftesbury, Francis Hutcheson, and Edmund Burke, the classic text is Immanuel Kant, *Critique of Judgment* (1790), especially "The Analytic of the Beautiful." A more recent treatment is Jerrold Levinson, "Pleasure and the Value of Works of Art," *The Pleasures of Aesthetics*, 11–24; originally published in *British Journal of Aesthetics* 32 (1992).

28. Jerome Stolnitz, "The Aesthetic Attitude," in Korsmeyer, *Aesthetics: The Big Questions*, 80.

29. For a fuller account of this last point, see Theodore Gracyk, "Valuing and Evaluating Popular Music," *Journal of Aesthetics and Art Criticism* 57 (1999): 205–20.

30. Macan, *Rocking the Classics*, chap. 4.

31. See Marcus Gray, *Last Gang in Town: The Story and Myth of the Clash* (New York: Henry Holt, 1995), 491–92.

32. Levinson, *Pleasures of Aesthetics*, 7.

33. Brand, "Disinterestedness and Political Art," 167.

34. Dick Hebdige, *Subculture: The Meaning of Style* (New York: Methuen, 1979), 17. Simon Frith explores this same theme in his recent work.

35. Tony Bennett, *Outside Literature* (Routledge, 1990), chap. 6. Suspicious of the idea that aesthetic pleasure involves a universality that transcends class interests, Bennett joins Terry Eagleton and Pierre Bourdieu in attacking Kant's theory of pure aesthetic response. All three ignore Kant's full theory of art and culture.

36. "This connection, however, must always be only indirect. In other words, we must think of taste as first of all connected with something else. . . . This something else may be something empirical, viz., an inclination inherent in human nature." Immanuel Kant, *Critique of Judgment*, trans. Werner S. Pluhar (Indianapolis: Hackett, 1987), 163, emphasis as in original (p. 296 in the standard Akademie pagination).

37. Ibid. (Akademie ed., 297). In contrast to works of art, the beauty of nature creates a direct, intellectual interest. So with both art and nature, Kant contends that a disinterested judgment of taste "is not based on any interest, yet it gives rise to one"; Kant, *Critique of Judgment*, 167, emphasis as in original (Akademie ed., 300).

38. Kant, 164 (Akademie ed., 297).

39. Simon Frith, *Sound Effects*, 164–65; Greil Marcus, "Life After Death," *Ranters and Crowd Pleasers: Punk in Pop Music, 1977–92* (New York: Doubleday, 1993), 210–15; Roland Barthes, *The Pleasure of the Text*, trans. Richard Miller (New York: Hill and Wang, 1975); and Barthes, "The Grain of the Voice," in Simon Frith and Andrew Goodwin, eds., *On Record: Rock, Pop, and the Written Word* (New York:

Pantheon, 1990), 293–300 (originally in *Image-Music-Text*, trans. Stephen Heath [New York: Hill and Wang, 1977]).

40. Frith, *Sound Effects*, 165. Making a different point, Frith quotes Pete Townshend's claim that the experience of "forgetting who we are at a rock concert, losing ourselves completely" is one of rock's great rewards (p. 80).

41. Marcus, *Ranters and Crowd Pleasers*, 210–11. Marcus is quoting from, and expanding on, Frith's explication of Barthes. Readers familiar with the history of aesthetics will recognize that this thesis recasts Kant's proposal that the pleasure of beauty involves a nonconceptual recognition of purposiveness without purpose: "Beauty is an object's form of purposiveness insofar as it is perceived in the object without the presentation of a purpose"; Kant, *Critique of Judgment*, sec. 17, emphasis deleted.

42. As quoted in Anthony DeCurtis, "Keith Richards," *Rolling Stone*, 28 May 1998, "The Blues Today" supplement, 5.

43. Patti Smith, "To Find a Voice," *Complete: Lyrics, Reflections, and Notes for the Future* (New York: Doubleday, 1998), xviii–xix. Elaine Scarry explores the "radical decentering" that we undergo in such experiences in *On Beauty and Being Just* (Princeton University Press, 1999), part 2.

44. For more on the notion of sympathetic participation, see Roger Scruton, *The Aesthetics of Music* (Oxford: Clarendon, 1997), chap. 11.

45. Scruton, 379. Scruton goes very wrong, I submit, in proposing that a "person with good taste turns instinctively away from certain things," such as pornography or the music of Nirvana (pp. 379 and 499).

46. Terri Sutton, "Women, Sex, and Rock 'n' Roll," in Evelyn McDonnell and Ann Powers, eds., *Rock She Wrote: Women Write About Rock, Pop, and Rap* (New York: Cooper Square Press, 1999), 380; originally published in *Puncture* (1989).

Sources of Chapter Titles and Subheadings

"Like a Rolling Stone," Bob Dylan, 1965.
"Long Distance Call," Muddy Waters, 1951.
"Not Fade Away," Buddy Holly, 1957.
"Don't Let Me Be Misunderstood," The Animals, 1965.
"They Don't Know," Kirsty MacColl, 1979.
"I Heard It Through the Grapevine," Gladys Knight and the Pips, 1967; Marvin Gaye, 1968.
"Around and Around," Chuck Berry, 1958.
"Adam Raised a Cain," Bruce Springsteen, 1978.
"Re-Make/Re-Model," Roxy Music, 1972.
"You've Really Got a Hold on Me," The Miracles, 1962; The Beatles, 1963.
"Nothing Compares 2 U," Sinéad O'Connor, 1990.
"I Can't Turn You Loose," Otis Redding, 1966.
"Don't Look Back," John Lee Hooker, 1963; Van Morrison with Them, 1965.
"Thank You for Talkin' to Me Africa," Sly and the Family Stone, 1971.
"Money Changes Everything," The Brains, 1980; Cyndi Lauper, 1983.
"Don't Play That Song," Ben E. King, 1962; Aretha Franklin, 1970.
"Shakin' All Over," Johnny Kidd and the Pirates, 1959; The Who, 1970.
"We Are Family," Sister Sledge, 1979.
"Message in the Music," O'Jays, 1976; Young Soul Rebels, 1992.
"What Do You Hear in These Sounds?" Dar Williams, 1997.
"Flyin' Saucer Rock 'n' Roll," Billy Riley, 1957.
"All or Nothing," Small Faces, 1966; "All or Nothin'," Tom Petty, 1991; "All or Nothin' at All," Bruce Springsteen, 1992.
"Speaking in Tongues," Talking Heads, 1983.
"Three Ways of Knowin'," Johnnie and Jack, 1955.
"Cross Road Blues," Robert Johnson, 1936; Cream, 1968.
"Free as a Bird," John Lennon, 1977; The Beatles, 1994.
"Act Naturally," Buck Owens, 1963; The Beatles, 1965.

277

"Exile in Guyville," Liz Phair, 1993.

Così Fan Tutte, Wolfgang Amadeus Mozart, 1790.

"Tutti Frutti," Little Richard, 1956.

"Mannish Boy," Muddy Waters, 1955; Rolling Stones, 1977.

"Boys Keep Swinging," David Bowie, 1979; Susanna Hoffs, 1991.

"Rebel Rebel," David Bowie, 1974; Rickie Lee Jones, 1993.

"Turn the Beat Around," Vicki Sue Robinson, 1976; Gloria Estefan, 1994.

"Sexx Laws," Beck, 1999.

"Middle of the Road," Pretenders, 1983.

"People Got to Be Free," The Rascals, 1968.

"Hello Stranger," Barbara Lewis, 1963.

"Eyesight to the Blind (Born Blind)," Sonny Boy Williamson, 1957; The Who, 1969.

"The Hunter Gets Captured by the Game," The Marvelettes, 1966; Jerry Garcia, 1974.

Index

279